TOP **10**
BERLIN

JÜRGEN SCHEUNEMANN

EYEWITNESS TRAVEL

Left **Berlin Reichstag** Right **A café in the Hackesche Höfe**

LONDON, NEW YORK,
MELBOURNE, MUNICH AND DELHI
www.dk.com

Produced by Dorling Kindersley Verlag, Munich
Reproduced by Connecting People, Starnberg &
Colourscan, Singapore
Printed and bound in China by Leo Paper Products
Ltd
First American Edition, 2002
11 12 13 14 10 9 8 7 6 5 4 3 2 1
Published in the United States by DK Publishing,
375 Hudson Street,
New York 10014
**Reprinted with revisions 2004, 2006, 2007,
2008, 2009, 2010, 2011**
**Copyright 2002, 2011 © Dorling Kindersley
Limited, London**

A catalog record for this book is available from the
Library of Congress

ISSN 1479-344X

ISBN 978-0-75666-921-8

Within each Top 10 list in this book, no
hierarchy of quality or popularity is implied. All 10
are, in the editor's opinion, of roughly equal merit.
Floors are referred to throughout in accordance
with German Usage; ie the "first floor" is the floor
above ground level.

Contents

Berlin's Top 10

Brandenburger Tor &
Pariser Platz   8

Reichstag   10

Unter den Linden   12

Potsdamer Platz   16

Museumsinsel   20

Kurfürstendamm   24

Kaiser-Wilhelm-
Gedächtnis-Kirche   26

Schloss Charlottenburg   28

Kulturforum   32

Zoologischer Garten   36

Historic Buildings   38

Modern Buildings   40

Moments in History   42

Churches & Synagogues   44

Museums   46

Art Galleries   48

Left **"East Side Gallery" on the Berlin Wall** Right **Façade of a house in Prenzlauer Berg**

Famous Berliners	50	Tiergarten & Federal District	96
Kneipen (Pubs)	52		
Bars & Lounges	54	Kreuzberg & Schöneberg	102
Performing Arts Venues	56		
Gay & Lesbian Attractions	58	Central Berlin: Unter den Linden	112
Shops & Markets	60		
Festivals & Fairs	62	Central Berlin: Scheunenviertel	122
Children's Attractions	64		
Lakes, Rivers & Canals	66	Central Berlin: Around Alexanderplatz	130
Sport & Fitness Venues	68		
Parks & Gardens	70	Prenzlauer Berg	138
Famous Hotels	72	Berlin's Southeast	144
Best Places to Eat	74	Potsdam & Sanssouci	152

Around Town

		Streetsmart	
Charlottenburg & Spandau	78	Practical Information	160
		Places to Stay	172
Grunewald & Dahlem	88	General Index	180

Left **The *Berlin* memorial on Tauentzienstraße** Right **The park of Schloss Sanssouci**

BERLIN'S
TOP 10

Berlin Highlights
6–7

Brandenburger Tor &
Pariser Platz
8–9

Reichstag
10–11

Unter den Linden
12–15

Potsdamer Platz
16–19

Museumsinsel
20–23

Kurfürstendamm
24–25

Kaiser-Wilhelm-
Gedächtnis-Kirche
26–27

Schloss
Charlottenburg
28–31

Kulturforum
32–35

Zoologischer Garten
36–37

Top 10 of Everything
38–75

BERLIN'S TOP 10

Berlin Highlights

Berlin is Germany's liveliest city and one of the most fascinating capitals in the world. You'll find no other place where art and culture, museums and theatres, entertainment and nightlife are more diverse and exciting than on the banks of the Spree River. Once reunited, Berlin quickly developed into a cosmopolitan city, and today there is an air of energy and vibrancy about it.

1 Brandenburger Tor and Pariser Platz

The Brandenburger Tor, Berlin's most famous sight, is located in Pariser Platz, where the famous Hotel Adlon and the embassies breathe a modern, stylish elegance *(see pp8–9)*.

2 Reichstag

No other building is a more potent symbol of Germany's history than the Reichstag *(below)*. Since its redesign by Sir Norman Foster in 1997–9, the structure has become one of the most popular sights in Berlin. Visitors are attracted by its vast egg-shaped dome, affording fantastic views across the city *(see pp10–11)*.

3 Unter den Linden

The magnificent, tree-lined boulevard *(below)* in the eastern part of the city has always been a central axis. Berlin's most important historic buildings are assembled here *(see pp12–15)*.

4 Potsdamer Platz

The new heart of the old metropolis beats on Potsdamer Platz, where exciting modern structures, such as the Sony Center, have been erected. With its restaurants, shops, film museum and cinemas, it is a unique world of entertainment *(see pp16–19)*.

Map labels: Moabit, Schlosspark, Spree, Spandauer Damm, Otto-Suhr-Allee, Kaiserdamm, Bismarckstrasse, Charlottenburg, Kantstrasse, Kurfürstendamm, Lietzenburger Strasse, Hansaviertel, Strasse des 17. Juni, Tegeler Weg, Beusselstr., Alt-Moabit, Levetzowstrasse, Lessingstr., Altona, Martin-Frankenstr., Hardenbergstrasse, Breitscheid Platz, Kurfü..., Tauentzienstrasse, Leibnizstrasse, Kaiser-Friedrich-Strasse, Stromstrasse

5 Museumsinsel

Among the museums in this important complex is the Pergamonmuseum, which houses the famous Pergamon Altar from ancient Greece (see pp20–23).

6 Kurfürsten-damm

Berlin's much visited strolling and shopping avenue is the main thoroughfare in the heart of the western city. Restaurants and stylish boutiques have increased the hustle and bustle along this grand boulevard (see pp24–5).

7 Kaiser-Wilhelm-Gedächtnis-Kirche

The tower ruins of the memorial church, built to commemorate Kaiser Wilhelm I, still stand today as a silent reminder of the horrors of war (see pp26–7).

9 Kulturforum

This complex of museums, which includes the famous Gemäldegalerie (gallery of paintings), the Kunstgewerbemuseum (museum of arts and crafts) and the Neue Nationalgalerie, as well as concert halls such as the Philharmonie, guarantees a unique cultural experience for visitors to Berlin (see pp32–5).

8 Schloss Charlottenburg

The historic rooms of the former Hohenzollern summer residence invite visitors to experience a slice of Prussian history, while the Baroque-style gardens, among the most beautiful in Germany, are perfect for strolling and sunbathing (see pp28–31).

10 Zoologischer Garten

Germany's oldest and most famous zoo and aquarium, in the centre of the city, boasts some 14,000 animals and over 1,800 different species (see pp36–7).

🔟 Brandenburger Tor & Pariser Platz

The best known of Berlin's symbols, the Brandenburg Gate stands proudly in the middle of Pariser Platz, asserting itself against the hyper-modern embassy buildings that now surround it. Crowned by its triumphant Quadriga sculpture, the famous Gate has long been a focal point in Berlin's history: rulers and statesmen, military parades and demonstrations – all have felt compelled to march through the Brandenburger Tor.

The Brandenburg Gate seen from the east

🍴 One of the best spots for a coffee or a bite to eat in Pariser Platz is Theodor Tucher, a café and restaurant that opens at 9am.

🎨 A small exhibition, housed in the northern side wing of the Brandenburger Tor, tells the history of the Gate.

- Pariser Platz
- Map F3, K3

- Tourist information, Brandenburger Tor
- Map F3, K3
- Apr–Nov: 9:30am–6pm daily; Nov–Mar: 10am–6pm daily
- (030) 25 00 25

Top 10 Sights

1. Brandenburger Tor
2. Quadriga
3. Hotel Adlon Berlin
4. DZ Bank
5. Akademie der Künste
6. French Embassy
7. Palais am Pariser Platz
8. Eugen-Gutmann-Haus
9. Haus Liebermann
10. American Embassy

1 Brandenburger Tor

Since its restoration in 2002, Berlin's symbol is now lit up more brightly than ever before. Built by Carl G Langhans in 1789–91 and modelled on the temple porticos of ancient Athens, the Gate has, since the 19th century, been the backdrop for many events in the city's turbulent history.

2 Quadriga

The sculpture, 6 m (20 ft) high above the Gate, was created in 1794 by Johann Gottfried Schadow as a symbol of peace. As a model for the laurel-crowned goddess of peace in the chariot, Schadow used his niece, who subsequently became famous throughout Berlin.

3 Hotel Adlon Berlin

Completed in 1997 and now favoured by visiting dignitaries, Berlin's most elegant hotel is a reconstruction of the original Hotel Adlon. This legendary hotel, destroyed in World War II, was host to the rich and famous, including Greta Garbo, Thomas Mann and Charlie Chaplin *(see p72)*.

4 DZ Bank

This modern building, designed by the American architect Frank Owen Gehry, combines the clean lines of Prussian architecture with some daring elements inside.

➔ *Opposite the Brandenburger Tor, check out The Kennedys museum (see p118).*

5 Akademie der Künste

Built between 2000 and 2005 and designed by Günter Behnisch and Manfred Sabatke, the building incorporates, behind a vast expanse of windows, the ruins of the old art academy, which was destroyed in World War II. Today it is an Academy of the Arts and features compelling exhibitions.

6 French Embassy

In 1999–2001, an elegant building was constructed by Christian de Portzamparc, on the site of the old embassy, which was destroyed in World War II. Its colonnades and tall windows, a homage to the former French Embassy palace, are particularly remarkable and worth seeing.

7 Palais am Pariser Platz

This complex by Bernhard Winking, a successful modern interpretation of Neo-Classical architecture, is slightly hidden to the north of the Brandenburger Tor. It is worth venturing inside where you will find a café, a restaurant and a souvenir shop around a pleasantly shaded courtyard.

8 Eugen-Gutmann-Haus

With its clean lines, the Dresdner Bank, built in the round by the Hamburg architects' team gmp in 1996–7, recalls the style of the New Sobriety movement of the 1920s. In front of the building, which serves as the Berlin headquarters of the Dresdner Bank, stands the famous original street sign for the Pariser Platz.

9 Haus Liebermann

Josef Paul Kleihues erected this building at the north end of the Brandenburger Tor in 1996–8, faithfully recreating an earlier building on the same site. The house is named after the artist Max Liebermann *(right)*, who lived here. In 1933, watching Nazi SA troops march through the Gate, he famously said: "I cannot possibly eat as much as I would want to puke out."

10 American Embassy

The last gap in the line of buildings around Pariser Platz was finally closed in 2008. A dispute between the embassy and the Berlin Senate delayed building for several years: an entire street was to be moved to satisfy the USA's security requirements. But in the end, the historical street stayed where it was.

For more on historical architecture in Berlin **see pp38–9**

🔟 Reichstag

Of all the buildings in Berlin, the Parliamentary Building is probably one of the most symbolic. The mighty structure, erected in 1884–94 by Paul Wallot as the proud manifestation of the power of the German Reich, was destroyed by arson in 1933 and bombed during World War II. In 1996, the artist Christo wrapped up the Reichstag and, in 1994–9, the British architect Sir Norman Foster transformed it into one of the most modern parliamentary buildings in the world. Today it is the official seat of the Bundestag, the German parliament.

Main entrance of the Reichstag

🍴 **If a meal at the Käfer restaurant exceeds your budget, many stalls in the vicinity of the Reichstag sell hot dogs.**

ℹ️ **Large numbers of visitors come to see the Reichstag cupola. It is best to avoid weekends or to start queuing half an hour before the opening time. Tuesday is the quietest day.**

- *Platz der Republik 1*
- *Map F3, K2*
- *Open 8am–midnight (last admission 10pm)*
- *(030) 22 73 21 52*
- *www.bundestag.de*

Top 10 Sights

1. The Cupola
2. Plenary Hall
3. Portico "Dem deutschen Volke"
4. Restored Façade
5. Restaurant Käfer
6. Installation "Der Bevölkerung"
7. Memorial for Delegates to the Reichstag
8. German Flag
9. Platz der Republik
10. Memorial for Victims of the Wall

The Cupola

The Reichstag cupola by Sir Norman Foster affords breathtaking views of Berlin. It is open at the top to air the building and – a touch of irony here – to allow for the dissemination of debates throughout the country. A ramp winds its way up to the top.

Plenary Hall

The plenary hall is the seat of the Deutscher Bundestag, the German parliament, which has convened here again since 20 April 1999. Technologically, the hall is one of the most advanced parliament buildings in the world. The federal eagle caused a row: considered too "fat", it had to be slimmed down.

Portico "Dem deutschen Volke"

The dedication "To the German People" was designed in 1916, against the will of Wilhelm II.

Sign up for DK's email newsletter on traveldk.com

4 Restored Façade
Despite extensive renovations, small bullet holes from World War II are still visible in the building's façade.

5 Restaurant Käfer
This luxury restaurant next to the cupola on the Reichstag's roof offers an excellent view of the historical centre of Unter den Linden. It is very popular and you may well have to wait for a seat *(see p101)*.

8 The German Flag
The giant German flag was first raised on the occasion of the official national celebrations of German reunification on 3 October 1990.

6 Installation "Der Bevölkerung"
Hans Haacke's work of art "To the People" is a counterpoint to the portico inscription opposite.

7 Memorial by Dieter Appelt
Unveiled in 1992, the memorial commemorates 97 Social Democratic and Communist Reichstag delegates who were murdered under the Third Reich.

9 Platz der Republik
Celebrations often take place on the lawn in front of the Reichstag, most recently in 1996, when the building was wrapped up by Christo.

Memorial for Victims of the Wall 10
Opposite the southern side of the Reichstag, a memorial recalls the Berlin Wall, which ran only a few steps away from this spot. One of the crosses commemorates Chris Gueffroy: shot in February 1989 when trying to escape, he was one of more than 100 people who died at the Wall.

The Reichstag Fire

When the Reichstag went up in flames on 27 February 1933, the Dutch Communist van der Lubbe was arrested and charged with arson. It is, however, much more likely that the Nazis had started the fire themselves. Adolf Hitler used the Reichstag fire as a pretext to get the "Enabling Act" passed by parliament. This allowed him to dispose of all his opponents, marking the beginning of a 12-year reign of terror.

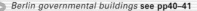

Unter den Linden

"As long as the lime trees still blossom in Unter den Linden, Berlin will always be Berlin," Marlene Dietrich once sang about this magnificent avenue. Today the lime trees blossom more beautifully than ever in the historical centre of Berlin, because the old buildings along the street have been extensively restored and modern architecture has created new highlights. The "Linden" – originally a royal bridle-path linking the Stadtschloss (the king's town residence) and Tiergarten – became Berlin's most fashionable street in the 18th century, and was synonymous with the city that was then the capital of Prussia.

Deutsches Historisches Museum in the Zeughaus

🔎 The largest selection of cakes in Berlin tempts visitors in the Café im Opernpalais. In summer, you can enjoy them outside.

• Map F/G3, K3/4

• Deutsches Historisches Museum, Unter den Linden 2 • 10am–6pm daily • (030) 20 30 40 • www.dhm.de • Admission charge

• St Hedwigskathedrale, Bebelplatz • 10am–5pm Mon–Sat, 1–5pm Sun • (030) 203 48 10 • www.hedwigs-kathedrale.de

• Staatsoper, Unter den Linden 7 • Box Office 10am–8pm Mon–Fri, 2–8pm Sun • (030) 20 35 45 55 • www.staatsoper-berlin.de • Admission charge

Top 10 Sights

1. Deutsches Historisches Museum in the Zeughaus
2. Staatsoper Unter den Linden
3. St Hedwigskathedrale
4. Humboldt-Universität
5. Neue Wache
6. Kronprinzenpalais
7. Bebelplatz
8. Opernpalais
9. Russian Embassy
10. Frederick the Great's Statue

Deutsches Historisches Museum

Germany's largest history museum, reopened in 2003, provides an overview of more than 1,000 years of German history. Housed in the Zeughaus – the royal arsenal built in 1706 – it is the oldest and, architecturally, the most interesting building in the avenue Unter den Linden *(see p14)*.

Staatsoper Unter den Linden

The richly ornamented State Opera House is one of Germany's most attractive. Neo-Classical in style, it was built by von Knobelsdorff in 1741–3 as Europe's first free-standing opera house, to plans devised by Frederick the Great himself *(see p56)*.

St Hedwigs-kathedrale

Designed by Georg W von Knobelsdorff in 1740–2 and modelled on the Pantheon in Rome, this is the seat of the Catholic archdiocese in Berlin. Frederick the Great commissioned the cathedral to appease Catholics in Berlin after conquering Silesia *(see p44)*.

Buses No. 100 and No. 200 run along the entire length of Unter den Linden, with bus stops at nearly all the famous sights.

Humboldt-Universität
4 Berlin's oldest and most highly regarded university was founded in 1890, on the
initiative of Wilhelm von Humboldt. Twenty-
nine Nobel Prize winners were educated
here, including Albert Einstein.

Neue Wache
5 The central German memorial for all
victims of war was created in the years
1816–8 and designed by Karl Friedrich
Schinkel. An enlarged reproduction of the
moving *Pietà* sculpture by Käthe Kollwitz
stands in the centre of the room.

Kronprinzenpalais
6 The Neo-Classical
Palais, built in 1732–3 by
Philipp Gerlach, was originally a residence for the
heirs to the Hohenzollern
throne. After World War I
it became an art muse-
um, and after 1948 the
East German government
housed state visitors
there. Until 2003 it was
used for exhibitions of the
Deutsches Historisches
Museum opposite.

Bebelplatz
7 Originally named
Opernplatz, this wide,
open space was designed
by Georg W von Knobels-
dorff as the focal point of
his Forum Fridericianum.
The elegant square was
meant to introduce some
of the splendour and
glory of ancient Rome to
the Prussian capital. In
May 1933, it became the
scene of the infamous
Nazi book burning.

Opernpalais
8 The charming build-
ing next to the Staats-
oper, built in 1733–7,
served as a palace for
the princesses.

Russische Botschaft
9 The gigantic Russian
Embassy, built in Stalinist
"wedding-cake style",
was the first building to
be constructed in Unter
den Linden after World
War II *(see also p118)*.

Frederick the Great's Statue
10 One of Christian Daniel
Rauch's grandest sculp-
tures, this statue shows
the "Old Fritz" (13.5 m/
45 ft high) on horseback,
wearing a uniform and tricorn hat *(see also p113)*.

→ *For more on Unter den Linden* see pp112–21

Old print roll from 1821 with views of the avenue Unter den Linden

Deutsches Historisches Museum

1 The Dying Warriors
The 22 reliefs by Andreas Schlüter, displayed on the walls of the courtyard rather than in one of the museum's exhibitions, portray the horrors of war in an unusually immediate way.

2 Martin Luther
Luther's portrait, by Lucas Cranach the Elder, is the focal point of exhibition rooms devoted to Martin Luther and the Reformation.

3 Europe and Asia
This group of Meissen porcelain figures reflects the fascinating relationship between the two continents.

4 Steam Engine
A full-sized steam engine from the year 1847 marks the entrance to the exhibition on the Industrial Revolution.

5 Clothes from the Camps
Among the many exhibits illustrating the years under Nazi rule is the jacket of a concentration camp inmate – a chilling reminder of the Third Reich.

6 Gloria Victis
The moving allegorical figure of Gloria Victis, created by the French sculptor Antonin Mercié, bears witness to the death of a friend during the final days of the Franco-Prussian War of 1870–71.

7 Soldiers Plundering a House
This painting by Sebastian Vrancx, dating from around 1600, depicts a scene from the wars of religion that tore the Netherlands apart during the 16th century.

8 Saddle
A valuable saddle, dating from the middle of the 15th century, is decorated with elaborately carved plaques made of ivory.

Gloria Victis Statue

9 The Berlin Wall
An original section of the Wall, together with the banners of a peaceful pro-unification demonstration in 1989, commemorates the fall of the Berlin Wall.

10 V2 Rocket
In the section on Nazi Germany is a V2 rocket engine – next to an 88-mm flak gun. The V2 was one of the *Wunderwaffen* ("wonder weapons") used at the end of World War II.

Portrait of Martin Luther in the Zeughaus

 For more on Berlin museums see pp46–7

Top 10 Events

1. **1573**
   Elector Johann Georg has a bridle path built, linking the Stadtschloss and Tiergarten
2. **1647**
   During the Great Elector's reign, the road is planted with "Linden" (lime trees)
3. **From 1740**
   Frederick the Great has grand buildings erected
4. **1806**
   Napoleon marches along Unter den Linden
5. **1820**
   The road becomes a grand boulevard
6. **1928**
   Unter den Linden and Friedrichstraße epitomize the world city
7. **1933**
   Troops celebrate Hitler's victory
8. **1945**
   The avenue is razed to the ground
9. **1948–53**
   Revival of the street
10. **October 1989**
    Demonstrations lead to the fall of East German regime

Zeughaus Unter den Linden

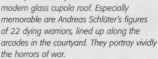

Schlüter's "Dying Warrior"

Originally the royal arsenal, the Zeughaus was built in 1706 in the Baroque style according to plans by Johann Arnold Nering. It is an impressive structure, with its main and side wings surrounding an historical central courtyard that is protected by a modern glass cupola roof. Especially memorable are Andreas Schlüter's figures of 22 dying warriors, lined up along the arcades in the courtyard. They portray vividly the horrors of war.

A cone-shaped glass annex, erected by the Chinese-born architect Ieoh Ming Pei in 2001 for special exhibitions and temporary shows, stands behind the museum.

The permanent exhibition in the main historical building includes a collection entitled "Images and Testimonials of German History". Highlighting the most important periods and events in the history of the country, the displays include a surprising variety of exhibits dating back to the days of the early Medieval German Empire through the period of the Reformation and the Thirty Years' War as well as the wars of Liberation and the failed Revolution of 1848, right up to the two World Wars and more recent events of the 20th century up to 1994.

The opening of the Reichstag in the White Salon of Berlin Schloss on 25 June 1888

Deutsches Historisches Museum: **www.dhm.de**

🔟 Potsdamer Platz

The heart of the new metropolis of Berlin beats on Potsdamer Platz. This square, where Berliners and tourists alike now flock to cinemas, restaurants and shops, was already a hub of urban life in the 1920s. After World War II, it became a desolate wasteland, but since the fall of the Berlin Wall, Potsdamer Platz – for a while Europe's largest building site – has become a city within the city, surrounded by imposing buildings which began to appear in the 1990s, and are still being added to today.

Reconstruction of the first traffic lights in Europe

Apart from visiting the famous Café Josty, make sure you do not miss Diekmann in the Weinhaus Huth.

- Potsdamer Platz
- Map F4, L2/3

- Filmmuseum Berlin
- Potsdamer Str. 2
- 10am–6pm Tue–Sun, 10am–8pm Thu
- (030) 300 90 30
- Admission charge

- Theater am Potsdamer Platz
- Marlene-Dietrich-Platz 1
- 8pm daily
- Admission charge

- Spielbank Berlin
- Marlene-Dietrich-Platz 1
- 11:30–3am daily
- (030) 25 59 90
- Admission charge

- Cinemaxx
- Potsdamer Str. 5
- 12:30pm–1:30am daily
- (01805) 24 63 62 99
- Admission charge

Top 10 Sights

1. Sony Center
2. Filmmuseum Berlin
3. Café Josty
4. Weinhaus Huth
5. Marlene-Dietrich-Platz
6. Potsdamer Platz Arkaden
7. Spielbank Berlin
8. Cinemaxx
9. DaimlerChrysler Quartier
10. Theater am Potsdamer Platz

Sony Center
The Sony Center *(right)* is the most ambitious, successful and architecturally interesting building in the new Berlin. The cupola structure, designed by Helmut Jahn and opened in 2000, is the European headquarters of the Sony company, and with its cinemas and restaurants it is also a social magnet.

Filmmuseum Berlin
This museum takes you backstage in the Hollywood and Babelsberg film studios. Exhibits include Marlene Dietrich's costumes *(see p18)*.

Café Josty
Café Josty harkens back to its legendary predecessor, a regular haunt for artists and intellectuals in the 19th century. Today's Café Josty is partially housed in the historic Kaisersaal (Emperor's Hall) of the former Grand Hotel Esplanade.

Weinhaus Huth
The only building on Potsdamer Platz to have survived World War II, the Weinhaus today accommodates restaurants and the fascinating art gallery Daimler Contemporary.

The best time to visit the Sony Center is in the early evening, when the inside of the Plaza is lit up.

5 Marlene-Dietrich-Platz

This square in front of the Stella-Musical-Theater is dedicated to the great actress. A brash *Flower Balloon* *(left)*, by the artist Jeff Koons, enlivens the centre of the square.

Locator Map

6 Potsdamer Platz Arkaden

The arcades draw visitors with over 130 shops, exclusive boutiques and popular restaurants on three storeys. The lower ground floor is a food court, serving dishes from around the world.

7 Spielbank Berlin

Berlin's casino *(below)* invites visitors to *faites vos jeux*. Apart from roulette, Black Jack is also played, and an entire floor is given over to gambling machines.

8 Cinemaxx

The Cinemaxx on Potsdamer Platz with its 17 screens is one of Berlin's largest cinemas. The bigger screens of the multiplex cinema show current Hollywood blockbusters, while the three smallest screens are for viewings of low-budget and German films. There is also a small bar serving drinks.

9 Daimler City

The Berlin headquarters of the famous car manufacturers was designed by Hans Kollhoff and Renzo Piano. Daimler's former software company, debis, was based in the building shown *left*.

10 Theater am Potsdamer Platz

Berlin's largest show stage, this venue has shown hits such as *Dirty Dancing* and *Mamma Mia!* The 1,300-seat theatre is often sold out.

For more on the Filmmuseum Berlin see p18

Left **S-Bahn sign** Centre **Café Josty sign** Right **Buddy Bears on Potsdamer Platz**

Exhibitions in the Filmmuseum

Film poster

1 Marlene Dietrich
This exhibition of the film star's estate includes costumes, touring luggage, photographs, letters and notes, posters and film clips.

2 Metropolis
This film, directed by Fritz Lang in 1927, has an alarming vision of a future world as its subject. Models and props from the film are on display.

3 Caligari
The best known German film of the 1920s, *The Cabinet of Dr Caligari* (1920), was a masterpiece of Expressionist filmmaking by Robert Wiene.

4 Leni Riefenstahl
This exhibition reveals the technical tricks used in the Nazi propaganda film *Olympia,* made by Leni Riefenstahl in 1936–8.

5 Film and National Socialism
This exhibition features documents relating to the propaganda uses of film, everyday cinema and the industry's victims: some film stars allowed themselves to be used by the Nazis, others refused to cooperate. The life and work of the actor Kurt Gerron, who was persecuted and murdered, is documented as an exemplary case.

6 Post-War Cinema
The story of films and film-making in East and West Germany, with props and costumes of popular stars of post-war German cinema such as Hanna Schygulla, Romy Schneider, Heinz Rühmann and Mario Adorf.

7 Artificial Worlds
The tricks employed by special effects studios, ranging from the first effects of the 1930s to computer animation.

8 Transatlantic
This exhibition of documents, letters, keepsakes and souvenirs retraces the careers of German film stars in Hollywood.

9 Pioneers and Divas
The infant days of cinema are featured here – as well as stars of the silent era such as Henny Porten and Asta Nielsen.

10 Exile
Documents relate the difficulties encountered by German filmmakers when making a new start in the USA in 1933–45.

Façade of the Filmmuseum Berlin

18

For more on Berlin museums see pp46–7

Top 10 Architects

1. Helmut Jahn (Sony Center)
2. Renzo Piano and Christian Kohlbecker (debis Headquarters, Musical-Theater, Spielbank, Weinhaus Huth)
3. José Rafael Moneo (Hotel Grand Hyatt, Mercedes-Benz Headquarters)
4. Hans Kollhoff (Daimler)
5. Giorgio Grassi (Park Colonnades)
6. Ulrike Lauber and Wolfram Wöhr (Grimm-Haus, Cinemaxx)
7. Sir Richard Rogers (Office Block Linkstraße)
8. Steffen Lehmann and Arata Isozaki (Office and Retail House Linkstraße)
9. Heidenreich & Michel (Weinhaus Huth)
10. Bruno Doedens and Maike van Stiphout (Tilla-Durieux-Park)

Europe's largest building site

In the 1920s, Potsdamer Platz was Europe's busiest square, boasting the first automatic traffic lights in the world. During World War II this social hub was razed to the ground. Untouched for almost 50 years, the empty square shifted back into the centre of Berlin when the Wall came down. During the 1990s, Potsdamer Platz became Europe's largest building site – millions of curious onlookers from around the world came to watch progress from the famous red info box. Altogether, around €17 billion were invested to create the present square.

Kollhoff-Tower

Moving the Esplanade

The Senate of Berlin stipulated that Sony should preserve the "Breakfast Room" and the "Emperors' Hall" of the Grand Hotel Esplanade, both protected following destruction in World War II. Accordingly, in 1996, the rooms were moved – 1,300 tons were loaded onto wheels and shifted by 75 m (246 ft) during the course of a week.

The historic Emperors' Hall is today incorporated into the modern Sony Center

Panoramapunkt is a viewing platform on the top floor of Kollhoff-Tower (open 11am–8pm daily).

Museumsinsel

Formed by the tributaries of the Spree river, Museumsinsel is an island in central Berlin that is home to the world's most diverse yet coherent museum complex. Built between 1830 and 1930, the museums, which hold the Prussian royal collections of art and archaeology, were turned into a public foundation in 1918. Heavily damaged in World War II, all museums have since been reconstructed and in 1999 the complex was declared a UNESCO World Cultural Heritage Site. Ongoing construction work will connect the individual museums. On the island's north side is the hugely impressive Berliner Dom.

Sarcophagi inside the Ägyptisches Museum

🅞 Some of the museums have cafés, but the Altes Museum café is convenient as it is a little closer to Karl-Liebknecht-Strasse, the island's main road.

🅞 It's best to reserve a whole day for the collections of Museumsinsel and take breaks in the parks nearby. Sundays can be very busy with long queues and large groups of visitors.

- Map G3, J5
- Most museums open 10am–6pm daily, until 8pm Thu
- (030) 266 42 4242
- €8–10 per museum; Museumsinsel day pass €14, 3-day pass €19, extra charge for some exhibitions • Admission free for children under 16
- www.museumsinsel-berlin.de

Top 10 Features

1. Pergamonmuseum
2. Bode-Museum
3. Neues Museum
4. Ägyptisches Museum
5. Alte Nationalgalerie
6. Altes Museum
7. James Simon Gallery
8. Colonnade Courtyard
9. Lustgarten
10. Berliner Dom

Pergamonmuseum

The Pergamonmuseum is one of the most important museums of ancient art and architecture in the world. Built between 1909 and 1930, it houses a vast collection of antiquities and temples *(see p22)*. The huge Ishtar gate *(right)* dates from the 6th century BC.

Bode-Museum

Located at the northern tip of Museumsinsel, the Bode-Museum is a stately structure dominated by a cupola *(above)*. The building holds the Sculpture Collection, the Museum of Byzantine Art and the Numismatic Collection, made up of a diverse collection of over 500,000 objects.

Neues Museum

Spectacularly revamped by British architect David Chipperfield, the building itself is as fascinating as the exhibits on show *(below)*. As well as the Ägyptisches Museum *(see p21)*, the Museum of Pre-and Early History is also housed here.

Alte Nationalgalerie

5 First opened in 1876, the Old National Gallery was beautifully restored in the 1990s *(left)* and now holds 19th-century sculptures and paintings *(see p48)*.

Ägyptisches Museum

4 Housed within the Neues Museum, this museum features portraits of Egyptian royals and monumental architecture *(see p46)*.

Altes Museum

6 The first building to be completed on Museum-sinsel in 1830, the Altes Museum resembles a Greek temple *(below)*. It houses the Classical Antiquities Collection *(see p39)*.

James Simon Gallery

7 Due to open in 2012, this new gallery, named in honour of James Simon (1851–1932), a generous patron of the Berlin State Museums, will serve as the central entrance building and visitor centre.

Colonnade Courtyard

8 This landscaped court-yard of columns, between the Alte Nationalgalerie and Neues Museum, frames and connects the museums. It provides an atmospheric venue for open-air concerts or space to relax.

Lustgarten

9 This "pleasure park", with a fountain in its centre, is located in front of the Altes Museum. Originally a herb garden, the area was transformed into a parade ground in 1713. Today, the lawns are popular with tired visitors *(see p39)*.

Berliner Dom

10 Easily the most over-whelming structure on the island, this Baroque-style cathedral *(above)* is unusually ornate for a protestant church. Services and organ concerts can be enjoyed in this exquisitely renovated church *(see p44)*.

Missing Treasures

During World War II, many of the island's exhibits were hidden in underground bunkers. Some pieces of "Priam's Gold", excavated from the site of ancient Troy by the German arch-aeologist Schliemann, were taken by the Red Army as war booty and remain in Moscow today. The Neues Museum highlights where there are gaps in the collection.

The impressive Pergamon Altar, excavated in the 19th century

Pergamonmuseum

1 Pergamon Altar
The colossal Pergamon Altar, dating from 160 BC, is the largest and most important treasure of the Berlin museums.

2 Ishtar Gate
The imposing Ishtar Gate and the Processional Way that led to it are fully preserved. The gate was built in ancient Babylon, during the reign of Nebuchadnezar II. Original faïence wall tiles depict the sacred lions.

3 Market Gate of Miletus
This vast gate (AD 120) is over 16 m (52 ft) high. To the right of the entrance, a hairdresser has carved an advertisement for his shop into the stone.

4 Assyrian Palace
The interior of this palace from the days of the Assyrian kings (12th century BC) has been completely restored and boasts impressive statues of lions.

5 The Goddess Athena
The beauty ideal prevalent in Greek antiquity is perfectly reflected in this statue's features.

6 The Goddess Persephone
The 5th-century BC Greek statue of the goddess of the underworld sports a mysterious smile, the expressive symbol of her divinity.

Goddess Persephone

7 Aleppo Room
Dating from the early 17th century, this small room features magnificent wooden cladding, taken from a Christian merchant's house in Syria. A beautiful example of Ottoman architecture.

8 Roman Mosaic
One of many on display, this Roman floor mosaic is magnificently executed and dates back to the 3rd or 4th century AD. It was excavated in Gerasa in Jordan.

9 Palace of Mshatta
A gift from Sultan Hamid II to Kaiser Wilhelm II, this desert palace, built in AD 744 in Jordan, has an elaborately decorated southern façade.

10 Temple of Athena
Dedicated to Athena of Nikephoros, this full-scale temple from the 2nd century BC has a simple yet elegant design.

Assyrian Palace

Top 10 Events

1. Plan for a public art collection created, 1810
2. The Altes Museum, Prussia's first public museum, opens, 1830
3. Completion of Neues Museum, 1859
4. Opening of Alte Nationalgalerie, 1876
5. Completion of Kaiser-Friedrich-Museum (Bode-Museum), 1904
6. Pergamonmuseum opens, 1930
7. Bombs destroy most of the museums, 1943
8. Most museums reopen after renovation, 1958
9. Museumsinsel declared a UNESCO Site, 1999
10. Neues Museum reopens, in 2009

Saving the Museumsinsel

The "island of museums" is a treasury of antique architecture – yet it has been slowly decaying. Since 1992 a total of €1.8 billion has been spent on the renovation and modernization of Museumsinsel. A "master plan" hatched by

The Palace of Mshatta

renowned architects, including David Chipperfield and O M Ungers, will transform the complex into a unique museum landscape – just as it was first conceived in the 19th century by Friedrich Wilhelm IV, when he established the "free instTution for art and the sciences". By 2014, all the museums will be linked by an "architectural promenade", creating a conceptual and structural link between the various parts. This promenade will consist of a variety of rooms, court-yards and vaults, as well as exhibition halls. The core of the complex will be a new central entrance building. After individual renovations, the museums are grad-ually reopening – the Neues Museum opened in 2009 and a fourth wing will be added to the Pergamon-museum, which should be completed by 2015. The Museumsinsel is a UNESCO World Heritage Site.

Pergamon and Asia Minor

From 241 until 133 BC, the antique city of Perg-amon was the capital of the Hellenistic Pergam-enian Empire, ruling the northwestern region of Asia Minor. Apart from many temples, the town, which is in Turkey and is now known as Bergama, also boasted a famous library.

A 17th-century carpet with floral motifs from western Anatolia

🔟 Kurfürstendamm

After years of decline, the Kurfürstendamm, or Ku'damm for short, has once again become a fashionable hot spot. Breathtaking architecture, elegant boutiques and a lively scene with street artists around Breitscheidplatz have made this shopping boulevard one of Berlin's most attractive and – at 3.8 km (2.5 miles) – also its longest avenue for strolling.

Corner of Kurfürstendamm and Joachimsthaler Straße

⬤ Only a few cafés in the Ku'damm area have survived: the most charming is Café Wintergarten in the Literaturhaus at the southern end of Fasanenstraße.

✪ It is best to avoid Ku'damm on Saturday mornings when the boulevard is teeming with locals and tourists out on shopping trips.

• Map B/C5, P3/4

• Tourist information
• Neues Kranzler-Eck, Kurfürstendamm 21
• 10am–8pm Mon–Sat, 10am–6pm Sun
• (030) 25 00 25

• Story of Berlin, Kurfürstendamm 207–8
• 10am–8pm daily (last admission at 6pm)
• (030) 88 72 01 00
• www.story-of-berlin.de

• Europa-Center, Tauentzienstr. 9
• 24 hours
(shops: 10am–8pm)
• (030) 348 00 88
• www.24EC.de

Top 10 Sights

1. Breitscheidplatz
2. Kaiser-Wilhelm-Gedächtnis-Kirche
3. Europa-Center
4. Neues Kranzler-Eck
5. Fasanenstraße
6. Ku'damm-Eck
7. Lehniner Platz
8. The Story of Berlin
9. Galerie Brusberg
10. Iduna-Haus

Breitscheidplatz

Here, in the heart of the western city, artists, Berliners and visitors swarm around J Schmettan's globe fountain, known by locals as "Wasserklops" (water meatball).

Kaiser-Wilhelm-Gedächtnis-Kirche

One of Berlin's most haunting symbols, the tower of the original church – destroyed during World War II – stands in the centre of Breitscheidplatz, serving as both memorial and reminder of the terrors of war *(see p26)*.

Europa-Center

The oldest shopping centre in West Berlin, originally opened in 1962, is still worth a visit. You will find a variety of shops, including a grocery store, a cinema and fashion boutiques.

Neues Kranzler-Eck

This glass and steel skyscraper was built in 2000 by the architect Helmut Jahn. The legendary Café Kranzler was retained as a bar in front of the office block. You will also find the tourist information centre here (see p163).

Fasanenstraße

A small street off Ku'damm, Fasanenstraße with its galleries, expensive shops and restaurants is one of Charlottenburg's most elegant areas (see pp80–81).

Ku'damm-Eck

This hotel/business complex (right) has a large video screen showing news and commercials.

Lehniner Platz

The square is home to the Schaubühne, built as Universum cinema in 1928 by Erich Mendelsohn, converted in 1978.

The Story of Berlin

This interesting multi-media show takes visitors on a tour of 800 years of Berlin's history – from the Great Elector to the capital of Prussia, from Willy Brandt to the Fall of the Wall. Underneath the museum a nuclear bunker can be visited.

THE STORY OF BERLIN
GESCHICHTEN EINER METROPOLE

Galerie Brusberg

This Neo-Classical building (right) provides a glimpse of Ku'damm's erstwhile splendour.

Iduna-Haus

The remarkable turreted house at this street corner (left) is one of few bourgeois houses preserved from the late 19th century. The richly ornamented, gleaming white Art Nouveau façade has been lavishly restored.

When Ku'damm was no more than a log road

In 1542, today's magnificent boulevard was just a humble "Knüppeldamm", or log road. It served the Electors as a bridle path, linking the town residence (Stadtschloss) and their hunting lodge (Jagdschloss). It was not until 1871 that the area around the Ku'damm developed into a fashionable "new west end". Chancellor Otto von Bismarck had the boulevard modelled on the Champs Elysées in Paris, and requested that his statue be erected in the street as a thank you. So far, however, the Berliners have failed to oblige him.

📑10 Kaiser-Wilhelm-Gedächtnis-Kirche

One of the most haunting symbols of Berlin, the ruins of the memorial church in the heart of the city's West End, have been irreverently nick-named "the hollow tooth". The Neo-Romanesque church was given the name of Kaiser Wilhelm Memorial Church in 1895, to honour Wilhelm I. Following damage by severe bombing raids in 1943, the ruins of the tower were left standing as a memorial. Next to it, Egon Eiermann erected a new church in 1957–63. Religious services are now conducted here.

The "hollow tooth" – the Tower Ruins

- There are fantastic views of the church from the Mövenpick Café in the Europa-Center opposite.

- If possible, visit the interior of the new church on a sunny day around lunch-time, when the blue glass window is at its most impressive.

- Breitscheidplatz
- Map D4, N4 • www.gedaechtniskirche.com
- (030) 218 50 23
- Church 9am–7pm, memorial hall 10am–4pm Mon–Sat
- Services 10am and 6pm Sun
- Admission free

Top 10 Sights

1. Tower Ruins
2. Kaiser's Mosaic
3. Mosaic of the Hohenzollerns
4. Coventry Crucifix
5. New Bell Tower
6. Main Altar
7. Tower Clock
8. The Orthodox Cross
9. Original Mosaics
10. Figure of Christ

Kaiser's Mosaic

One of the mosaics that have been preserved depicts Emperor Heinrich I on his throne, with imperial orb and sceptre *(below)*. Originally decorated through-out with scenes from German imperial history, the church interior was meant to place the Hohenzollerns within this tradition.

Tower Ruins

Only the tower of the memorial church survived the destruction of World War II that razed much of Berlin to the ground. Today only 63 m (206 ft) high, it once rose to 113 m (370 ft). The hole in the tower's roof has a ragged edge, hence the nickname "hollow tooth". The restoration of the tower ruins is set to run until the end of 2011.

Mosaic of the Hohenzollerns

The surprisingly coloured mosaic of the Hohenzollerns adorns the vestibule of the church ruins. It depicts Emperor Wilhelm I together with Queen Luise of Prussia and her entourage.

Coventry Crucifix
This small crucifix was forged from old nails that were found in the ruins of Coventry Cathedral. It commemorates the bombing of Coventry, England, by the German Luftwaffe in 1940.

New Bell Tower
The hexagonal bell tower rises 53 m (174 ft) high next to the tower ruins, on the site of the old church's main nave.

Main Altar
The golden figure of Christ created by Karl Hemmeter is suspended above the modern main altar in the church. In the evening light, the windows behind the altar glow an overwhelming dark blue.

Tower Clock
The tower bears a clock based on a Classical design, with Roman numerals. At night, it is lit in blue by modern light-emitting diodes to match the lighting inside the new church.

The Orthodox Cross
A gift from the Russian Orthodox bishops of Volokolomsk and Yuruyev, this cross was given in memory of the victims of Nazism.

A Church with Two Lives

The Kaiser-Wilhelm-Gedächtnis-Kirche has the Berliners to thank for its preservation: in 1947, the Senate had planned to demolish the Tower Ruins for safety reasons. In a referendum only about ten years later, however, one in two Berliners voted for its preservation. And so the idea came about to build a new church next to the ruin and to preserve the vestibule of the old church as a striking memorial hall to the horrors of war.

Original Mosaics
Mosaics showing Prussian dukes are preserved on the walls and ceilings all along the stairways.

Figure of Christ
Miraculously, the vast, plain sculpture of Christ, which is suspended from the ceiling, survived the bombing of the church.

For more on Berlin churches **see pp44–5**

Schloss Charlottenburg

The construction of Schloss Charlottenburg, designed as a summer residence for Sophie Charlotte, wife of the Elector Friedrich III, began in 1695. Between 1701 and 1713 Johann Friedrich Eosander added a cupola and the Orangerie was extended. Today, it has been extensively renovated.

Schloss Charlottenburg

🍴 The Orangery Café (left of the main entrance) has an attractive garden.

⭐ At weekends, the palace park is over-crowded, but a midweek early-evening stroll can be very romantic (open 6am–dusk).

• Spandauer Damm
• Map A/B3 • Admission charge in all museums
• Two-day ticket for all museums: €12

• Altes Schloss •
10am–5pm Tue–Sun (to 6pm summer) • Neuer Flügel • 10am–5pm Wed–Mon
• (030) 32 09 11

• Belvedere • Apr–Oct: noon–5pm Tue–Fri; Nov–Mar: noon–5pm Tue–Sun

• Neuer Pavillon
• Re-opens 2012 following renovation

• Mausoleum • Apr–Oct: 10am–6pm (noon–4pm Nov–Mar) Tue–Sun
• (030) 32 09 14 46

• Museum Berggruen
• Schlossstr. 1
• 10am–6pm Tue–Sun
• (030) 34 35 73 15

Top 10 Sights

1. Altes Schloss
2. Porzellankabinett
3. Schlosskapelle
4. Monument to the Great Elector
5. Neuer Flügel
6. Schlossgarten
7. Belvedere
8. Neuer Pavillon
9. Mausoleum
10. Museum Berggruen

Altes Schloss
The Baroque tower of the oldest part of the palace (1695) by Johann Arnold Nering is crowned by Richard Scheibe's golden statue of Fortuna.

Porzellankabinett
The small, exquisite mirrored gallery has been faithfully restored to its original glory. Valuable porcelain items from China and Japan are on display.

Schlosskapelle
The luxurious splendour of the palace chapel recalls the once magnificent interior design of the palace, before it was destroyed in World War II. But appearances can be deceptive: apart from the altar which is preserved in its original form, the entire chapel – including the king's box – is a costly reconstruction.

Monument to the Great Elector

The equestrian monument of Friedrich Wilhelm I is considered to be one of his most dignified portraits. Made in 1696–1703 by Andreas Schlüter, it originally stood on the Rathausbrücke, near the destroyed Stadtschloss.

Neuer Flügel

Built between 1740 and 1747 by Georg Wenzeslaus von Knobelsdorff, the new wing contains Frederick the Great's private quarters.

Palace Layout

Schlossgarten

The palace park, originally Baroque in style, was redesigned by Peter Joseph Lenné between 1818 and 1828 as an English-style landscape garden.

Belvedere

Friedrich Wilhelm II liked to escape to the romantic Belvedere, a summer residence built in 1788 by Carl Gotthard Langhans, which served as a tea pavilion. Today it houses a collection of precious Berlin porcelain objects.

Neuer Pavillon

This Italianate villa behind the palace, designed by Schinkel for Friedrich Wilhelm III in 1825, was inspired by the Villa Reale del Chiatamone in Naples. The pavilion clearly shows the Hohenzollern's love of the Italian style.

Mausoleum

Slightly hidden, this Neo-Classical building *(above)* by Schinkel, is the final resting place for Queen Luise and other Hohenzollerns.

Museum Berggruen

Situated in the Western Stüler Building, opposite Schloss Charlottenburg, this modern art gallery houses the permanent exhibition "Picasso and his Time", featuring more than 100 works that span the artist's career. Other highlights of the collection include works by Matisse, Klee and Giacometti *(see p49)*.

For more on Charlottenburg see pp78–83

Left **The new wing** Centre **Frederick the Great's Watteau painting** Right **Neuer Pavillon**

Palace Rooms

Goldene Galerie

The festival salon in the Neuer Flügel, 42 m (138 ft) long, was designed, in the Rococo style, by G W von Knobelsdorff for Frederick the Great. The richly ornamented room has a cheerful appearance.

Eichengalerie

The wooden panelling of the so-called oak gallery is carved with preciously gilded portraits of the Hohenzollern ancestors.

Gris-de-Lin-Kammer

This small chamber in Friedrich's second palace apartment is decorated with paintings, including some by his favourite artist, Antoine Watteau. The room was named after its violet-coloured damask (*gris-de-lin* in French) wall coverings.

Schlafzimmer Königin Luise

Queen Luise's bedchamber, designed in 1810 by Karl Friedrich Schinkel, features the clear lines typical of the Neo-Classical style. The walls are clad in silk fabrics and wallpaper.

Winterkammern

Friedrich Wilhelm II's early Neo-Classical rooms contain fine paintings, wall carpets and superb furniture of the time.

Goldene Galerie

Bibliothek

Frederick the Great's small library has outstanding elegant bookcases and an unusual, light green colour scheme.

Konzertkammer

Furniture and gilded panelling in the concert hall have been faithfully recreated as during Frederick the Great's time. Here hangs *Gersaint's Shop Sign*, which the king bought directly from the artist Watteau and is considered to be one of the artist's most important works.

Grünes Zimmer

The green room in Queen Elisabeth's quarters gives an excellent impression of royal chambers furnished in the 19th-century Biedermeier style.

Rote Kammer

The elegant chamber, decorated entirely in red and gold, is adorned by portraits of King Friedrich I and Sophie Charlotte.

Friedrich I's Audienzkammer

The ceiling paintings and Belgian tapestries in Friedrich I's reception chamber depict allegorical figures symbolizing the fine arts and the sciences. There are also magnificent lacquered cabinets, modelled on Asian originals.

Sign up for DK's email newsletter on traveldk.com

Top 10 Hohen-zollern rulers

1 Friedrich Wilhelm (the Great Elector, 1620–88)
2 Friedrich I (1657–1713)
3 Friedrich Wilhelm I (1688–1740)
4 Friedrich II (the Great) (1712–86)
5 Friedrich Wilhelm II (1744–97)
6 Friedrich Wilhelm III (1770–1840)
7 Friedrich Wilhelm IV (1795–1861)
8 Wilhelm I (1797–1888)
9 Friedrich III (1831–88)
10 Wilhelm II (1859–1941)

The Hohenzollern and Berlin

In 1412, the Hohenzollern dynasty, not originally resident in the Berlin area, was asked by the Luxemburg King Sigismund to liberate the province of Brandenburg from the men

Prussia's first king: Friedrich I

ace of robber barons. Burggraf Friedrich of Hohenzollern from Nuremberg was so successful in this enterprise that he was made an Elector in 1415 – this is where the histories of the Hohenzollerns and Berlin first became entwined, a relationship that was to last for 500 years. Right from the start, the family attempted to limit the powers of the town. Culture flourished under its rulers, especially under the Great Elector, who brought 20,000 Huguenot craftsmen to Berlin, as well as founding an art gallery and several schools. Friedrich Wilhelm I, father of Frederick the Great, transformed Berlin into a military camp, with parade grounds and garrisons, and scoured the town for tall men to join his body guard. In the 19th century, however, relations between Berlin and the Hohenzollerns became decidedly less cordial.

Frederick the Great in Charlottenburg

Frederick II had two apartments furnished for himself in the palace, and he took a strong personal interest in the design of the Neuer Flügel in 1740–7. From 1745, after the end of the Second Silesian War, he stayed at the palace less and less often, preferring his palace at Sanssouci, although larger festivities in the presence of the King still took place at Charlottenburg.

Frederick the Great

The Altes Schloss, designed in 1695 by Johann Arnold Nering

For more on historical architecture in Berlin **see pp38–9**

Kulturforum

The Kulturforum is a unique complex of museums, concert halls and libraries, based at the south-eastern end of the Tiergarten. Every year, some of the most outstanding European art museums, as well as the famous concert hall of the Berlin Philharmonic Orchestra, attract millions of visitors who are interested in culture and music. The Kulturforum, based in the former West Berlin, has been growing since 1956, as a counterpoint to the Museumsinsel in the former East Berlin. Here visitors can admire some of the best examples of modern architecture in the capital.

Neue Nationalgalerie in the Kulturforum

🍴 Enjoy a break around the quiet back of the Nationalgalerie.

🎟 A day ticket (€8) gives admission to all museums.

• Map E4, L1/2

• Gemäldegalerie, Matthäikirchplatz 4/6 • 10am–6pm daily (to 10pm Thu) • (030) 266 29 51 • Adm charge

• Neue Nationalgalerie, Potsdamer Str. 50 • 10am–6pm Tue–Wed & Fri (to 10pm Thu), 11am–6pm Sat & Sun • (030) 266 29 51 • Adm charge

• Kunstgewerbemuseum, Herbert-von-Karajan-Str. 10 • 10am–6pm Tue–Fri, 11am–6pm Sat & Sun • (030) 266 29 51 • Adm charge

• Musikinstrumentenmuseum, Ben-Gurion-Str. • 9am–5pm Tue–Wed & Fri (to 10pm Thu), 10am–5pm Sat & Sun • (030) 25 48 10 • Adm charge; free Thu eve

Top 10 Sights

1. Gemäldegalerie
2. Neue Nationalgalerie
3. Philharmonie
4. Kunstgewerbemuseum
5. Musikinstrumentenmuseum
6. Kammermusiksaal
7. Kupferstichkabinett
8. St Matthäuskirche
9. Staatsbibliothek
10. Kunstbibliothek

Gemäldegalerie

Berlin's largest art museum boasts some of the finest masterpieces of European art. They are displayed in the modern Neubau, built in 1998 by the architects Heinz Hilmer and Christoph Sattler. The superb collection includes paintings by Holbein, Dürer, Gossaert, Bosch, Vermeer, Brueghel the Elder, Titian, Caravaggio, Rubens, Rembrandt and many others.

Neue Nationalgalerie

Based in a building by Mies van der Rohe, the gallery exhibits mainly 20th-century art, with an emphasis on German Expressionism, such as Karl Schmitt-Rottluff's *Farm in Daugart* (1910) *(see also p48)*.

Philharmonie

This tent-like building, designed by Hans Scharoun in 1960–3, was the first new structure in the Kulturforum. Considered one of the best concert halls in the world, it is the seat of the Berlin Philharmonic Orchestra. It is also known, jokingly, as "Circus Karajani", after Herbert von Karajan (1908–89) who conducted the Philharmonic Orchestra for many years. Sir Simon Rattle has been the conductor since 2002.

For more on Berlin museums see pp46–7

4 Kunstgewerbe-museum

Craft objects from the Middle Ages to the present day and from around Europe are on show here, including valuable items like this Baroque clock and the Guelphs' treasure (see also p47).

5 Musikinstrumen-tenmuseum

Concealed behind the Philharmonie is this fascinating little museum of musical instruments. More than 750 exhibits, particularly of early instruments such as harpsichords, are on show (see also p47), as well as a 1929 Wurlitzer.

6 Kammer-musiksaal

The smaller relative of the larger Philharmonie, this concert hall is one of Germany's most highly regarded venues for chamber music. It was built in 1984–8, to a design by Hans Scharoun, carried through by his pupil Edgar Wisniewski.

7 Kupferstich-kabinett

The Gallery of Prints and Drawings holds more than 520,000 prints and 110,000 drawings from all periods and countries, including this portrait of Dürer's mother (see also p49).

8 St Matthäuskirche

This church is the only historical building to have been preserved in the Kulturforum. Built by F A Stüler in 1844–6, it is also a venue for art installations as well as a hall for classical concerts.

9 Staatsbibliothek

Built in 1967–78 according to plans by Hans Scharoun, the National Library has a collection of five million books, manuscripts and journals, making it one of the largest German-language libraries in the world.

10 Kunstbibliothek

The unassuming Art Library holds, among other items, a vast collection of art and advertising posters. It also hosts temporary exhibitions on architecture and art as well as design shows.

Left **Merchant Georg Gisze** Centre **Venus and the Organ Player** Right **Portrait of Holzschuher**

Gemäldegalerie

1 Portrait of Hieronymus Holzschuher
Albrecht Dürer painted this portrait of the mayor of Nuremburg in 1529.

2 Portrait of the Merchant Georg Gisze
This painting by Hans Holbein (1532), showing the merchant counting his money, reflects the rise of the wealthy citizen during the Renaissance.

3 Madonna with Child and Singing Angels
A 1477 painting by Sandro Botticelli depicts the Madonna and Child, surrounded by angels carrying lilies.

4 The Birth of Christ
Martin Schongauer's altar painting (c.1480) is one of only a few religious paintings by the artist that have been preserved.

Victorious Eros

5 Victorious Eros
Caravaggio's painting (1602), after Vergil's model, shows Eros, the god of love, trampling underfoot the symbols of culture, glory, science and power.

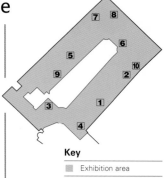

Botticelli's Madonna

Key

■ Exhibition area

6 Portrait of Hendrickje Stoffels
In a 1656–7 portrait of his lover Hendrickje Stoffels, Rembrandt's focus is entirely on the subject.

7 The French Comedy
This painting by Antoine Watteau belonged to Frederick the Great's collection.

8 The Glass of Wine
Skilfully composed by Vermeer (1658–61), this scene shows a couple drinking wine.

9 Venus and the Organ Player
This Titian (1550–52) reflects the playful sensuality typical of the Italian Renaissance.

10 Dutch Proverbs
More than 100 proverbs were incorporated into this painting by Pieter Brueghel (1559).

For more on Berlin's art galleries see pp48–9

Top 10 Architects

1 Hans Scharoun (Philhar-wmonie)
2 Mies van der Rohe (Neue Nationalgalerie)
3 James Stirling (Wissenschaftszentrum)
4 Heinz Hilmer (Gemäldegalerie)
5 Christoph Sattler (Gemäldegalerie)
6 Friedrich August Stüler (St. Matthäuskirche)
7 Edgar Wisniewski (Kammermusiksaal)
8 Rolf Gutbrod (Kunstgewerbemuseum)
9 August Busse (altes Wissenschaftszentrum)
10 Bruno Doedens (Henriette-Herz-Park)

Architecture in the Kulturforum

The Kulturforum was planned to fill the large area between Potsdamer Straße and Leipziger Platz that had been destroyed during World War II. The original idea for a varied townscape of museums and parks is credited to the Berlin architect Hans

Sculpture by Henry Moore

Scharoun, who had designed plans for this in the years 1946 and 1957. It was also Scharoun who, with the construction of the Philharmonie in 1963, set the character of the Kulturforum: the tent-like, golden roofs of the music hall, the Kammermusiksaal and the Staatsbibliothek, all designed by Scharoun and – after his death – realized by his pupil Edgar Wisniewski, are today among Berlin's best-known landmarks. All the buildings are characterized by the generous proportions of their rooms. In their day, the Scharoun buildings were highly controversial but today they are considered to be classics of modern architecture.

Mies van der Rohe's Nationalgalerie
The Neue Nationalgalerie, built to plans by Mies van der Rohe in 1965–8, is the only museum in the world designed by this Bauhaus architect. Having emigrated to the USA in 1937, van der Rohe returned to Berlin for its construction.

The Philharmonie, designed by Hans Scharoun – famed for its superb acoustics

Zoologischer Garten

Berlin's Zoological Garden is Germany's oldest zoo and, with nearly 1,500 different species, it is one of the best-stocked in the world. Animals have been kept and bred here, in the northwest of the Tiergarten district, since 1844. A total of about 15,000 animals live in the zoo, ranging from saucer jellyfish to the Indian elephant. Some enclosures are interesting buildings in their own right. In summer, a visit to the zoo is a favourite day out for Berliners, and many animals, such as the panda and baby gorillas, have become celebrities.

The Elephant Gate – the Zoo's main entrance

🅒 There is a café and self-service restaurant with a terrace inside the zoo, to the right of the Elephant Gate.

🅒 A day at the zoo is not complete without a visit to the aquarium. The basins and terraria teem with life, as do the zoo enclosures. A combined ticket for €18 entitles you to visit both zoo and aquarium.

Hardenbergplatz 8 and Budapester Str. 34 • (030) 25 40 10 • Map D4, N5 • www.zoo-berlin.de • Jan–Mar: 9am–5pm daily; Apr–mid-Sep: 9am–7:30pm daily; mid-Sep–Oct: 9am–7pm daily; Nov–Dec: 9am–5pm daily • Admission charge

Top 10 Zoo Sights

1. Panda Bears
2. Monkey House
3. Polar Bears: Knut
4. Giraffe House
5. Nocturnal Animal House
6. Elephant House
7. Aviaries
8. Crocodile Hall
9. Aquarium
10. Amphibians' Section

Monkey House
Monkeys and apes are at home in this house, and here you can watch gorillas, orang-utangs and chimpanzees swinging from tree to tree and playing in the straw. The Eastern Lowland Gorillas are very popular.

Panda Bears
Bao-Bao the Giant Panda (one of the most endangered species in the world) is one of the great stars of the Berlin Zoo. He was presented to Germany by China as an official gift in 1980. His female partner Yan Yan, who was on loan from China, died in 2007.

Polar Bears
The polar bear Knut is another star of the zoo. Born in 2006 and now fully grown, he was the first polar bear born here in over 30 years.

4 Giraffe House

The African-style Giraffe House is the oldest house (1871–2). Visitors enjoy watching the giraffes as they nibble the leaves of a tree or bend down, in slow motion, to take a drink.

5 Nocturnal Animal House

This house, in the cellar of the Predatory Animal House, houses the creatures of the night, including nocturnal reptiles and birds. Here you can admire striped bandicoots, fruit bats and slender loris. Asleep during the day, their hearing is outstanding and their eyes may light up uncannily in the dark.

6 Elephant House

These good-natured pachyderms have a healthy appetite: fully grown male Indian elephants devour up to 50 kg (110 lb) of hay a day! Two elephants have been born in captivity.

7 Aviaries

Nowhere else in the city can you hear such singing, tweeting and whistling – cockatiels, parrots, hornbills and humming-birds sound off in the Bird House aviaries.

8 Crocodile Hall

Not for the timid: in the crocodile hall visitors cross a small wooden footbridge, only 2 m (6 ft) above the dozing creatures. Opened in 1913, it was the first zoo enclosure accessible to the public.

9 Aquarium

The greatest draw in the aquarium, where Caribbean and Amazonian habitats have been recreated, are the blacktip reef sharks and green morays. The electric eel, able to generate up to 800 volts, and the sting-rays are also popular.

10 Amphibians' Section

Poisonous snakes, bird spiders and reptiles as well as other amphibians crawl and slither around behind glass on the second floor of the aquarium. A particularly spectacular event is the feeding of the spiders.

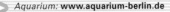

Aquarium: **www.aquarium-berlin.de**

Left **Statues at Altes Museum** Centre **Schloss Bellevue** Right **Portico of the Konzerthaus**

Historic Buildings

Brandenburger Tor
More than a mere symbol, the Brandenburg Gate is synonymous with Berlin (see pp8–9).

Schloss Charlottenburg
This palace boasts Baroque and Rococo splendours and a beautiful park, making it one of the most attractive in Germany (see pp28–31).

Schloss Bellevue
Built according to plans by Philipp Daniel Boumann in 1785–90, this palace was the residence of the Hohenzollerns until 1861. Since 1994 the stately building with its Neo-Classical façade has been the official residence of the President of the Federal Republic. The modern, egg-shaped Presidential Offices stand immediately next to the old palace. ◊ Spreeweg 1 • Map E4 • Not open to the public

Reichstag
The seat of the Deutscher Bundestag, the German parliament, with its spectacular cupola, is a magnet for visitors (see pp10–11).

Berliner Rathaus
Berlin's Town Hall, also known as "Red Town Hall" because of the red bricks from Brandenburg Province with

Southern façade of the Berliner Rathaus

which it is built, harks back to the proud days when Berlin became the capital of the new Empire. Built in 1861–9 according to designs by Hermann Friedrich Waesemann, the town hall was one of Germany's largest and most magnificent buildings, built to promote the splendour of Berlin. The structure was modelled on Italian Renaissance palaces, and the tower is reminiscent of Laon cathedral in France. The exterior was decorated with *Die Steinerne Chronik* (the stone chronicle) in 1879, depicting scenes from the city's history (see p131). ◊ Rathausstraße 15 • Map G3, K6 • 8am–6pm daily

Konzerthaus
The Concert Hall, one of Karl Friedrich Schinkel's masterpieces, was formerly known as *Schauspielhaus* (theatre). The building has a portico with Ionic columns, and a large number of statues of allegorical and historical personages, some riding lions and panthers, as well as deities, muses and bacchants. ◊ Gendarmenmarkt 2 • Map L4 • noon–7pm Mon–Sat; noon–4pm Sun • (030) 203 09 21 01

Hackesche Höfe
This complex of 19th-century warehouses consists of nine interlinked courtyards,

some of which are decorated in Art-Nouveau style, originally by August Endell. In the early 1990s the complex was completely renovated. The first courtyard is particularly attractive: coloured glazed tiles with geometric patterns decorate the house from the foundations up to the guttering. In the last courtyard, trees are grouped around an idyllic well. The Hackesche Höfe is one of Berlin's most popular hot-spots; restaurants, cafés, a cinema and the Chamäleon variety show attract visitors from afar. *Rosenthaler Str. 40–41 • Map G3, J5 • 9am–2am Tue–Sat*

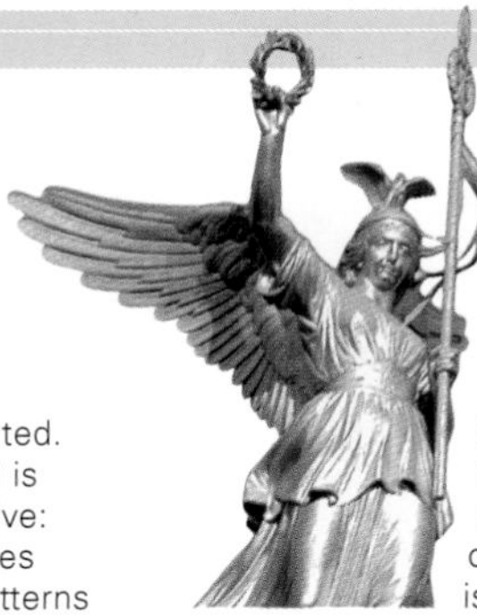
Victoria, the goddess of victory, on the Siegessäule

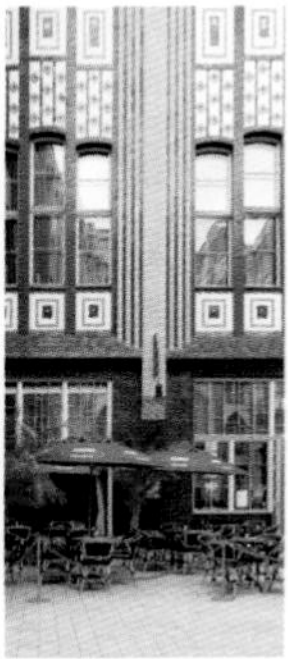
Hackesche Höfe

8 Siegessäule

The Victory Column in Tiergarten, 62 m (203 ft) high, is topped by the statue of Victoria. It is being refurbished *(see p97)*.

9 Altes Museum and Lustgarten

The façade of the Old Museum, possibly one of the most attractive Neo-Classical museums in Europe, is remarkable for the shiny red marble used in its construction, which is visible behind 18 Ionic columns. Built in 1830 according to plans by Karl Friedrich Schinkel, it was at the time one of the first buildings to be created specifically as a museum. Originally it was to house the royal collection of paintings; today it is home to a collection of antiquities. In front of the museum, on Museumsinsel, are the gardens designed by Peter Joseph Lenné. Conceived as the king's herb garden, it is today decorated with a granite bowl by Gottlieb Christian Cantian, weighing 70 tons, and a fountain *(see p114)*.

10 Zeughaus

Designed by J A Nering as the first Berlin Baroque building, the former Royal Prussian Arsenal is now the Deutsches Historisches Museum *(see pp12–15)*, with a modern addition by I M Pei.

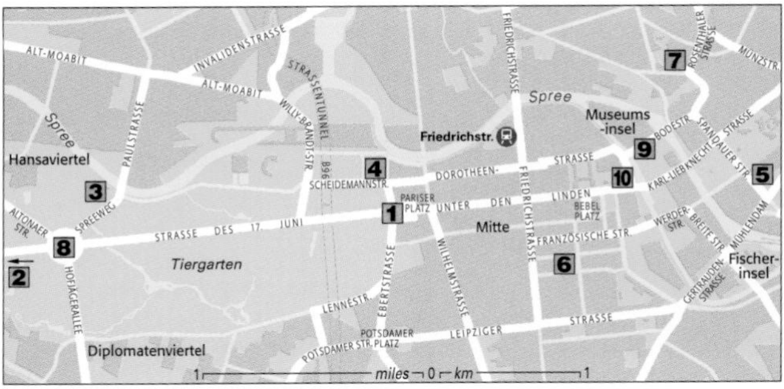

For more about historic buildings see Unter den Linden pp12–15

Left **Neue Nationalgalerie in the Kulturforum** Right **Nordic Embassies**

🔟 Modern Buildings

1 Sony Center
One of Berlin's largest structures is the spectacular Sony Center *(see p16)*.

2 Neue Nationalgalerie
This impressive low building with its huge windows was built in 1965–8 according to plans by Mies van der Rohe. It was the first building to be designed by the pioneering Bauhaus architect after his emigration to the USA. He was able to make use of his earlier designs for the Havana headquarters of the Bacardi company, which had been abandoned after the Cuban Revolution *(see pp32, 48)*. ⊗ *Potsdamer Str. 50 • Map E4 • 10am–6pm Tue–Wed, until 10pm Thu, 10am–6pm Fri, 11am–6pm Sat & Sun*

3 Bundeskanzleramt
Berliners are not too fond of the Chancellor's modern offices, although this is the only government building to have been designed by a Berlin architect. Axel Schultes developed a vast, elongated office complex, which extends north of the Reichstag, in a bend of the Spree, even stretching across the river. In the centre of the

The modern Bundeskanzleramt

hyper-modern building stands a gleaming white cube with round windows, which Berliners quickly nicknamed "washing machine". Critics describe the design as pompous, while civil servants dislike their small offices. The interior of the building is decorated with valuable modern paintings. The Chancellor's office on the 7th floor has a view of the Reichstag. ⊗ *Willy-Brandt-Str. 1 • Map J/K2 • Not open to the public*

Ludwig-Erhard-Haus

4 Ludwig-Erhard-Haus
The seat of the Berlin Stock Exchange, Ludwig-Erhard-Haus was designed by the British architect Nicholas Grimshaw in 1994–8. Locals call it the "armadillo", because the 15 giant metal arches of the domed building recall the giant animal's armour. ⊗ *Fasanenstr. 85 • Map N4 • 8am–6pm Mon–Fri*

The Kant-Dreieck in Charlottenburg

5 Philharmonie and Kammermusiksaal

Two modern concert halls in the Kulturforum were designed by Hans Scharoun in 1961 and 1987 respectively – the Chamber Music Hall was completed according to Scharoun's plans by his pupil Edgar Wisniewski. Both buildings are renowned for their excellent acoustics as well as for their tent-like roof structures *(see also pp32–5 and 56–7).*

6 Hauptbahnhof

Europe's largest train station sits on the site of the historic Lehrter Bahnhof. This impressive glass and steel structure doubles as a retail and hospitality hub. ⊗ *Hauptbahnhof • Map J2*

7 Quartiere 205–207 Friedrichstraße

The Galeries Lafayettes and the Friedrichstadtpassagen are based within these three office blocks by architects Nouvel, Pei and Ungers *(see p119).*

8 Nordische Botschaften

No other embassy building has caused as much of a stir as the five embassies of the Scandinavian countries: the green shutters open and close depending on the amount of available light. ⊗ *Klingelhöferstr. • Map N6 • Not open to the public*

9 DZ Bank on Pariser Platz

This elegant building by Frank Owen Gehry combines Prussian and modern architecture. The giant dome inside is particularly remarkable *(see p8).* ⊗ *Pariser Platz 3 • Map K3 • 10am–6pm Mon–Fri*

10 Kant-Dreieck

The aluminium sail on top the KapHag-Group's headquarters, built by Josef Paul Kleihues in 1992–5, has become a symbol of the new Berlin. Originally, the structure was to be built one-third higher than it is now, but the plans were vetoed by the Berlin Senate. ⊗ *Kantstr. 155 • Map N4 • 9am–6pm Mon–Fri*

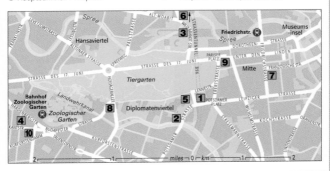

For more on architecture in Potsdamer Platz **see pp16–19**

Left **At Checkpoint Charlie** Centre **Grafitti on the Wall** Right **Marlene Dietrich in the "Blue Angel"**

Moments in History

1 1685: Edict of Potsdam

Berlin's history as a cultural capital began in 1685, when the far-sighted Great Elector announced in the Edict of Potsdam that around 20,000 Huguenots would be taken in by Berlin. Many were excellent craftsmen and scientists, who, having fled Catholic France because of their Protestant beliefs, brought a new age of cultural ascendancy to the provincial town.

Statue of the Great Elector

2 1744: Frederick the Great

Although "Old Fritz", as Frederick the Great was nicknamed, preferred the isolation of Sanssouci to the bustle of Berlin, in 1740 he began to transform the city into a new metropolis. In particular, the "Forum Fridericianum" in Unter den Linden brought new splendours to the town, and masterpieces such as the national opera house helped transform Berlin into one of the most important European cities.

Frederick playing the flute in Sanssouci

3 1928: Golden Twenties

Between 1919 and 1933, Berlin flourished culturally and became an important metropolis. Film, theatre, cabaret shows and thousands of restaurants and bars transformed the town into an international centre of entertainment. In the realms of fine art and architecture, too, Berlin set new standards.

May 1945: Berlin in ruins

4 1945: Surrender

Signed in Berlin-Karlshorst on 8 May 1945, Germany's unconditional surrender marked more than the end of World War II. The previous Jewish population of 161,000 had virtually disappeared and Berliners called their city "the empire's fields of rubble".

5 1953: Workers' Uprising in East Germany

On 17 June 1953, construction workers in Frankfurter Allee demonstrated against an increase in the average rate

Old Photos of Berlin: **www.luise-berlin.de/Historie/indexhis.htm**

1953: workers on a frieze in Frankfurter Allee

of production. Soviet tanks suppressed the rebellion while, in West Berlin, the uprising was interpreted as a demonstration for German unification.

6 1961: Building of the Wall

The building of the Berlin Wall, which commenced during the night of 12 August 1961, was a traumatic event for many Berliners. Many families were torn apart by the concrete wall and more than 100 people were to be killed over the following 30 years at the border dividing East and West.

7 1963: "I am a Berliner"

No other politician was as enthusiastically received in Berlin as the US President John F. Kennedy. On 17 July 1963, in front of Rathaus Schöneberg, he declared to the cheering crowd: "I am a Berliner". Berliners had forgiven the US for staying silent when the Wall was built. Kennedy confirmed once more that the Western Allies would stand by Berlin and support the town, just as they had done during the blockade of 1948–9, when the US and Britain air-lifted food to the "island" of West Berlin.

8 1968: The late Sixties

During the late 1960s, West Berlin students transformed Germany. Rudi Dutschke and

others proposed political change and a reappraisal of Germany's Nazi past. The movement came to an untimely end when Dutschke was injured in an assassination attempt in April 1968.

9 1989: Fall of the Wall

The fall of the Berlin Wall in November 1989 heralded a new dawn. For the first time in 30 years, Berliners from both halves of the divided city were able to visit each other. The town celebrated all along Ku'damm and in front of the Brandenburg Gate.

Celebrations after the Fall of the Berlin Wall

When the Wall was built, Willy Brandt, then governing mayor of West Berlin, had promised: "Berlin will survive!" He was right.

10 1991: Berlin becomes the capital of Germany

In 1991, Berlin was officially declared the capital of the reunified Federal Republic of Germany. Allied Forces left the city during 1994, but it was only when the Bundestag, the German parliament, moved here from Bonn on 19 April 1999 that Berlin became the "real" capital. Today, all the main ministries, the Bundesrat (upper house), and the Chancellor's and the President's offices are based in Berlin.

1991: Berlin becomes the capital

For famous Berliners see pp50–51

Left **St Hedwigskathedrale** Centre **Berliner Dom interior** Right **Main altar in Marienkirche**

🔟 Churches & Synagogues

1 Berliner Dom

Berlin Cathedral, the largest and most lavish church in town, was reopened in 1993, after almost 40 years of restoration. Designed by Julius Raschdorf in 1894–1905, the building reflects the empire's aspirations to power. In particular, the imperial stairs, made from black marble, are a manifestation of the proximity of the Hohenzollern town residence opposite the cathedral. Members of this ruling dynasty are buried in the crypt. The main nave, topped by a 85-m (279-ft) high dome is remarkable. The church is dominated by a magnificent 20th-century Neo-Baroque pulpit and the giant Sauer organ *(see also pp20–23)*. ⊗ *Am Lustgarten • Map K5 • Apr–Sep: 9am–8pm Mon–Sat, noon–8pm Sun; Oct–Mar: 9am–7pm Mon–Sat, noon–7pm Sun • (030) 20 26 91 19*

The interior of Nikolaikirche

tower, added in 1790 by Carl Gotthard Langhans. The font (1437) and the fresco *Dance of the Dead* (1485) are among the church's oldest treasures. The richly ornamented Baroque pulpit was created by Andreas Schlüter in 1703. ⊗ *Karl-Liebknecht-Str. 8 • Map J6 • 10am–6pm Mon–Sat, noon–6pm Sun; Services 10:30am Sun • Admission charge*

2 St Hedwigs-kathedrale

Berlin's largest Catholic church was commissioned by Frederick the Great in 1747–73 after his conquest of Silesia *(see pp12–15)*. ⊗ *Bebelplatz • Map K4 • 10am–5pm Mon–Sat, 1–5pm Sun • (030) 203 48 10*

Font in Marienkirche

4 Nikolaikirche

Berlin's oldest sacred building, the Church of St Nicholas was built in 1230, in the Nikolaiviertel. The present church, with its red-brick twin towers, dates from around 1300. It is particularly famous for the portal on the west wall of the main nave, created by Andreas Schlüter. It is adorned with a gilded relief depicting a goldsmith and his wife. The church was rebuilt in 1987 and completely restored in 2009. ⊗ *Nikolaikirchplatz • Map K6 • 10am–6pm Tue–Sun*

3 Marienkirche

Work started in 1270 on the Church of St Mary, which nestles at the foot of the Fernsehturm. Gothic and Baroque in style, it has an impressive Neo-Gothic

Neue Synagoge – Centrum Judaicum: **www.cjudaicum.de**

Kaiser-Wilhelm-Gedächtnis-Kirche

A landmark in West Berlin, the Kaiser Wilhelm Memorial Church successfully combines modern architecture with the ruins of the church tower (see pp26–7).

Neue Synagoge

Berlin's largest synagogue, built originally in 1859–66, was demolished in World War II but completely reconstructed in 1988–95. Its magnificent dome is visible from afar (see p123).
Ⓢ Oranienburger Str. 29–30 • Map G3, J4 • (030) 88 02 83 00 • Admission charge

Dome of the Neue Synagoge

Friedrichswerdersche Kirche

This small brick church was built by Karl Friedrich Schinkel in 1824–30, in the Neo-Gothic style. Originally it was meant to serve the German and French communities of the Friedrichswerder district. Today, the Schinkel Museum is based here.
Ⓢ Werderscher Markt

The nave of Friedrichswerdersche Kirche

Synagoge Rykestraße

The small synagogue looks the same today as when it was originally built over 100 years ago (see p141).

Christi-Auferstehungs-Kirche

The only Russian-Orthodox church in Berlin, the Church of Christ's Ascension is known for its green onion domes.

Services are still held in Russian, following Orthodox rituals.
Ⓢ Hohenzollerndamm 166 • Map B6 • Only during service 10am & 6pm Sat, 10am Sun

Französischer Dom

At 66 m (216 ft) high, this Baroque tower, which dates back to 1701–5, is a magnificent ornamental structure for the church serving Berlin's Huguenot community. Ⓢ Gendarmenmarkt 5 • Map L4 • noon–5pm Tue–Sun • (030) 20 64 99 22

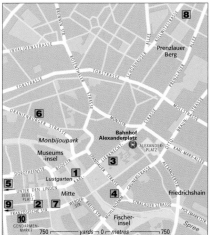

For more on Berlin's historic architecture see pp38–9

45

Left **Detail from the Pergamon Altar frieze** Right **Tapestry in the Kunstgewerbemuseum**

⁰10 Museums

1 Pergamonmuseum
This impressive museum is a vast treasure trove of antiquities *(see pp20–23)*.

2 Ägyptisches Museum
The star exhibit in the Egyptian Museum, part of the Neues Museum, is the beautiful bust of Nefertiti, wife of Akhenaton. The long-necked limestone bust, discovered in 1912, was copied all over ancient Egypt. Also worth seeing is the "Berlin Green Head", a small bust from the 4th century BC. The

Bust of Nefertiti

museum also holds numerous mummies, sarcophagi, murals and sculptures.
§ *Museumsinsel, Bodestr. 1 • Map K5 • 10am–6pm daily, until 10pm Thu • (030) 266 424 242 • Admission charge*

3 Deutsches Historisches Museum
Germany's largest history museum uses unique exhibits, documents and films to take

The Jewish Museum

the visitor on a journey through German history, from the Middle Ages to the present day. Special exhibitions are devoted to particular themes *(see pp12–15)*.

4 Dahlem Museums
These three museums are a fantastic resource of exotic and historic European cultures. The Museum of Ethnology is devoted to the cultures of the Pacific, North and South America and Africa. The Museum of Asian Art has exquisite collections from China, Japan, India and Southeast Asia. The Museum of European Cultures explores everyday life within Europe's cultural and historical contexts. Its collections will eventually move to the Humboldt-Forum *(see p89)*.

5 Jüdisches Museum
The Jewish Museum, housed in a spectacular building designed by Daniel Libeskind, documents the German–Jewish relationship through the centuries. There are special exhibitions on the influence of Berlin Jews on the town's cultural life, and on the life of the Enlightenment philosopher Moses Mendelssohn. An empty room commemorates the loss of Jewish culture. There is also an exciting programme of special events *(see p103)*.

Brachiosaurus in the Natural History Museum

6 Deutsches Technikmuseum

The fascinating Museum of Technology, on the site of a former station, has fascinating hands-on displays on the history of technology *(see p103)*.

7 Kunstgewerbemuseum

European crafts from over five centuries are on display at this museum. Its most valuable exhibits are the treasure of the Guelphs from Braunschweig and the silver treasure of the town council in Lüneburg. The museum also holds valuable Italian tin-glazed earthenware, Renaissance faïence and German Baroque glass and ceramics. Popular displays show Neo-Classical porcelain and furniture, Jugendstil art and Tiffany vases, as well as 20th-century designs. The museum is closed for renovation until 2012. ◈ Matthäikirchplatz • Map L1/2 • 10am–6pm Tue–Fri, 11am–6pm Sat & Sun • (030) 266 29 02 • Admission charge

Harlequin Group, c.1740, in the Kunstgewerbemuseum

8 Museum für Naturkunde

With over 60 million exhibits, the Natural History Museum is one of the largest of its kind. One of the star features is the world's largest dinosaur skeleton, a brachiosaurus found in Tanzania in 1909. There are six more dinosaur skeletons as well as many fossils of mussels, birds and mammals. Together, they take the visitor back to prehistoric times. It is also worth making a visit to the glittering exhibition of meteorites and minerals. ◈ Invalidenstr. 43 • Map F2 • 9:30am–6pm Tue–Fri, 10am–6pm Sat & Sun • (030) 20 93 85 91 • Admission charge

9 Haus am Checkpoint Charlie

The museum at the former Allied checkpoint documents events at the Berlin Wall *(see p103)*.

10 Musikinstrumenten-museum

Some 750 musical instruments can be heard in this museum, including such famous ones as Frederick the Great's harpsichord. Don't miss the silent-film organ which still works (first Sat in the month, noon). ◈ Ben-Gurion-Str. 1 • Map L2 • 9am–5pm Tue–Fri, until 10pm Thu, 10am–5pm Sat & Sun • Admission charge

Left *The Adoration of the Shepherds* Centre *Cupid Victorious* Right **Hamburger Bahnhof**

🔟 Art Galleries

1 Gemäldegalerie
Berlin's best art museum, the Gemäldegalerie focuses on European art of the 13th to 19th centuries, such as Caravaggio's *Cupid Victorious (above)*, and works by Dürer, Rembrandt and Rubens *(see pp34–5)*.

2 Neue Nationalgalerie
The National Gallery's collection includes modern German art and classics of the 20th century. It often holds spectacular temporary exhibitions. ◈ *Potsdamer Str. 50 • Map E4 • 10am–6pm Tue, Wed & Fri, 10am–10pm Thu, 11am–6pm Sat & Sun • (030) 266 29 51 • Admission charge*

3 Alte Nationalgalerie
The Old National Gallery, built by Friedrich August Stüler in 1866–76 on the Museumsinsel, holds a collection of 19th-century (and mainly German) paintings, including works by Adolf von Menzel, Wilhelm Leibl, Max Liebermann and Arnold Böcklin.

Mao by Warhol, in the Hamburger Bahnhof

The gallery also has sculptures by Schadow, Rauch and Reinhold Begas *(see pp20–21)*. ◈ *Bodestr. 1–3 • Map J5 • 10am–6pm Tue–Sun, until 10pm Thu • (030) 20 90 58 01 • Admission charge*

4 Hamburger Bahnhof
A "museum of the present day", the historic Hamburg Station houses modern paintings, installations and multi-media art. One of its highlights is the Erich Marx Collection, with works by Joseph Beuys. Apart from famous artists like Andy Warhol, Jeff Koons and Robert Rauschenberg, it also owns works by Anselm Kiefer, Sandro Chiao and others. ◈ *Invalidenstr. 50–51 • Map F2 • 10am–6pm Tue–Fri, 11am–8pm Sat, 11am–6pm Sun • (030) 39 78 34 11 • Admission charge*

The Glass of Wine by Jan Vermeer, in Gemäldegalerie

Head of a Faun by Picasso (Berggruen)

Museum Berggruen
Heinz Berggruen, born in Berlin in 1914, emigrated but returned to Berlin in 1996. His collection, including works from Picasso's "blue period", is based in a historic building by Stüler. There is free admission from 2pm to 6pm on Thursdays *(see p28)*.

Bauhaus-Archiv
Few schools have exercised as much influence on 20th-century architecture and design as the Bauhaus, founded in 1919 by Walter Gropius. On show in the museum are furniture, sketches, everyday objects and paintings. ◈ *Klingelhöfer-str. 14 • Map N3 • 10am–5pm Wed–Mon • (030) 254 00 20 • Admission charge*

Deutsche Guggenheim
Sponsored by the Deutsche Bank, the museum hosts temporary exhibitions, often showing modern art from the US *(see p113)*. ◈ *Unter den Linden 13–15 • Map K4 • 10am–8pm daily, till 10pm Thu • Admission charge (free Mon)*

Berlinische Galerie
Huge collections of mostly German, east European and Russian painters, photographers, graphic designers and architects from the 20th century, such as Baselitz, Grosz and Kirchner. ◈ *Alte Jakobstr. 124–128 • Map G4 • 10am–6pm Wed–Mon • (030) 78 90 26 00 • Admission charge*

Bröhan-Museum
A collection of Art-Nouveau and Art-Deco objects from around Europe is on display here. There are also paintings by Berlin artists. ◈ *Schlossstr. 1a • Map B3 • 10am–6pm Tue–Sun • (030) 32 69 06 00 • Adm charge (free 1st Wed of month)*

Art Deco vase in the Bröhan-Museum

Kupferstichkabinett
Prints and calligraphies, including works by Botticelli, Dürer, Rembrandt, Goya, Daumier and the Dutch Old Masters. ◈ *Matthäi-kirchplatz 8 • Map L1 • 10am–6pm Tue–Fri, 11am–6pm Sat & Sun • (030) 266 424 214 • Adm charge*

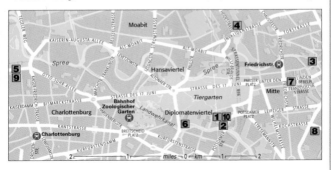

Left **Philosopher G W F Hegel** Centre **The brothers Grimm** Right **Conductor von Karajan**

🔟 **Famous Berliners**

1 Marlene Dietrich

The famous filmstar (1901–92), born in Schöneberg, began her career in Berlin in the 1920s. Her breakthrough came with the film *The Blue Angel* (1931). She lies buried in the Friedenau cemetery in Steglitz. Her personal possessions are exhibited in the Filmmuseum Berlin in the Sony Center on Potsdamer Platz.

2 Albert Einstein

In 1914, the physicist Albert Einstein (1879–1955) became the director of the Kaiser Wilhelm-Institute for Physics. He was awarded the Nobel Prize for Physics in 1921 for his Theory of Relativity, first developed in 1905. Einstein mostly lived and worked in Potsdam, but stayed closely connected with Berlin through his lectures and teaching activity. In 1933 Einstein, who was Jewish, had to emigrate from Germany to the USA where he stayed until his death.

Albert Einstein taught in Berlin

3 Bertolt Brecht

Born in Augsburg, Bavaria, Bertolt Brecht (1898–1956) wrote some of his greatest works,

Brecht's study

such as the *Threepenny Opera,* in a small apartment in Charlottenburg. In the Third Reich, the playwright emigrated to the US, but he returned to Germany after World War II and founded the Berliner Ensemble in East Berlin in 1949. Until his death, Brecht lived in Chausseestraße in Berlin-Mitte, with his wife, Helene Weigel. His renovated apartment has been turned into a museum.

4 Herbert von Karajan

This famous Austrian conductor (1908–1989) was head of the Berlin Philharmonic Orchestra from 1954 until 1989. During this time he helped create the orchestra's unique sound, which remains legendary until this day. Herbert von Karajan was both revered and feared by his musicians because of his genius and his fiery temperament. Berliners still refer to the Philharmonie as "Circus Karajani".

Share your travel recommendations on traveldk.com

5 Robert Koch

Robert Koch

Like few other physicians of his day, Robert Koch (1843–1910) laid the foundations and shaped the face of modern medicine with his pioneering discoveries. The Director of the Institute for Infectious Diseases, Koch also taught and researched at the Charité Hospital. In 1905 he received the Nobel Prize for Medicine for his discoveries in the field of microbiology.

6 Theodor Fontane

A Huguenot, Fontane (1819–98) was one of the most important 19th-century novelists in Germany. He also worked as a journalist for more than 20 years, penning many of his articles and essays in the Café Josty on Potsdamer Platz. Fontane is particularly well known for his *Walks in the Province of Brandenburg*, in which he describes the mentality of the people, historic places and the Brandenburg landscapes.

7 Käthe Kollwitz

The sculptor and painter Käthe Kollwitz (1867–1945) portrayed the social problems of the poor, and her work provides a powerful, haunting commentary on human suffering. Kollwitz spent a large part of her life in a modest abode in the square that is now named after her, in the Prenzlauer Berg district. A monument recalls how she captured the lives of poor Berlin families, burdened with large numbers of children, and of social outcasts. Her *Pieta* now adorns the Neue Wache *(see p13)*.

Sculpture by Kollwitz

8 Jacob and Wilhelm Grimm

The brothers Jacob (1785–1863) and Wilhelm (1786–1859) Grimm are well known around the world, thanks to their collection of classic fairy tales including *Little Red Riding Hood* and *Hansel and Gretel*. Equally important, however, was their linguistic output, the *German Grammar* and *German Dictionary* which are standard reference works even today.

9 Georg Wilhelm Hegel

The influential philosopher Hegel (1770–1831) taught at Humboldt University from 1818 until his death.

10 Felix Mendelssohn Bartholdy

The composer (1809–47), a grandson of Moses Mendelssohn, was also the conductor of the Staatskapelle (state orchestra) at the opera house in Unter den Linden. His grave is found in one of the cemeteries in front of the Hallesches Tor in Kreuzberg.

Felix Mendelssohn Bartholdy

For moments in history in Berlin see pp42–3

Left **Zum Nußbaum** Centre **Bar am Lützowplatz** Right **Tables outside Zwiebelfisch**

🔟 Kneipen (Pubs) & Bars

1 Green Door

This Berlin classic never goes out of style. A young urban crowd enjoys some of the best drinks and cocktails money can buy in Germany, mingling at the minimalist retro-style bar and along the curved, green walls. At weekends, the place is packed to bursting. There's an outdoor bell, but the door policy is pretty liberal as long as you look sober.

Ⓢ *Winterfeldstr. 50 • Map D4/5 • 6pm–3am Sun–Thu, 6pm–4am Fri & Sat • (030) 215 25 15*

2 Newton-Bar

To see and be seen is the name of the game in this elegant venue. Service is charming and the fastest in town, and in summer there's even a fold-down bar on the pavement outside. Heavy leather armchairs make for comfortable sitting, and the walls are adorned with enlarged photographs of nudes by Helmut Newton, after whom the bar is named. Don't miss out on the superb Caribbean and Latin-American cocktails.

Ⓢ *Charlottenstr. 57 • Map L4 • 10am–3am daily • (030) 202 95 40*

Green Door's interior

Berliner Weiße

3 E & M Leydicke

This slightly dated winery is still a big hit with tourists as well as groups of pupils and students. Try the sweetish strawberry and raspberry wines.

Ⓢ *Mansteinstr. 4 • Map E6 • 7pm–1am daily • (030) 216 29 73*

4 Bar am Lützowplatz

The "Lützow-Bar", as this sleek and impressive location is simply called, is a veritable Berlin classic and boasts the city's longest bar counter. The interior is truly astounding and the well-dressed bar staff with their white dinner jackets, as well as the outstanding cocktails they mix, make this a must for any visitor.

Ⓢ *Lützowplatz 7 • Map M6 • 5pm–4am daily • (030) 262 68 07*

5 Victoria Bar

This homely bar, with its understated 1960s-retro ambiance and subdued lighting, is a great place for a relaxing drink and has become a firm favourite among the well-to-do artsy crowd. The cocktails are mixed by the renowned barman Stefan Weber, accompanied by sophisticated lounge music.

Ⓢ *Potsdamer Str. 102 • Map E5 • 6:30pm–4am Fri & Sat, 6:30pm–3am Sun–Thu • (030) 25 75 99 77*

Green Door

Zum Nußbaum
One of only a few traditional pubs in the historic Nikolaiviertel worth checking out, the Nußbaum serves draught beer and traditional Berlin food. ◎ *Am Nußbaum 3 • Map K6 • noon–midnight • (030) 242 30 95*

Zwiebelfisch
A classic of the ageing Charlottenburg scene, where the last survivors of the 1968 student revolt generation come to reminisce. The artists in the photographs on the walls are former patrons. In the summer, there are tables outdoors on Savignyplatz. ◎ *Savignyplatz 7–8 • Map N3 • noon–6am daily • (030) 312 73 63*

Café M
Noisy yet laid back, the Café M Kneipe in Schöneberg is (in) famous. If you find the rock music too loud, try the tables outside. ◎ *Goltzstr. 33 • Map E5 • 8am–late daily (from 9am Sat & Sun) • (030) 216 70 92*

Kumpelnest 3000
A very popular venue in a former brothel, complete with chintz wallpaper. They serve a delicious Caipirinha as well as other cocktails, but for most of the clientele its real attraction is as a great place for people-watching. ◎ *Lützowatr. 23 • Map E5 • 7pm–5am daily • (030) 261 69 18*

Vienna Bar
Adjoining the well-known Paris Bar restaurant, this has become a big hit with the fancy Charlottenburg crowd. Enjoy the superb cocktails, great German and Austrian wines along with a small selection of Austrian food, while chatting the night away. ◎ *Kantstr. 152 • Map C4 & N3 • 11am–4am daily • (030) 31 01 50 90*

Victoria Bar

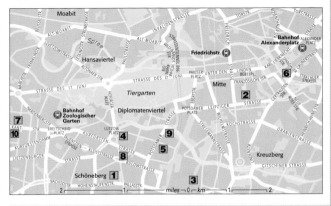

For Berlin bars **see pp54–5**

Left **Clärchen's Ballhaus** Centre **Spindler & Klatt** Right **Felix**

🔟 Bars, Lounges & Clubs

1 Tresor Club
Berlin's first techno club, Tresor Club opened in 1991 in the basement vault-rooms of the former Wertheim department store. Today, this institution is located in a giant former power station, situated over three floors including the +4 Bar, which has views of the old power station ruins. The club continues to deliver the latest in electronic music with a full programme of visiting musicians and DJ sets. ✪ Köpenicker Straße 70 • Map H4 • from midnight Wed, Fri & Sat • (030) 62 90 87 50

40 Seconds

2 40 Seconds
The stunning, sweeping view of the skyline is the defining feature of this classy club, restaurant and bar. Welcoming a hip "in" crowd in their late 20s to mid-30s, 40 Seconds has less attitude than comparable lounges and offers amazingly good, light food and sublime drinks. ✪ Potsdamer Str. 58 • Map E5 • from 11pm Fri & Sat • (030) 89 06 42 41

3 Weekend
This rooftop club with great views of the glittering high-rises on Alexanderplatz is a young, trendy and surprisingly down-to-earth house and electro pop club, frequented by a music-oriented, fashionable twenty-something crowd. ✪ Alexanderstr. 7 • Map H3 & J6 • from 11pm Thu–Sat • (030) 24 63 16 76

4 Felix
The Felix, in the basement of the Adlon, is the jewel in the crown of Berlin's nightlife, welcoming the city's hippest crowd. Getting in is as hard as finding a quiet spot in the stylish dance club, but on special weeknights, quieter jazz programmes are offered. During international events staged in Berlin, the Felix is a sure thing for spotting celebrities. ✪ Behrenstr. 72 • Map F4 & K3 • from 7pm (kitchen until 10:30pm) Thu–Sat • (030) 301 11 71 52

5 Spindler & Klatt
This event space doubles as a regular lounge with restaurant, but it is most famous for special events, mainly dance nights and funky parties. ✪ Köpenicker Str. 16 • from 8pm (kitchen until 1am) Mon–Sat • (030) 69 56 67 75

6 Sage Club
As one of the city's oldest and most successful clubs, the Sage Club (which also hosts the notorious, all-nude Kit Kat Club

Sign up for DK's email newsletter on traveldk.com

events) is a sure bet for a thrilling night out. It has a stylish interior and an impressive state-of-the-art sound system. ❧ *Brückenstraße 1 • Map H4 • from 7pm Thu, from 11pm Sat & Sun (Kit Kat Club) • (030) 278 98 30*

Ice-cold Mojito cocktail

7 Cookies

After several moves, Cookies has finally found its perfect home in the basement of the elegant Westin Grand Hotel, which is now the permanent location for a die-hard clubbing scene encompassing house, techno, hip-hop and indie styles. ❧ *Westin Grand Hotel, Friedrichstr./ Unter den Linden • Map F3 & K4 • from 7pm Tue & Thu • (030) 27 49 29 40*

8 Sophienclub

This is one of the oldest of the East Berlin clubs. The Sophienclub is tucked away right next to the Hackesche Höfe complex *(see p123)* and attracts an enthusiastic, alternative rock and pop crowd, as well as being popular with students. It is

undoubtedly one of the liveliest and often most packed clubs in the city. ❧ *Rosenthaler Str. 40 • Map G3 & J5 • from 10pm Tue–Sat • (030) 282 45 52*

9 Clärchen's Ballhaus

The Ballhaus is the last survivor of the 1920s "Tanzcafés" where classic society dances are still fashionable. Despite its rustic interior and its many long-time, mostly working-class clientele, the Ballhaus also attracts a younger hip crowd who enjoy the quirky atmosphere and old-fashioned hits. ❧ *Auguststr. 24 • Map G2 • from noon daily • (030) 282 92 95*

10 Watergate

Located on the river Spree with beautiful views of the illuminated Warschauer Brücke, the Watergate, with its stunning LED dance floor, is one of Berlin's cutting-edge clubs, featuring the latest in house, techno and drum 'n' bass styles. ❧ *Falckensteinstr. 49 • from midnight Wed, Fri & Sat • (030) 61 28 03 95*

Watergate

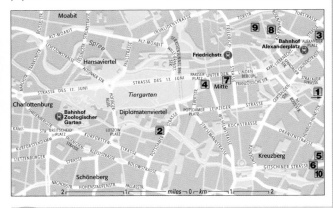

For pubs see pp52–3

Left **Deutsches Theater** Centre **Friedrichstadtpalast** Right **Theatre performance**

🔟 Performing Arts Venues

1 Staatsoper Unter den Linden

Both the theatre troupe and the orchestra of the venerable Berlin Opera enjoy top reputations. Nowhere else can you see so many top stars of classical music. During refurbishment (until 2013), performances will take place at Schillertheater, Bismarckstr. 110. ✆ (030) 20 35 45 55

The Berlin Philharmonic Orchestra

2 Philharmonie

Germany's "temple" of classical music still presents the best performers in the world. Designed by Scharoun, the concert hall has unique acoustics, much appreciated by artists and audience alike. Concerts by the Berlin Philharmonic Orchestra are very popular and are often sold out for weeks ahead *(see pp32–5)*. ✆ Herbert-von-Karajan-Str. 1 • Map L2 • Box Office: 3–6pm Mon–Fri, 11am–2pm Sat & Sun • (030) 25 48 89 99

3 Deutsche Oper

Berlin's most modern opera house, with its elegant retro-design, was built in 1961 on the site of the former Deutsches Opernhaus, which was destroyed during World War II. The controversial 88 slabs of washed-out concrete, chosen by Architect Fritz Bornemann for the main façade, replaced the classic columned portico that once stood here and led critics to accuse the building of lacking artistic formation. Opera, ballet and concerts are held here along with an extensive children's programme. ✆ Bismarckstrasse 35 • Map B4/M2 • (030) 34 38 43 43

4 Chamäleon-Varieté

The lack of technology is more than made up for with much wit and ingenuity by the small, alternative Chamäleon stage. If you are seated in the front row, you are likely to get pulled onto the stage. ✆ Rosenthaler Str. 40–1, Hackesche Höfe • Map J5 • 8pm Tue–Fri, 7pm, 10pm Sat, 7pm Sun • (030) 40 00 59 30

5 Bar jeder Vernunft

This venue, whose name means "devoid of all reason", is Berlin's most popular comedy theatre. The cabaret offers a humorous and, at times, romantic programme of songs and *chansons*, reviews, cabaret, slapstick and comedy, all under the roof of an amazing mirror tent dating from the 1920s. Many stars of the international and German cabaret scene can be seen regularly among the performers here: for example Tim Fischer, Georgette Dee, the Pfister Sisters and Gayle Tufts, as well as older stars such as Otto

Sander. 🚫 *Schaperstr. 24 (car park Freie
Volksbühne)* • *Map C5* • *Box office open
noon–7pm Mon–Sat, 3–7pm Sun & hols*
• *(030) 883 15 82*

Theater des Westens

Inside the mirror tent: Bar jeder Vernunft

Deutsches Theater
Performances at the
German Theatre, one of the
best German-language venues,
include mainly classic plays in
the tradition of Max Reinhardt.
Experimental theatre by young
playwrights is performed at the
DT Baracke. 🚫 *Schumannstr. 13* • *Map
J3* • *7:30pm daily* • *(030) 28 44 12 25*

Theater des Westens
In addition to producing its
own shows, such as *La Cage
aux Folles*, this theatre also
shows guest productions such
as *Les Misérables* and *Hair*.
🚫 *Kantstr. 12* • *Map N4* • *7:30pm
Tue–Fri, 2:30pm & 7:30pm Sat & Sun*
• *(01805) 44 44*

Friedrichstadtpalast
The long-legged dancers in
Friedrichstadtpalast are as popular
today as they were in the 1920s
in their legendary former venue,
which was damaged during World
War II. Long celebrated as the
"world's greatest variety show",
the performances have today
become even more spirited and
entertaining. 🚫 *Friedrichstr. 107* •
Map J4 • *Box office (030) 23 26 23 26*

Hebbel am Ufer
The Hebbel am Ufer theater
has attained cult status in Berlin,
thanks to its modern and varied
programme of concerts, dance
and song. Top performers from
around the world appear here.
🚫 *Halleches Ufer 32* • *Map F5* •
performances daily • *(030) 259 00 40*

Volksbühne
Frank Castorf has trans-
formed this former Socialist
stage into a theatre, which has
become famous for its classy,
and at times controversial
performances. 🚫 *Rosa-Luxemburg-
Platz* • *Map H2* • *(030) 24 06 57 77*

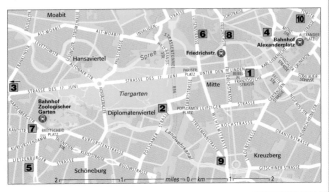

Deutsches Theater: www.deutschestheater.de

Left **Tom's Bar** Centre **Façade of the Connection** Right **The Mann-o-Meter**

🔟 Gay & Lesbian Attractions

Christopher Street Day on Ku'damm

Christopher Street Day
Every summer, Germany's largest gay festival, Christopher Street Day, transforms Berlin into a giant street party, with thousands of gays and lesbians parading from Kurfürstendamm down the Straße des 17. Juni to Siegessäule. At night, the party continues in the city's many gay clubs and Kneipen. ✪ *Kurfürstendamm, Straße des 17. Juni • Map P3/4 • 4th weekend in June*

Siegessäule
Berlin's oldest and best-selling gay magazine is named after the Victory Column, Berlin's landmark. This colourful monthly magazine includes all sorts of useful information, a round-up of what's on, small ads and interviews from the city's gay scene. ✪ *Free in gay cafés and shops*

Siegessäule front covers

Mann-o-Meter
Berlin's best-known advice centre for gays offers help and advice of all kinds. Apart from psychological support in relation to Aids, safe sex and coming out, its counsellors offer help in finding accommodation, give support to those in troubled relationships and provide legal advice. Mann-o-Meter is also a good starting point for gay visitors to Berlin who wish to find out about the gay scene – and, last but not least, the café is also a good place to meet people. ✪ *Bülowstr. 106 • Map E5 • 5–10pm Mon–Fri, 4–10pm Sat & Sun • (030) 216 80 08*

SchwuZ
"SchwuZ" in Kreuzberg is one of the best venues for gay parties in Berlin. At weekends, this is where a young crowd hangs out, dancing, chatting, drinking and enjoying the entertainment. The parties are often themed – details can be found in gay magazines such as *Siegessäule* or *Sergej*. ✪ *Mehringdamm 61 • Map F5 • from 11pm Fri & Sat • (030) 62 90 88 10 • Admission charge*

Tom's Bar
One of the traditional pubs in Berlin, in the centre of the city's gay heart in Motzstraße, Tom's Bar is not for those who are

shy and timid; Tom's Bar is a well-known pick-up joint. Below the (rather dark and dingy) Kneipe is a darkroom. ✆ *Motzstr. 19 • Map D5 • from 10pm daily • (030) 213 45 70*

Inside the Prinz-Eisenherz bookstore

6 Prinz-Eisenherz-Buchhandlung

Germany's oldest openly gay bookstore stocks the entire range of German and international gay and lesbian publications. Its knowledgeable bookshop assistants will track down rare or out-of-stock titles at your request. The bookshop also hosts frequent literary readings. ✆ *Lietzenburger Str. 9A • Map N3 • 10am–8pm Mon–Sat • (030) 313 99 36*

7 Connection

Connection is perhaps not the best, but certainly one of the most popular gay discos in Berlin. Late at night, this is where gays mainly from the scene meet and dance to house and techno rhythms. In the base-ment under the club is a labyrinth of darkrooms. ✆ *Fugger-str. 33 • Map D5 • from 11pm Fri & Sat • (030) 218 14 32 • Admission charge*

8 Café Berio

A long-time favourite among Berlin's scene, the Café Berio is an old-fashioned café that has been turned totally gay. In the summer its terrace is a great place to have breakfast while people watching. ✆ *Maaßenstr. 7 • Map E5 • 8am–1am Fri & Sat, 8am–midnight Sun–Thu • (030) 216 19 46*

9 Schwules Museum

The small Gay Museum is situated in Kreuzberg. It docu-ments, through temporary exhi-bitions, the high and low points of gay and lesbian life since the 19th century. Next to the muse-um is an archive, a small library and a venue for cultural events. ✆ *Mehringdamm 61 • Map F5 • 2–6pm Mon, Wed–Fri, Sun, 2–7pm Sat • (030) 69 59 90 50 • Admission charge*

10 SO 36

This famous – and infamous – dance venue for young gays has been extremely popular for many years. The Sunday night club "Café Fatal" is legendary, when old German chart hits and dance tunes are played. ✆ *Oranienstr. 190 • Map H5 • for current programmes and opening hours check their website • www.so36.de • (030) 61 40 13 06*

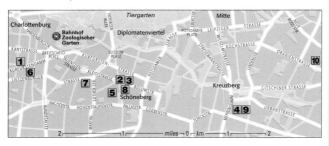

Left **Inside Quartier 206** Centre **Food department Galeries Lafayette** Right **In Winterfeldtplatz**

10 Shops & Markets

1 Kaufhaus des Westens (KaDeWe)

Whatever you are looking for, you will find it here, in Europe's largest tem-

The KaDeWe

ple of consumption. On eight floors, the venerable KaDeWe (department store of the West) offers more than three million products. On its gourmet floor, West Berlin's former "shop window", you can choose from 1,800 cheeses, 1,400 breads and pastries and 2,000 cold meats. The window displays and inner courtyards are also worth a visit in themselves (see also p170).
Ⓢ Tauentzienstr. 21–24 • Map D4, P5 • (030) 212 10 • 10am–8pm Mon–Thu, 10am–9pm Fri, 9:30am–8pm Sat

2 Galeries Lafayette

This small French department store specializes in classic womens- and menswear on one level, and young fashion upstairs. French delicacies are sold in the food department (see also p119).

3 Antik- und Flohmarkt Straße des 17. Juni

Berlin's largest art and antiques market specializes in antique

furnishings and fittings, cutlery and porcelain, books, paintings, clothing and jewellery. The traders are professionals and demand high prices, but in return you are assured of buying something splendid. With its street artists and buskers, the market is an ideal weekend spot for a bit of browsing, dawdling and people-watching (see p85).
Ⓢ Straße des 17. Juni • Map M4 • 10am–5pm Sat & Sun

4 Department Store Quartier 206

This fashion store is one of the most exclusive in town. Here, the man-about-town can purchase his Gucci or DKNY ties, while the lady tries on Versace or Calvin Klein gear on three floors in the Friedrich-stadtpassagen (see p119).
Ⓢ Friedrichstr. 71 • Map L4 • (030) 20 94 62 40 • 10:30am–7:30pm Mon–Fri, 10am–6pm Sat

5 Stilwerk

Style is writ large in this trendy shop. Stilwerk is not a department store, however, but

The famous glass cone at Lafayette

Kaufhaus des Westens: www.kadewe.de

Façade of the Stilwerk shopping centre

a shopping centre, specializing in designer furniture, lamps and fittings – basically anything good and expensive *(see also p85)*.
◈ *Kantstr. 17 • Map C4 • (030) 31 51 50 • 10am–8pm Mon–Fri, 10am–6pm Sat*

Gipsformerei Staatliche Museen

If you fancy a Schinkel statue for your home or an elegant Prussian sculpture from the palace gardens, you'll find moulded plaster reproduction in all shapes and sizes here. ◈ *Sophie-Charlotten-Str. 17–18 • Map A3 • (030) 326 76 90 • 9am–4pm Mon–Fri, till 6pm Wed*

Königliche Porzellan-Manufaktur (KPM)

Prussia's glory and splendour to take away – traditional KPM

porcelain for your dining table at home. Apart from elegant porcelain dinner services, figures and accessories made in the Berlin factory are also on sale.
◈ *Wegelystr. 1 • Map M4 • (030) 39 00 90 • 10am–6pm Mon–Sat*

Markt am Winterfeldtplatz

The trendiest and also the most attractive weekly food and clothing market in Berlin has developed into a hotspot of the Schöneberg crowd. This is the place for meeting up on Saturday mornings *(see p107)*.

Türkenmarkt am Maybachufer

Berlin's largest weekday Turkish market lures visitors with its smells and dishes from *A thousand-and-one-nights*. Bartering is expected *(see p107)*. ◈ *Maybachufer • Map H5 • noon–6:30pm Tue–Fri*

Berliner Antik- und Flohmarkt

Numerous antique and junk shops are hidden underneath the S-Bahn arches at Friedrichstraße Station. Much of it is overpriced, but occasionally you will find a bargain. ◈ *Friedrichstr., S-Bahn arches • Map J4 • (030) 208 26 45 • 11am–6pm Wed–Mon*

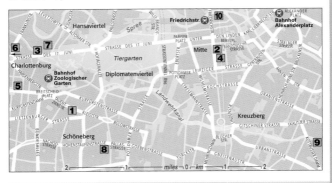

Left **Popkomm** Centre **Christopher Street Day Parade** Right **The Berlin Marathon**

🔟 Festivals & Fairs

1 Berliner Filmfestspiele
The Berlinale is the only top German film festival, and is attended by Hollywood stars and German starlets alike. Until 1999, the film festival took place all around the Zoo-Palast cinema; today the traditional festival draws thousands of cinema fans to the area around Potsdamer Platz. *Filmhaus Potsdamer Platz • Map L2 • 2nd and 3rd week in February • www.berlinale.de*

Zoo-Palast cinema during the Berlinale

2 Internationale Funkausstellung (IFA)
The latest in entertainment technology and high-tech toys are on show at the IFA (International Broadcasting Exhibition) in the ICC. *Messe Berlin, ICC • Map A5 • (030) 303 80 • every year in Aug or early Sep • Admission charge*

3 Popkomm
As one of Europe's biggest music and entertainment trade shows, the trendy Popkomm attracts top acts and thousands of music fans for its mix of concerts, talks and parties at the Messe and in clubs around the city. *Messe Berlin • Map A5 • (030) 30 38 30 09 • mid- to late September*

4 Christopher-Street-Parade
This gay parade celebrates alternative lifestyles. Up to 500,000 gays and lesbians from around the world boisterously dance, drink and celebrate in the streets of Central Berlin *(see also p58)*. *Kurfürstendamm and Straße des 17. Juni • Map P3/4 • (030) 23 62 86 32 • 3rd or 4th weekend in June*

5 Berliner Festspiele
See a variety of classical concerts, exhibitions, theatrical performances, jazz and literature, all organized around a particular theme. *Various venues • throughout the year • www.berlinerfestspiele.de*

6 Lange Nacht der Museen
For one night, one ticket gives access to all the city's museums until well after midnight. Many institutions also put on special events, and street artists and

IFA and Grüne Woche at the Messe

Karneval der Kulturen

sellers entertain the public, who normally wait in long queues.
* Berlin museums • (030) 24 74 98 88
• last weekend in January or August
• www.lange-nacht-der-museen.de

Grüne Woche
The largest gourmet feast in the world, Green Week is a tasty agricultural and gastronomical fair for everyone. Nowhere else can you enjoy a culinary journey around the world in such a condensed space.
* Messe Berlin, ICC • Map A5
• (030) 303 80 • 2nd half of January
• Admission charge

Fashion Week
Top designers and local talent present their new collections. * Various venues • Jan/ Feb & Jul • www.fashion-week-berlin. com/en/ • Admission charge

Karneval der Kulturen
Multicultural Berlin cele-brates for three days in the colourful Kreuzberg district in a cheerful street carnival parade.
* Kreuzberg • Map G/H5/6 • Whitsun

Internationale Tourismusbörse (ITB)
The world's largest tourism fair offers up-to-date information to the general public, often at elaborately designed stalls. The night-time shows put on by many of the exhibiting countries are especially popular.
* Messe Berlin • Map A5 • (030) 303 80
• March • Admission charge

Sports Highlights

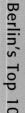

Berlin-Marathon
The most exuberant marathon in the world attracts thousands of runners.
* Straße des 17. Juni • 2nd or 3rd Sunday in September

Berlin Parade
Inline-skaters from around the world meet for "blading". * Straße des 17. Juni • www. berlinparade.com

Sechstagerennen
The Six Day Race is one of Berlin's most venerable sports events. * Velodrom
• 1st half of January

German Open
Top-quality ladies' tennis, usually sold out.
* Tennisclub Rot-Weiß • May

Berliner Neujahrslauf
The New Year's Day Run is a race for those who are fit and not afraid of the cold.
* Brandenburger Tor • Map K3
• 1st January

Internationales Stadionfest (ISTAF)
The biggest athletics festival in Germany. * Olympiastadion
• 1st or 2nd Sun in June

DFB-Pokalfinale
German's soccer Cup Final is played to a crowd of 76,000 fans every year.
* Olympiastadion

Deutsches Traberderby
The derby for professional trotter races. * Trabrennbahn Mariendorf • 1st week in August

Beach Volleyball World Tour
Volleyball Grand Slam tournament. * Hauptbahnhof
• one week in June

Berliner Motorradtage
The international meeting of bikers is a noisy event.
* Kurfürstendamm • end March

Left **Filmpark Babelsberg** Centre **Roller-skating in Berlin** Right **Deutsches Technikmuseum**

⁊⁄₁₀ Children's Attractions

1 Deutsches Technikmuseum

The technology museum is a giant playground for children, excellent for learning through play. There are locomotives to clamber over, windmills to play with and the exhibition "Spektrum", where older children can conduct their own physics and chemistry experiments *(see p103)*.

2 Labyrinth Kindermuseum

Berlin's Museum for Children is particularly suitable for children at the preschool stage and in the early school years. Three or four themed exhibitions each year deal with subjects in a child-friendly and entertaining way – for example "Snoops and Detectives". Every exhibition is interactive, allowing children to join in and experiment, becoming independent through their experiences in play. ✎ *Osloer Str. 12 • 1–6pm Tue–Fri, 1–6pm Sat, 11am–6pm Sun • (030) 800 931 150 • Admission charge*

3 Grips-Theater

This famous Berlin theatre for children and young people has been showing the hit musical *Linie 1* since 1986. The play, which is best suited to older children and adolescents, tells of the exciting life in the big city, using a U-Bahn line running from Kreuzberg to the Ku'damm as a metaphor. All shows are in German. ✎ *Altonaer Str. 22 • Map D3 • Phone for performance times • (030) 397 47 40 • Admission charge*

4 Museum für Naturkunde

Berlin's museum of natural history has the biggest dinosaur skeleton on show anywhere in the world. The collections here are well presented *(see p47)*.

5 Zoologischer Garten

If you are visiting Berlin with children you should not miss out on the Zoo. Particular favourites are the Monkey House (with baby gorillas and chimpanzees) and the Baby Zoo, where children are allowed to touch and feed the young of various animal species *(see pp36–7)*.

Giraffe House in the Zoo

6 Filmpark Babelsberg

Exciting shoot-outs, a walk-on film set with a U-boat, a town on an island and a small town in the Wild West are the most popular attractions at the film park – and not just with the children. A tour of the former UFA-Film studios lets visitors look behind the scenes: children try out make-up and costumes and admire the "sandman", a TV figure popular with children in East Germany since 1959. Everywhere in the

Share your travel recommendations on traveldk.com

park you will encounter props and figures from well-known German films. "Special effects" are demonstrated on the visitors in an imaginative exhibition. The "World of Horror" chills more than just children's spines. ⊗ Großbeerenstr., Potsdam • Mar–Nov: 10am–6pm daily; Jul–Aug: 10am–8pm daily. Closed Mon–Fri in Sep • (0331) 721 27 50 • Admission charge

The Sandman in Filmpark Babelsberg

7 ZEISS-Großraum-planetarium
Artificial stars, planets and nebulae take you to far-away galaxies under the silvery dome of the Planetarium *(see p142)*.

8 Legoland
This is the world's first indoor Legoland. Apart from the rides (best for children under 8), thousands of LEGO bricks can be turned into replicas of Berlin sights. There is also a 4D cinema and a café. ⊗ Potsdamer Str. 4 • Map L2 • 10am–7pm daily (last admission 5pm) • (030) 301 04 00 • Admission charge

9 Puppentheater-museum
The small but excellent and inspirational Puppet Museum specializes in dolls and puppets. Children are allowed to perform their own puppet shows and have a go at being puppet theatre directors. ⊗ Karl-Marx-Str. 135 • Map H6 • 9am–4pm Mon–Fri, 11am–4:30pm Sun • (030) 687 81 32 • Admission charge

10 AquaDom and Sea Life Berlin
In the Sea Life centre, visitors are invited on a journey from the Spree River and Lake Wannsee to the depths of the oceans. A mirror maze and fish feeding sessions add to the fun along the way. The biggest attraction awaits at the end of the journey – a lift ride up through the centre of the AquaDom – the world's largest cylindrical aquarium with over 1,500 tropical fish. ⊗ Spandauer Str. 3 • Map K5 • 10am–7pm daily (last admission 6pm) • (01805) 66 69 01 01 • www.sealife europe.com • Admission charge

Giant AquaDom aquarium

For more on sports & leisure in Berlin see pp68–9

Left **Neuer See** Centre **Landwehrkanal** Right **Pleasure boat on Wannsee**

Lakes, Rivers & Canals

Großer Wannsee
Wannsee has long been a popular destination for Berliners, and it is well worth visiting Strandbad Wannsee. Europe's largest inland beach, it attracts some 40,000 visitors a day who sunbathe on its beautifully white, artificial beach and swim in the lake. This is also a great place for people-watching, and in the summer you will see yachts, wind surfers and jet skis. In the middle of the large lake is Pfaueninsel (Peacock Island), which can be reached by ferry.
◈ Am Großen Wannsee

Teufelssee
The dark green waters of the Devils' Lake may conjure up evil, yet this is actually one of Berlin's cleanest lakes. It is also one of the most relaxed and easy-going places – nudists, gay Berliners and dog lovers enjoy peace and tranquillity on the reed-covered banks in the middle of the Grunewald woods.
◈ Teufelsberg, Grunewald

Großer Müggelsee
Covering 766ha (1,900 acres), Berlin's largest lake, situated in the far southeast of the city, is up to 8 metres (26 feet) deep. Berliners have nicknamed it the "large bathtub" – a good description, for thousands of Berliners congregate here in the heat of summer for a refreshing dip. You can also row, sail or surf on the lake (see p146).

Schlachtensee
After Wannsee, Schlachtensee is the second most popular lake in Berlin. The small, elongated lake attracts mainly young people. To avoid the crowds on the sunbathing lawn right next to Schlachtensee S-Bahn station, just follow the embankment path around to the right. There you will find many small and slightly concealed green spaces perfect for sunseekers. The best time to go is during the week.
◈ Am Schlachtensee

Spree River
One of Berlin's many epithets is that of "Athens on the Spree", so named because of its cultural heritage and the slowly meandering river. In total, the Spree measures 398 km (249 miles), of which 46 km (29 miles) run through Berlin. Its banks are attractive for rest and recreation, and guided boat tours, romantic evening cruises and walks along the riverside are pleasant ways to spend the day.
◈ Mitte, Tiergarten • Map J/K 1–6

Boat trip to the Spree bend

Houseboats on Landwehrkanal

Lietzensee

6 The Bohemian population of Charlottenburg considers this their "local lake". It is not suitable for swimming, but idyllic meadows around the lake are ideally suited for sunbathing and snoozing. The shaded lakeside walks in the middle of the city are also popular with dog owners. In the evening, the few cafés on the east side offer a great view of the illuminated Funkturm.
◈ Am Kaiserdamm • Map A4

Krumme Lanke

7 Although Krumme Lanke is commonly thought not to be clean enough for bathing, some people now think otherwise. In fact, it seems cleaner (though also colder) than the water in Schlachtensee.
◈ Am Fischerhüttenweg

Landwehrkanal

8 Built in 1845–50, this is Berlin's oldest artificial waterway. The canal connects the Upper and the Lower Spree, running east to west through the western part of the centre. Take a boat trip along the canal and you will see some of Berlin's most attractive bridges. At some places, it is possible to lie on the green banks of the canal in the middle of the city, for example at the Paul-Lincke-Ufer in Kreuzberg.
◈ Lützowplatz • Map M/N5

Tegeler See

9 The northernmost lake in Berlin is situated in an elegant residential area. A particularly attractive

walk is Greenwich Promenade, from Tegeler Hafen (harbour) to Schwarzer Weg. A small, slightly hidden lakeside path leads from here to the other side of the lake and to a peninsula. Here stands the Villa Borsig, built in 1905 for a family of industrialists. Today it is owned by a foundation and is closed to the public. If you continue southward along Schwarzer Weg, you will get to the Tegeler See lido. ◈ Alt-Tegel

Ship's bell

Neuer See

10 Visitors will be surprised to discover the tranquil New Lake in the middle of the city, well hidden at the western end of the vast Großer Tiergarten park. On its banks is the Café am Neuen See *(see p101).* A boat trip or a walk around the lake is a pleasant way to while away an afternoon.
◈ Großer Tiergarten • Map M3

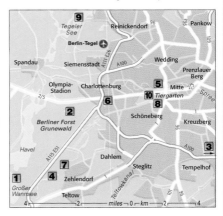

For parks and gardens in Berlin see pp70–71

Left **Inline-Skating in the Tiergarten** Centre **Trabrennbahn Mariendorf** Right **At Sport Oase**

Sport & Fitness Venues

Olympiastadion
The Olympic Stadium is worth a visit even if no particular sports events are scheduled. The giant edifice, constructed by Werner Mach for the Olympic Games in 1936, reflects the architectural style typical of the Nazi period. Two statues by Arno Breker flank the main entrance. Opposite the 80,000-seater stadium are the Maifeld, inspired by the architecture of ancient Rome, and a belltower from where you have fantastic views of Berlin. The stadium itself was renovated and partially covered in 2000–4. Berlin's premier-league football club, Hertha BSC, plays its home games here. An exhibition documents the history of the stadium *(see p84)*.

Hertha BSC playing in the Olympiastadion

Galopprennbahn Hoppegarten
Horse races take place against the historical backdrop of the Union Club 1867's traditional race track, considered to be the most attractive track between Moscow and Paris. In the audience, horse- and betting-mad Berliners mingle with the city's upper classes. *Goetheallee 1, Dahlwitz-Hoppegarten • races 2pm selected Sat & Sun • (03342) 389 30 • www.hoppegarten.com*

Trabrennbahn Mariendorf
Exciting trotting races such as the annual derby for the "Blue Ribbon" take place on the Trabrennbahn in Mariendorf. *Mariendorfer Damm 222 • races 6pm Mon & Fri, 1pm Sun • (030) 740 12 12*

Velodrom
This futuristic, silvery sports arena is the focal point for Berlin's cyclists. Every year in January, this is where the legendary Sechstagerennen (Six Day Race) takes place. *Paul-Heyse-Str. 26 • times vary depending on event • (030) 44 30 44 30*

Cycling
The large green spaces in Berlin and Potsdam are ideal for cycling excursions. Districts such as the Scheunenviertel or Dahlem are also well suited for exploration by bike. There are several places where you can hire a bicycle – for example, in the centre at Friedrichstraße station *(see p162)*.

Interior of the Neukölln swimming baths

Stadtbad Neukölln

The most attractive swimming baths in Berlin date back to the late 19th century. These luxuriously fitted Art-Nouveau baths make swimming a rather special experience. ⊙ *Ganghoferstr. 3 • 2–5pm Mon, 6:45–8am, 2–10pm Tue & Thu, 6:45–8am, 5–6:30pm Wed (also 2–5pm women only), 6:45–8am, 10am–10pm Fri; 8am–10pm Sat & Sun • Closed in summer • (030) 68 24 98 12*

Sport Oase

This charming badminton and squash centre is based in a former Schultheiss brewery. It has four halls with 23 courts on several levels; and there is also a bar. ⊙ *Stromstr. 11–17 • Map D3 • 8am–11pm Mon–Thu, 8am–10pm Fri, 10am–8pm Sat, 9am–10pm Sun • (030) 390 66 20*

Fitness First

In the western centre of the city, this gym for women guarantees a relaxed and cheerful atmosphere for exercise on standard equipment as well as many specialist classes. The staff are very helpful. ⊙ *Tauentzienstr. 13a • Map P5 • 7am–11pm Mon–Fri, 10am–8pm Sat & Sun • (030) 21 45 94 42*

Inline-Skating Tiergarten

The paths and tracks in the northern half of the Großer Tiergarten park, as well as around the perimeters of Straße des 17 Juni, are excellent for inline-skating away from the traffic. Skating in the busy city streets – though practised – is officially forbidden. ⊙ *Tiergarten • Map M5/6*

Aspria

Berlin's premier health and wellness club offers everything from a full-sized swimming pool and sauna to a beauty salon, a health-orientated restaurant, massages, and a rooftop relaxation area. ⊙ *Karlsruher Str. 20 • 6am–11pm Mon–Fri, 8am–10pm Sat & Sun • (030) 89 06 88 80 • Admission charge*

Yoga at Aspria

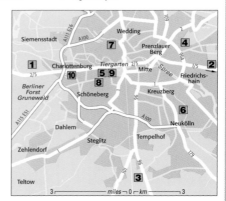

miles 0 *km* 3

(Map: Siemensstadt, Wedding, Charlottenburg, Tiergarten, Prenzlauer Berg, Mitte, Friedrichshain, Berliner Forst Grunewald, Schöneberg, Kreuzberg, Dahlem, Neukölln, Steglitz, Tempelhof, Zehlendorf, Teltow)

Left **Britzer Schloss and Park** Centre **Neuer See** Right **Schlosspark Charlottenburg**

🔟 Parks & Gardens

1 Großer Tiergarten

Tiergarten – the green lungs of Berlin – is the most famous park in the city. It covers an area of 203 ha (500 acres) and is situated right in the centre of town. Originally designed, in 1833–40, by Peter Joseph Lenné as a hunting estate for the Elector, in the latter half of the 19th century the park became a recreation ground for all Berliners. Today it attracts a happy crowd of cyclists, joggers, sunbathers and Turkish families having barbecues, especially at weekends. 🗺 *Tiergarten • Map M5/6*

2 Schlosspark Charlottenburg

The Palace Park is one of the most attractive and charming green spaces in Germany. Immediately behind Schloss Charlottenburg is a small but magnificent Baroque garden, and beyond this extends a vast park, dating back to the early 19th century. It was landscaped in the English style and boasts artificial lake and river landscapes, small hidden buildings and idyllic shaded groves on the banks of ponds and streams. The park is ideally suited for strolling, and it is also a favourite place for sunseekers *(see also pp28–31)*. 🗺 *Schloss Charlottenburg, Spandauer Damm • Map A/B3 • from sunrise to sunset daily*

3 Grunewald and Teufelsberg

The Grunewald, or "green forest" as the public woods in the southwest of Berlin were known originally, is the least built-up area of woodland in the city. Parts of Grunewald are very quiet and isolated indeed, and there are even wild boar in the woods – which can be a nuisance to people who have gardens in the nearby district of Zehlendorf. Grunewald is excellent for hiking and horse-riding. 🗺 *Grunewald*

Statue of Luise on Pfaueninsel

4 Pfaueninsel

Peacock Island, an island in the middle of Wannsee that can be reached only by ferry, is probably the most romantic spot in Berlin. In the 19th century, the island served as a love nest for King Friedrich Wilhelm II. His charming folly of a palace ruin was in keeping with the tastes of the time. Today dozens of proud peacocks live in the area around the building *(see p89)*.

5 Botanischer Garten

The 19th-century Botanical Garden is a paradise of flowers and plants in the southwest of the city. The vast area with 15 greenhouses was built in the late 19th century around gentle hills and picturesque ponds. In the Great Palm House by Alfred Koerner you can see spectacular orchids and giant Victoria water lilies, reaching a diameter of over 2 m (6 ft). The museum introduces visitors to the world of microbiology. ⌖ *Unter den Eichen 5–10 (garden), Königin-Luise-Str. 6 (museum and garden)* • *9am to sunset daily (garden); 10am–6pm daily (museum)* • *(030) 83 85 01 00* • *Admission charge*

Flowering hibiscus in Botanischer Garten

6 Viktoriapark and Kreuzberg

The old municipal park, originally designed in 1888–94 as a recreation area for local workers, is today one of Berlin's most popular green spaces. The meadows around Kreuzberg, which rises to 30 m (98 ft), are great for sunbathing. On top of the mountain, a monument recalls the Prussian Wars of Liberation (see p105).

7 Volkspark Friedrichshain

The oldest park in Berlin (1840) is an artificial landscape of lakes and meadows and two wooded heaps of rubble, one of which is jokingly called "Mount Klamott", meaning Mount Rubble. There is also a fountain with statues of the most popular fairy tale characters (see p146).

8 Tierpark Friedrichsfelde

This second, larger zoo is situated in the idyllic palace park of Friedrichsfelde. Some 950 animal species live in the park; the elephants are particularly worth seeing (see p147).

9 Treptower Park

The 19th-century landscape garden on the banks of the Spree has become famous for the Soviet Memorial, which stands next to the graves of 5,000 Red Army soldiers (see p146).

10 Britzer Schloss and Park

The Palace in Britz, dating from 1706, has been furnished with historical furniture from the Gründerzeit (after 1871). It is situated in a lovely park. ⌖ *Alt-Britz 73* • *11am–6pm Tue–Sun (palace), 9am to sunset daily (garden)* • *(030) 60 97 92 30* • *Admission charge*

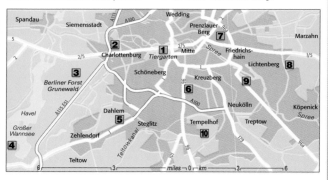

For waterside recreation grounds see pp66–7

Left **Brandenburger Hof** Centre **Inside the Bristol Kempinski** Right **Lobby of the Regent Berlin**

Famous Hotels

Inside the famous Hotel Adlon

1 Hotel Adlon Berlin

Berlin's top hotel ranks as one of the finest in Europe. A reconstruction of the historic Adlon hotel, it opened in 1997 and has become popular with celebrities and politicians from around the globe. Even if you are not going to stay here, you could have a cup of tea or coffee in the magnificent lobby. Ⓢ *Unter den Linden 77 • Map K3 • (030) 226 10 • www.hotel-adlon.de • €€€€€*

2 Regent Berlin

Concealed behind the ultra-modern façade of this hotel is a late 19th-century building with thick carpets, sparkling chandeliers and tasteful wallpaper. Comfort of an international standard and discreet service are guaranteed. Ⓢ *Charlottenstr. 49 • Map K4 • (030) 203 38 • www.theregent berlin.com • €€€€€*

3 Grand Hyatt

Japanese minimalism is the style that was chosen for this modern building on Potsdamer Platz. The spacious rooms overlook the Marlene-Dietrich-Platz, but if this is too mundane for you, you can always enjoy the fantastic views of the entire city from the hotel's Olympus Wellness-Club. Ⓢ *Marlene-Dietrich-Platz 2 • Map F4 • (030) 25 53 12 34 • www.berlin.grand.hyatt.com • €€€€€*

4 Schlosshotel im Grunewald

This small and very expensive palace hotel is situated in a quiet part of Grunewald, some distance from the centre. The hotel is popular with filmstars and celebrities wishing to get away from the crowds. Karl Lagerfeld designed the interior – and for a mere €1,500 you can even rent his permanent bedroom suite. Ⓢ *Brahmsstr. 10 • (030) 89 58 40 • www.schlosshotelberlin.com • €€€€*

5 Kempinski Hotel Bristol Berlin

The grand old lady of West Berlin hotels, the splendid Kempinski is beginning to show her age a little, but the cosmopolitan glamour is still there and no hotel in town is better. All the rooms are furnished with a timeless elegance, while the lobby and bar are panelled in dark wood. In the Kempinski-Grill you can enjoy a glass of Sekt right on the Ku'damm while watching less fortunate mortals. A place where you can be pampered and spoilt *(see p179)*.

Regent Berlin porter

Hackescher Markt

One of Berlin's best hotels, the charming Hackescher Markt, is situated right in the popular Mitte district. Service and furnishings are of a four-star standard, yet the prices are moderate. Best of all is the hotel's central location in one of Berlin's liveliest areas: it is only a few steps away from the Hackesche Höfe and the Scheunenviertel. ⊗ *Große Präsidentenstr. 8 • Map J5 • (030) 28 00 30 • www.loock-hotels.com • €€*

Ritz-Carlton Berlin

The Ritz-Carlton Berlin near Potsdamer Platz is an ultra-luxurious gem hidden behind a modern façade reminiscent of New York's Rockefeller Center. The lobby with its marble columns and tons of gold leaf is a stunning setting for the Curtain Club and the Desbrosses brasserie. Its rooms are sumptuously decorated, all decorated to Prussian Neo-Classical designs – there are even telescopes to enjoy the cityscape. ⊗ *Potsdamer Platz 3 • Map F4 • (030) 33 77 77 • www.ritzcarlton.com • €€€€€€*

Ritz-Carlton Berlin

Sofitel Berlin Gendarmenmarkt

A quiet and elegant hotel with great views over the historic square, the relatively small Sofitel has real style and offers excellent service. All the rooms are first-class and feature elegant furnishings *(see p179)*.

Savoy Hotel

Greta Garbo used to stay at the Savoy, and the style of days gone by is celebrated throughout. Many filmstars are regulars in this hotel, which is justly proud of its service. The Savoy is famous for its Times Bar. ⊗ *Fasanenstr. 9–10 • Map N4 • (030) 31 10 30 • www.hotel-savoy.com • €€€*

Brandenburger Hof

An elegant town hotel, based in a 19th-century manor house. The lobby is traditionally furnished and the rooms are in a sobre Bauhaus-style. The Michelin-starred Quadriga restaurant specializes in French cuisine. ⊗ *Eislebener Str. 14 • Map P4 • (030) 21 40 50 • www. brandenburger-hof.com • €€€€*

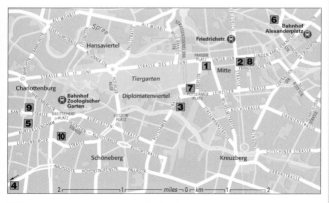

For hotel price categories see p173

Left **Bocca di Bacco** Centre **Outdoor tables at Lutter & Wegner** Right **The popular Vau**

🔟 Best Places to Eat

1 Vau

The best of international and Austrian cooking is served by Kolja Kleeberg at the stylishly designed Vau. The restaurant has been awarded a well-deserved Michelin star. ◉ *Jägerstr. 54–55 • Map L4 • noon–2:30pm, 7–10:30pm Mon–Sat • (030) 202 97 30 • €€€€€–€€€€€€*

2 Vox

The exquisite food in this elegant hotel restaurant is a sleek and modern fusion of Asian and international dishes, with an emphasis on Japanese (sushi) dishes and French-Italian fare. In summer, reserve one of the outside tables. Open for breakfast. ◉ *Marlene-Dietrich-Platz 2 • Map F4 • 6:30–10:30am, 6:30pm–midnight daily; also noon–2:30pm Mon–Fri • (030) 25 53 17 72 • €€€€*

3 Hugo's

The Michelin-starred Hugo's is Berlin's most affable gourmet restaurant, with impeccable service and stunning views of the city. Wood panelling and plush leather set the tone, while the international cuisine reveals the light touch of German chef Thomas Kammeier. The wine list is to die for, and there are private rooms for those who prefer intimate dining. ◉ *Budapester Str. 2 • Map N5 • 6–10:30pm Mon–Sat • (030) 26 02 12 63 • €€€€€*

Inside Hugo's

4 Bocca di Bacco

Berlin's hippest Italian restaurant offers fresh fish and exceptional meat creations such as *Bresaola di Cavallo* (horse meat with salad and nuts). ◉ *Friedrichstr. 167–8 • Map K4 • noon–midnight Mon–Sat, 6pm–midnight Sun • (030) 20 67 28 28 • €€€–€€€€*

5 Borchardt

Everyone of importance, including German chancellors, dines at Borchardt. The historic room is furnished in Wilhelminian style (featuring tall columns, wall mosaics and tile flooring) – an appropriate setting for the classic French cooking served here. Without a reservation, however, even top politicians can't get a table. ◉ *Französische Str. 47 • Map K4 • 11:30am–midnight daily • (030) 81 88 62 62 • €€€€*

6 Weinbar Rutz

This rising star in Berlin's gourmet scene has slowly worked towards its first, well-deserved Michelin star by offering consistently high-quality fish and hearty meat dishes based on local recipes, but served with a creative twist. The Rutz is cosy and informal. The prodigious wine list has over 700 wines. ◉ *Chausseestr. 8 • Map F2 • from 6:30pm Tue–Sat (wine bar from 4pm) • (030) 24 62 87 60 • €€€€–€€€€€*

The super-trendy Borchardt restaurant

Fischers Fritz
7 This high-profile establishment is the only restaurant in Berlin with two Michelin stars. Chef Christian Lohse prepares some of the most spectacular seafood dishes in the country. ⊗ *Hotel Regent Berlin, Charlottenstr. 49 • Map K4 • noon–2pm, 6:30–10:30pm daily • (030) 20 33 63 63 • €€€€*

Facil
8 This Michelin-starred restaurant, in a green oasis on top of the Madison hotel, is a study in understated elegance. Chef Michael Kempf creates stylish Mediterranean dishes with a French accent. ⊗ *Potsdamer Str. 3 • Map L2 • noon–3pm, 7–11pm Mon–Fri • (030) 590 05 12 34 • €€€€–€€€€€*

Lutter & Wegner Gendarmenmarkt
9 In this old building, formerly the Berliner Sektkellerei (supposedly the place where sparkling wine, or *sekt*, was invented), Austrian cuisine is the star. Try the best *Wiener schnitzel* in town, accompanied by a classic warm potato salad, at consistently good prices. In the summer, there are tables outdoors. ⊗ *Charlottenstr. 56 • Map L4 • 11am–3pm daily • (030) 202 95 40 • €€€*

Das Speisezimmer
10 Hidden in the courtyard of an old locomotive factory, this unpretentious restaurant is run by celebrity TV chef Sarah Wiener. The philosophy is "fresh and local", and the light and affordable cuisine mixes influences from Austria and Italy. ⊗ *Chausseestr. 8, 2nd courtyard • Map F2 • noon–11pm Mon–Fri, 6–11pm Sat & Sun • (030) 814 529 430 • no credit cards • €€–€€€*

Vox restaurant

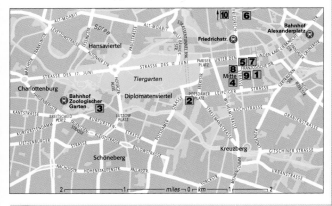

For restaurants in Berlin districts **see pp87, 93, 101, 109, 121**

AROUND TOWN

Charlottenburg &
Spandau
78–87

Grunewald &
Dahlem
88–93

Tiergarten &
Federal District
96–101

Kreuzberg &
Schöneberg
102–109

Central Berlin:
Unter den Linden
112–121

Central Berlin:
Scheunenviertel
122–129

Central Berlin:
Around Alexanderplatz
130–137

Prenzlauer Berg
138–143

Berlin's
Southeast
144–149

Potsdam &
Sanssouci
152–157

BERLIN'S TOP 10

Left **On Savignyplatz** Centre **Front door in Charlottenburg** Right **On Breitscheidplatz**

Charlottenburg & Spandau

SOPHISTICATED CHARLOTTENBURG IS A HAUTE *bourgeoisie enclave and was the only district of Berlin that did not rub shoulders with the Wall. The historical streets off Ku'damm feature small cafés, restaurants, art galleries and boutiques, based in stout residential houses from the beginning of the 20th century. These streets and Charlottenburg's proud town hall remind us that this district was once the richest town in Prussia, which was only incorporated into the city of Berlin in 1920. Spandau, on the other hand, is rural in comparison, a part of Berlin with a special feel. Spandau's Late Medieval old town and the citadel make this district on the other side of the Spree and Havel seem like a small independent town.*

Prussian Eagle in Spandau

🔟 Sights

1	Kurfürstendamm	**6**	Savignyplatz
2	Schloss Charlottenburg	**7**	Fasanenstraße
3	Zoologischer Garten	**8**	Funkturm and Messegelände
4	Zitadelle Spandau	**9**	Newton-Sammlung
5	Spandau Old Town	**10**	Käthe-Kollwitz-Museum

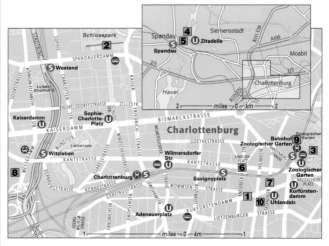

1 Kurfürstendamm

The famous Berlin boulevard, the pride of Charlottenburg, is today a lively and fashionable avenue *(see pp24–5)*.

2 Schloss Charlottenburg

The Baroque and English-style gardens of this Hohenzollern summer residence are ideal for a stroll *(see pp28–31)*.
🔊 *Spandauer Damm • Map A/B3 • opening hours see p28 • (030) 32 09 11 • Admission charge*

Inside Nikolaikirche, Spandau Old Town

3 Zoologischer Garten

This is Germany's oldest and most important zoological garden, combined with an aquarium *(see pp36–7)*.

4 Zitadelle Spandau

The only surviving fortress in Berlin, the citadel, at the confluence of the Havel and Spree Rivers, is strategically well placed. The star-shaped moated fortress, built in 1560 by Francesco Chiaramella da Gandino, was modelled on similar buildings in Italy. Its four powerful corner bastions, named Brandenburg, König (king), Königin (queen) and Kronprinz (crown prince) are especially remarkable. A fortress stood on the same site as early as the 12th century, of which the Juliusturm survives – a keep that served as

Zitadelle Spandau

a prison in the 19th century. At the time, Berliners used to say, "off to the Julio", when they sent criminals to prison. Later the imperial war treasures were kept here – the reparations paid by France to the German Empire after its defeat in the Franco-Prussian War of 1870–71. The Bastion Königin houses a museum of municipal history.
🔊 *Am Juliusturm • 10am–5pm daily • (030) 354 944 200 • Admission charge*

5 Spandau Old Town

When walking around Spandau Old Town, it is easy to forget that you are still in Berlin. Narrow alleyways and nooks and crannies around Nikolaikirche are lined by Late Medieval houses, a sign that Spandau was founded in 1197 and is thus older than Berlin itself. Berlin's oldest house, the Gothic House, dating back to the early 16th century, stands here, in Breite Straße 32.
🔊 *Breite Straße, Spandau*

Spandau and Berlin

West Berliners consider the Spandauers to be rather different sorts of people, provincial and rough, and not "real" Berliners at all. But the Spandauers can reassure themselves that Spandau is 60 years older than Berlin, and proudly point to their independent history. The mutual mistrust is not just a consequence of Spandau's geographical location, isolated from the remainder of the city by the Havel and Spree Rivers. It is also due to the incorporation of Spandau in 1920. Today, still, Spandauers say they are going "to Berlin", even though the centre of the city is only a few stops away on the U-Bahn.

Left **A plaque in Savignyplatz** Centre **Literaturhaus Fasanenstraße** Right **Villa Grisebach**

Savignyplatz

One of Berlin's most attractive squares is right in the heart of Charlottenburg. Savignyplatz, named after a 19th-century German legal scholar, is the focal point of Charlottenburg's reputation as a district for artists and intellectuals and as a trendy residential area for dining out and entertainment. The square has two green spaces, either side of Kantstraße. It was built in the 1920s as part of an effort to create parks in the centre of town. Small paths, benches and pergolas make it a pleasant place for a rest. Dotted all around Savignyplatz are restaurants, street cafés and shops, especially in Grolman-, Knesebeck-, and Carmerstraße, all three of which cross the square. Many a reveller has lost his way here after a night's celebrating, which is why the area is jokingly known as the "Savignydreieck" (the Savigny Triangle). North of Savignyplatz it is worth exploring some of the

Balconies in Savignyplatz

most attractive streets in Charlottenburg – Knesebeck-, Schlüter- and Goethestraße. This is still a thriving Charlottenburg community; the small shops, numerous bookstores, cafés and specialist retailers are always busy, especially on Saturdays. South of the square, the red-tiled S-Bahn arches also lure visitors with their shops, cafés and bars; most of all the Savignypassage near Bleibtreustraße and the small passageway between Grolman- and Uhlandstraße on the opposite side of the square.

🔎 *An der Kantstraße • Map N3*

Fasanenstraße

This elegant street is the most attractive and trendiest street off Ku'damm. Designer shops, galleries and restaurants are tucked away here, a shoppers' paradise for all those who regard Kurfürstendamm as a mere retail strip catering for the masses. The junction of Fasanenstraße and Ku'damm is one of the liveliest spots in Berlin. One of the best known places

The Jewish House, in Fasanenstraße

Statue in Savignyplatz

Around Town – Charlottenburg & Spandau

Kempinski Hotel Bristol Berlin, Fasanenstraße

is the "Bristol Berlin Kempinski" *(see p72)* at the northern end of Fasanenstraße. The Lübbecke & Co bank opposite cleverly combines a historic building with a new structure. Next to it are the Jüdisches Gemeindehaus (Jewish Community House, *see p84*) and a little farther along, at the junction with Kantstraße, is the Kant-Dreieck *(see p41)*. Berliner Börse (stock exchange), based in the ultra-modern Ludwig-Erhard-Haus *(see p40)*, is just above, at the corner of Hardenbergstraße. The southern end of the street is dominated by residential villas, some of which may seem a little pompous, as well as the Literaturhaus, Villa Grisebach, one of the oldest art auction houses in Berlin, and the Käthe-Kollwitz-Museum *(see p83)*. There are also some very expensive fashion stores here, as well as a few cosy restaurants. At its southern end, the street leads to picturesque Fasanenplatz, where many artists lived before 1933.

Ⓢ *Charlottenburg • Map N/P4*

Shops in Fasanenstraße

A Day in Charlottenburg

Morning

Begin your tour of Charlottenburg at Breitscheidplatz and stroll down **Kurfürstendamm** *(see pp24–5)* in a westerly direction. Turn left into **Fasanenstraße** to visit the **Käthe-Kollwitz-Museum** *(see p83)* and to see the **Literaturhaus**. You could stop for a mid-morning breakfast at **Café Wintergarten** *(see p86)* in the Literaturhaus, before going back up Fasanenstraße in a northerly direction. On the left you will pass the **Kempinski Hotel Bristol Berlin**, and on the right you can see the Jewish House and the Ludwig-Erhard-Haus. Diagonally opposite, on the other side of Kantstraße, stands the **Theater des Westens** *(see p57)*. Continue along Kantstraße on the left side until you reach the shopping centre **Stilwerk** *(see p60–61)*, a place no one has ever been known to leave without buying something!

Afternoon

A good place for lunch is the restaurant **Soultrane** in Stilwerk shopping centre. Afterwards, continue along Kantstraße to **Savignyplatz**. Now explore the small streets around the square, Grolman-, Carmer-, Knesebeck- and Mommsenstraße. Small shops invite you to browse and spend your money, and the **Café Savigny** *(see p86)* is a good place for a fruit flan with whipped cream and a cup of coffee. For the early evening, **Dressler** *(see p87)* is recommended, here you will find a range of dishes typical of a real French brasserie.

Ehrenhalle in the Messegelände

8 Funkturm and Messegelände

The 150-m (492-ft) high Funkturm (TV tower), reminiscent of the Eiffel Tower in Paris, is one of the landmarks of Berlin that can be seen from afar. Built in 1924 to plans by Heinrich Straumer, it served as an aerial and as an air-traffic control tower. The viewing platform at 125 m (410 ft) provides magnificent views, while the restaurant, situated at 55 m (180 ft), overlooks the oldest part of the complex, the exhibition centre and the surrounding pavilions. The giant building in the

The History of Charlottenburg

The magnificent Charlottenburger Rathaus (town hall) on Otto-Suhr-Allee is a reminder of the time when this district of 200,000 people was an independent town. Charlottenburg, named after the eponymous palace, arose in 1705 from the medieval settlement of Lietzow. Towards the end of the 19th century, Charlottenburg – then Prussia's wealthiest town – enjoyed a meteoric rise following the construction of the Westend colony of villas and of Kurfürstendamm. Thanks to its numerous theatres, the opera and the Technical University, the district developed into Berlin's west end during the 1920s.

east is the Hall of Honour built to designs by Richard Ermisch in 1936, in the colossal Fascist architectural style.

On the opposite side rises the shiny silver ICC, the International Congress Centrum, built in 1975–9 by Ralf Schüler and Ursulina Schüler-Witte. It is still considered one of the most advanced conference centres in the world, with 80 rooms for more than 5,000 visitors. Berlin's vast exhibition grounds are among the largest in the world, covering an area of 160,000 sq m (40 acres). These play host to, among others, Grüne Woche (green week, an agricultural fair), Internationale Tourismusbörse (international tourism fair) and Internationale Funkausstellung (international TV fair). ◈ *Messedamm 22 • Map A4/5 • 11am–9pm Mon, 10am–11pm Tue–Sun (tower) • (030) 303 80 • Admission charge*

The Berliner Funkturm

9 Newton Sammlung

Helmut Newton (1931–2004), the world-famous

photographer, has finally returned to his home city. This museum presents his private belongings; it also has changing exhibitions that show his early fashion and nude photography as well as photos of the famous, rich and beautiful since 1947. ⊛ *Jebensstr. 2 • Map C4 • 10am–6pm Tue & Wed, 10am–10pm Thu, 10am–6pm Fri–Sun • (030) 31 86 48 56 • Admission charge (free Thu from 6pm)*

Käthe-Kollwitz-Museum

The museum is dedicated to the work of the Berlin artist Käthe Kollwitz (1897–1945), who documented the misery of workers' lives in 1920s Berlin in numerous prints, graphics and sketches. After losing a son and a grandson in World War I, she concentrated on the themes of war and motherhood. The museum holds some 200 of her works, including several self-portraits. ⊛ *Fasanenstr. 24 • Map P4 • 11am–6pm daily • (030) 882 52 10 • Admission charge*

Mother and Child by Käthe Kollwitz

A Day in Spandau

Morning

Start with a journey on the U-Bahn. From the centre of town, take a U2 train in the direction of Ruhleben, and at Bismarckstraße station change to the U7 train in the direction of Rathaus Spandau. Ten minutes later you will have reached the centre of **Spandau Old Town** *(see p79)*, where you can visit Breite Straße and Nikolaikirche.

Before returning to Charlottenburg, visit the **Zitadelle Spandau** *(see p79)*. There, in the museum café, you can also enjoy a late breakfast. Return by U-Bahn. This time, get off the train at the Wilmersdorfer Straße station, one of the few pedestrianized areas in Berlin. This is a particularly good area for shopaholics and bargain hunters.

Afternoon

From Wilmersdorfer Straße a 20-minute walk along Kaiserdamm in a westerly direction will take you to the **Funkturm** and the **Messegelände** with the "Ehrenhalle". You could have lunch at the **Funkturm-Restaurant**, and enjoy the magnificent views. Nearby, the Haus des Rundfunks (broadcasting house) and the **Georg-Kolbe-Museum** *(see p84)* are worth visiting. After your museum visit, if you still have some time and energy, you could take bus M49 from here to the **Olympiastadion** *(see p68)*. In the evening, return to Charlottenburg and Savignyplatz by S75 from S-Olympiastadion. Here you can enjoy the famed Franconian cooking at **Florian** *(see p87)*.

Left **In the Deutsche Oper** Centre **Denkmal Benno Ohnesorg** Right **In the Theater des Westens**

Best of the Rest

1 Olympiastadion
Built for the 1936 Olympic Games, the stadium is an example of Fascist architecture *(see p68)*. ❀ *Olympischer Platz • 9am–7pm daily (Jun–Sep: to 8pm; Nov–Mar: to 4pm) • (030) 30 68 81 00*

2 Georg-Kolbe-Museum
Sculptures by Georg Kolbe (1877–1947) are exhibited in his home and workshop. ❀ *Sensburger Allee 25 • 10am–6pm Tue–Sun • (030) 304 21 44 • Admission charge*

3 Le-Corbusier-Haus
The apartment block where the French architect Corbusier lived was built for the 1957 Interbau trade fair. Designed to alleviate the acute housing shortage after World War II, it was highly innovative in its day. ❀ *Flatowallee 16*

4 Jüdisches Gemeindehaus
Berlin's Jewish community house stands on the site of the Charlottenburg synagogue. Damaged during "Reichskristallnacht" on 9 November 1938, it was mostly destroyed during World War II. Only the portal remains. ❀ *Fasanenstr. 79–80 • Map P4 • 9am–5pm Mon–Thu, 9am–3pm Fri • (030) 88 02 82 06*

5 Theater des Westens
This theatre is based in an attractive building from 1895–6. It is regarded as one of Germany's best musical theatres *(see p57)*. ❀ *Kantstr. 12 • Map N4 • Call for show times • 0180 544 44*

6 Deutsche Oper
The German Opera, opened in 1961, specializes in Italian and German classics. ❀ *Bismarckstr. 34–37 • Map B4 • (030) 34 38 43 43 • Admission charge*

7 Denkmal Benno Ohnesorg
Alfred Hrdlicka's sculpture from 1971 commemorates the student Benno Ohnesorg, who was shot dead here during a demonstration on 2 April 1967. ❀ *Bismarckstr. • Map B4*

8 Technische Universität
Berlin's Technical University was founded in 1879. ❀ *Straße des 17. Juni • Map C4 • 8am–8pm Mon–Fri • (030) 31 40*

9 Universität der Künste
The School of Art is one of the best German universities for the fine arts, architecture and design. ❀ *Hardenbergstr. 32–33 • Map N4 • 8am–6pm Mon–Fri • (030) 318 50*

10 Erotik-Museum
Historic and new erotica. ❀ *Kantstr. 5 • Map N4 • 9am–midnight daily (from 11am Sun) • (030) 886 06 66 • Admission charge (over 18 years only)*

Left **Zille-Hof** Centre **Butter Lindner** Right **Tee Gschwendner**

🔟 Shops & Markets

1 Stilwerk
A shopping centre specializing in stylish designer home furnishings *(see p60)*. ◈ *Kantstr. 17 • Map C4 • (030) 31 51 50*

2 Antik- und Flohmarkt Straße des 17. Juni
Berlin's largest antiques, art and flea market, selling excellent items *(see p60)*. ◈ *Straße des 17. Juni • Map M4 • 10am–5pm Sat & Sun*

3 Peek & Cloppenburg
Offering five floors of men's, women's and children's clothing, this is one of Berlin's most popular department stores. ◈ *Tauentzienstr. 19 • Map P5 • 10am–8pm Mon–Sat • (030) 21 29 00*

4 Hallhuber
This huge upscale clothing store offers the latest designer labels for both men and women (DKNY, Paul Smith and the like) as well as its own less expensive house label. ◈ *Tauentzienstr. 18a • Map P4 • (030) 21 91 32 49*

5 Bücherbogen
Berlin's leading arts and photography bookseller is tucked away within three arches under the S-Bahn viaduct. ◈ *Savignyplatz • Map N3 • (030) 31 86 95 11*

6 Jil Sander
Simple, elegant designer fashions for men and women are for sale at this cool boutique. ◈ *Kurfürstendamm 185 • Map P4 • (030) 886 70 20*

7 Butter Lindner
This traditional Berlin store specializes in fresh, home-made foods and delicatessen. Of its numerous branches, one of the most attractive ones is in Charlottenburg. ◈ *Knesebeckstr. 92 • Map P3 • 8am–6pm Mon–Fri, 8am–1:30pm Sat • (030) 313 53 75*

8 Hellmann Menswear
Ladies' and gentlemen's fashions made from the best materials, including Hellmann's own collection and clothes from well-known designers. ◈ *Kurfürstendamm 53 • Map P3 • 10am–7pm Mon–Fri, 10am–6pm Sat • (030) 882 25 65*

9 Tee Gschwendner
This tiny store is a haven for tea lovers, and upstairs you can try out a new flavour in their own tea room. ◈ *Kurfürstendamm 217 • Map P4 • 10am–8pm Mon–Fri, 10am–6pm Sat • (030) 881 91 81*

10 Zille-Hof
Old Berlin bric-à-brac market, with a vast, if expensive, selection. ◈ *Uhlandstr. 19 • Map P4 • 8am–5:30pm Mon–Fri (to 1pm Sat) • (030) 313 43 33*

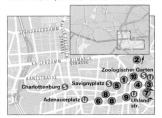

→ *For more on shopping see p170*

Left **Café Wintergarten** Centre **Berliner Kaffeerösterei** Right **Café Filmbühne am Steinplatz**

Cafés

1 Café Wintergarten im Literaturhaus
One of Berlin's most beautiful cafés is based in the conservatory of an old city mansion. In summer guests can sit outside, in the Literaturhaus garden.
◈ *Fasanenstr. 23 • Map P4 • 9:30am–1am daily • (030) 882 54 14*

2 Café Savigny
This gay and lesbian café, with traditional 19th-century interior, has a relaxed atmosphere; the tarts are particularly worth trying. ◈ *Grolmanstr. 53–54 • Map N3 • 9am–1am daily • (030) 32 89 06 61*

3 Einstein Coffeeshop
Probably the most popular outlet of this up-market chain. This revamped café heaves with the rich and beautiful of Charlottenburg. ◈ *Kurfürstendamm 50a (off Ku'damm) • Map P4 • 7:30am–9pm Mon–Fri, 7:30am–8:30pm Sat, 9am–8pm Sun*

4 Berliner Kaffeerösterei
A cosy mix of coffee bar and traditional café, offering coffee beans from around the world, breakfast snacks and cakes. ◈ *Uhlandstraße 173 • Map C5 • 8am–8pm Mon–Fri, 9am–8pm Sat, 10am–6pm Sun • (030) 88 67 79 20*

5 Café Filmbühne am Steinplatz
Other cafés may sell better cakes, but this coffee shop excels thanks to its student atmosphere.
◈ *Hardenbergstr. 12 • Map N3 • 9am–midnight daily • (030) 312 65 89*

6 Café Hardenberg
The Technical University's student café has a great atmosphere and reasonable prices. ◈ *Hardenbergstr. 10 • Map N3 • 9am–1am daily • (030) 312 26 44 • no credit cards*

7 Café Balzac
This is one of several cafés modelled on the US Starbucks chain. ◈ *Hardenbergstr. 11 • Map M3 • 7:30am–7pm Mon–Fri, 9am–6pm Sat, 9:30am–6pm Sun • no credit cards*

8 Café Aedes
This modern café, located in an S-Bahn arch, forms part of an architectural gallery. ◈ *Else-Ury-Bogen/ Savignyplatz • Map N3 • 8am–midnight Mon–Fri, 9am–midnight Sat & Sun • (030) 31 50 95 35*

9 Café Kleine Orangerie
A small garden café at the Charlottenburg Palace. ◈ *Spandauer Damm 20 • Map A3 • 10am–10pm daily (summer) • (030) 322 20 21*

10 Schwarzes Café
Alternative rock café, offering all-day breakfasts. ◈ *Kantstr. 148 • Map N4 • Open around the clock • (030) 313 80 38*

Note: *All restaurants accept credit cards and offer vegetarian dishes unless stated otherwise.*

Price Categories

For a three-course meal for one with half a bottle of wine (or equivalent meal), taxes and charges included

€	under €20
€€	€20–30
€€€	€30–45
€€€€	€45–60
€€€€€	over €60

Left **At Ana e Bruno's** Centre **Kuchi, on Kantstrasse**

🔟 Restaurants

1 Francucci's

A well-kept secret, this popular Tuscan restaurant has excellent pizza, home-made pasta and creative meat and fish dishes. ◎ *Kurfürstendamm 90 • Map B5 • noon–midnight daily • (030) 323 33 18 • €€€*

2 Alt-Luxemburg

Chef Karl Wannemacher (one Michelin star) dishes up good international and German food. ◎ *Windscheidstr. 31 • Map P1 • 5pm–midnight Mon–Sat • (030) 323 87 30 • €€€€*

3 Eiffel

A large but still charming French restaurant with some traditional Berlin dishes and outside tables. ◎ *Kurfürstendamm 105 • Map P1 • 9am–1am daily • (030) 891 13 05 • €€*

4 Lubitsch

A small, elegant restaurant, serving German and Italian "fusion" food. ◎ *Bleibtreustr. 47 • Map N/P3 • 10am–midnight Mon–Sat, 6pm–midnight Sun • (030) 882 37 56 • €€*

5 Florian

Trendy and popular with film lovers; southern German food. ◎ *Grolmanstr. 52 • Map N3 • 6pm–3am daily • (030) 313 91 84 • €€*

6 First Floor

An award-winning gourmet restaurant with German and French food. ◎ *Budapester Str. 45 • Map N5 • noon–3pm, 6:30–11pm Tue–Sat • (030) 25 02 10 20 • €€€€*

7 Dressler

Everything at Dressler's looks, smells and tastes as it would in a real French brasserie. In winter, the game and poultry dishes are well worth trying. ◎ *Kurfürstendamm 207–208 • Map C5 • 8am–1am daily • (030) 883 35 30 • €€€*

8 Austeria

This homely seafood restaurant has an outstanding choice of oysters. ◎ *Kurfürstendamm 184 • Map C5 • 11am–1am daily • (030) 881 84 61 • €€€*

9 Kuchi

Thanks mainly to its exqui-site sushi and mixed Asian hot dishes, this minimalist restaurant has a loyal clientele and ranks among the best sushi bars in town. ◎ *Kantstr. 30 • Map M3 • noon–11pm daily • (030) 31 50 78 15 • no credit cards • €€*

10 Ana e Bruno

Friendly and extremely tasteful, Ana e Bruno is one of the best Italian restaurants in Berlin. ◎ *Sophie-Charlotten-Str. 101 • Map A3 • 5pm–midnight daily • (030) 325 71 10 • €€€*

⟶ *For more on restaurants in Berlin see **pp74–5***

87

Left **Landing stage Wannsee** Centre **Castle ruins on Pfaueninsel** Right **Jacobsbrunnen Pfaueninsel**

Grunewald & Dahlem

B ERLIN'S GREEN SOUTH, *which includes the districts of Grunewald and Dahlem, is dotted with numerous lakes, rivers, small castles, private estates and residential villas, leafy roads and cafés for daytrippers. Grunewald and Dahlem have managed to preserve their rural character, although affluent and famous Berliners have always built their houses here. There are many attractions in Berlin's southwest: visitors can enjoy extensive walks in the Grunewald forest, or ferry across the picturesque lake to Pfaueninsel, an island with romantic castle ruins – and a favourite destination for locals. The swimming baths at Wannsee, Europe's largest inland beach, welcomes up to 40,000 visitors a day for fun, games and a dip in the water and on its beautiful white beaches. The museum complex in Dahlem, too, with its outstanding ethnographic and art collections, is worth visiting. Meanwhile, the Alliiertenmuseum and the Haus der Wannsee Konferenz recall a more painful period in Berlin's history.*

A peacock on Pfaueninsel

 Sights

1 Dahlem Museums
2 Pfaueninsel
3 Schloss Klein-Glienicke
4 Gedenkstätte Haus der Wannsee-Konferenz
5 Strandbad Wannsee
6 Alliiertenmuseum
7 Mexikoplatz
8 Dahlem Villas
9 Jagdschloss Grunewald
10 Museumsdorf Düppel

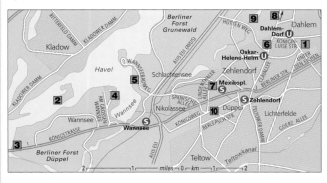

Around Town – Grunewald & Dahlem

1 Dahlem Museums

These three museums, dedicated to foreign cultures and peoples, hold one of Germany's best ethno-cultural collections. The Ethnological Museum has about one million items from around the world, including full-scale wooden huts and boats from the island populations of the South Pacific and a large collection of ceramic and stone sculptures from the Mayas, Aztecs and Incas. Highlights of the Museum of Asian Art include Japanese painting, Chinese porcelain, Buddhist cave paintings and early Indian sculptures. The Museum of European Cultures boasts a vast collection of ethnographically and culturally important objects from all over the continent. ◈ *Lansstr. 8 (Museum of European Cultures reopens mid-2011 at Arnimallee 25) • 10am–6pm Tue–Fri, 11am–6pm Sat & Sun • Ethnological Museum: (030) 830 14 38; Museum of Asian Art: (030) 830 13 82; Museum of European Cultures: (030) 83 90 12 87 • Admission charge*

Exhibit in a Dahlem Museum

2 Pfaueninsel

Visitors are enchanted by the romantic palace ruins and the eponymous peacocks that run around here. The Wannsee island, which can only be reached by ferry, is one of the most charming spots for a walk in Berlin *(see also p70)*. ◈ *Pfaueninselchaussee • 10am–sunset daily • (030) 80 58 68 30 • Admission charge (castle)*

3 Schloss Klein-Glienicke

One of the most beautiful Hohenzollern palaces in Berlin, this romantic castle with its extensive park was built by Schinkel in 1824–60 as a summer residence for Prince Carl of Prussia. The landscape garden, designed by Peter Joseph Lenné, hides many secrets – for example pavilions called "Große" and "Kleine Neugierde" (large and small curiosity), a garden house and a teahouse, a casino right on the water (a former apartment for guests) as well as the Orangerie (a greenhouse). ◈ *Königstr. 36 • May–Oct: 10am–6pm Sat & Sun; Nov–Apr: 10am–5pm Sat & Sun (with tour only) • (0331) 969 42 00 • Admission charge*

4 Gedenkstätte Haus der Wannsee-Konferenz

It is hard to believe that something as abhorrent as the Holo-caust could have been planned at this elegant villa in a picturesque spot on Wannsee. Built in 1914–15 by Paul Baumgarten in the style of a small Neo-Baroque palace for the businessman Ernst Marlier, it was here that the Nazi elite, among them the infamous Adolf Eichmann, met on 20 January 1942 to discuss the details of the mass extermination of Jews. An exhibition at the memorial documents both the conference and its consequences as well as the history of the villa. ◈ *Am Großen Wannsee 56–58 • 10am–6pm daily • (030) 805 00 10 • Free admission*

Neo-Baroque Gedenkstätte Haus

Gryffin at Schloss Klein-Glienicke

Villa at No. 23 Toni-Lessler-Straße

flanked by elegant semi-circular Art-Nouveau apartment blocks, and in front of these stands Berlin's last remaining Art-Deco-style S-Bahn station. The yellow buildings are covered in green shingles and, in summer, the balconies are richly decked with greenery and flowers. Some of Berlin's most magnificent mansion houses line both sides of Argentinische and Lindenthaler Allee. Many celebrities live in the area around the square. ✒ *Mexikoplatz*

⑤ Strandbad Wannsee

Europe's largest inland beach is a surprisingly picturesque spot on the edge of the large city, attracting up to 40,000 visitors a day. The renovated swimming baths were built in 1929–30 as a recreation area for workers in the neighbouring districts *(see p66)*.
✒ *Wannseebadeweg 25* • *Apr–Sep: 10am–7pm Mon–Fri, 8am–8pm Sat & Sun* • *(030) 70 71 38 33* • *Admission charge*

⑥ Alliiertenmuseum

Visitors stroll around this museum reminiscing and recalling the 50 or so years of partnership between Western Allies and West Berliners. The museum, based in a former US barracks, employs uniforms, documents, weapons and military equipment to tell the story of Berlin's postwar history, though not only from the military point of view.
✒ *Clayallee 135* • *10am–6pm daily exc Wed* • *(030) 818 19 90* • *Free admission*

⑦ Mexikoplatz

Idyllic Mexikoplatz in the southern district of Zehlendorf is one of the most atmospheric and architecturally fascinating squares in Berlin. The two round green spaces in the centre are

⑧ Dahlem Villas

Some of Berlin's most attractive villas, dating back to the 19th century, are found in the streets surrounding the Grunewald S-Bahn station. Especially worth seeing are Nos. 15 and 11 in Winklerstraße, the latter of which was built by Hermann Muthesius in the style of an English country mansion. Villa Maren, at No. 12 next door, is a beautiful example of the Neo-Renaissance style. The villas on Toni-Lessler-Straße and on Furtwänglerstraße are also worth a detour. ✒ *Am Großen Wannsee*

Villa at No. 11 Winklerstraße

Jagdschloss Grunewald

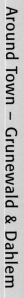

A Day in the South

Morning

Start your morning walk through Berlin's southern districts by taking the S-Bahn (line S1) to **Mexikoplatz**. Here you can admire the beautiful villas and the lovely green square before dropping in to **Café Krone** in Argentinische Allee for a late breakfast. After refreshments, continue on foot or by bus (No. 118) southwards to the open-air museum **Museumsdorf Düppel**. From there, return by bus via Argentinische Allee to the **Alliierten-museum**. From the museum you can stroll across Königin-Luise-Straße and through the picturesque streets right up to the beer garden **Luise** *(see p93)* near the Free University, where you may like to have lunch.

Afternoon

Start your afternoon walk at the **Dahlem Museums** *(see p89)*. Once you have enjoyed this cultural break, continue by U-Bahn (U3, Dahlem-Dorf) to Krumme Lanke, and from there, on foot, to the S-Bahn station Mexikoplatz. The S-Bahn will take you to Wannsee S-Bahn station, from where you can reach all the sights in southwestern Berlin. When the weather is right, visit **Strandbad Wannsee**, or visit the **Haus der Wannsee-Konferenz** *(see p89)* and then admire the park and **Schloss Klein-Glienicke** *(see p89)*. After your walk, allow yourself to be tempted by coffee and cake or supper at the **Goldener Greif in Schloss Klein-Glienicke** *(see p93)*. Your best option for the return journey is the S-Bahn from Wannsee.

9 Jagdschloss Grunewald

The small gleaming white palace in Grunewald underwent major restoration in 2009. The oldest palace in the city area, it dates back to 1542 and served as a hunting lodge for the Electors. The castle, built in the Renaissance and Baroque styles, houses a small collection of German and Dutch paintings. ⊗ *Hüttenweg 100, Grunewaldsee • (030) 813 35 97 • Admission charge*

10 Museumsdorf Düppel

The open-air museum at Düppel is a reminder of the fact that Berlin once consisted of a series of villages, with one of the oldest settlements dating back to the 13th century. The lively museum is animated by actors, who are dressed and act out daily life as it would have been during the Middle Ages. There are fascinating live demonstrations of ancient crafts such as bread-baking, pottery and basket-weaving. Plants are grown as in medieval times for their various uses. ⊗ *Clauertstr. 11 • Apr–Oct: 3–7pm Thu, 10am–5pm Sun • (030) 802 66 71 • Admission charge*

At Museumsdorf Düppel

Left **Onkel-Tom-Siedlung** Centre **St-Annen-Kirche** Right **Outside the Free University Berlin**

⑩ Best of the Rest

1 Open Air Museum Domäne Dahlem
Learn about modern organic farming techniques at this historic working farm. ✆ Königin-Luise-Str. 49 • 10am–6pm Mon, Wed–Sun • (030) 666 30 00 • Admission charge

2 Grunewaldturm
This red Neo-Gothic brick tower was built in 1897 as a memorial to Kaiser Wilhelm I. ✆ Havelchaussee

3 Onkel-Tom-Siedlung
The "Uncle Tom's Hut" settlement, developed in 1926–32 according to designs by Bruno Taut and others, was intended to create a modern housing estate for workers, unlike their old narrow, dark tenement blocks. ✆ Argentinische Allee

4 Free University
The campus of Berlin's largest university, founded in 1948 as a rival to East-Berlin Humboldt University, covers large parts of Dahlem. It is worth looking at the 1950s Henry-Ford-Bau and the Philological Library, designed by Sir Norman Foster. ✆ Habelschwerdter Allee 45 • Library: 9am–10pm Mon–Fri (to 5pm Sat & Sun)

5 Teufelsberg
Both the hill and the lake, the dark green Teufelssee, are popular destinations for a day out, for flying kites and biking. Swimming and sunbathing at the lake is mainly nude.

6 St-Peter-und-Paul-Kirche
This charming stone church, built in 1834–7 by F A Stüler, resembles Russian-Orthodox churches and is used for marriage ceremonies. ✆ Nikolskoer Weg 17 • 11am–4pm daily • (030) 805 21 00

7 Blockhaus Nikolskoe
The log cabin, built in 1819, was a present from King Friedrich Wilhelm III to his daughter Charlotte and his son-in-law, future Tsar Nicholas I. The restored wooden Russian-style dacha is now a restaurant. ✆ Nikolskoer Weg 15 • 10am–8pm daily (to 10pm summer) • (030) 805 29 14

8 Heinrich von Kleist's Tomb
The German playwright Kleist and his companion Henriette Vogel committed suicide by shooting themselves in 1811; they are buried here together (near the S-Bahn overpass). ✆ Bismarckstr. 3, Am Kleinen Wannsee

9 St-Annen-Kirche
This 14th-century Gothic church has attractive murals depicting scenes from the life of Saint Anna, as well as late-Gothic figures of saints and a Baroque pulpit. ✆ Königin-Luise-Str./Pacelliallee

10 Teltower Damm
The main shopping street of Zehlendorf has managed to preserve its village character and its 1768 Baroque church. ✆ Zehlendorf, at S-Bahn station Zehlendorf

Price Categories

For a three-course		
meal for one with half	**€**	under €20
a bottle of wine (or	**€€**	€20–30
equivalent meal), taxes	**€€€**	€30–45
and charges included	**€€€€**	€45–60
	€€€€€	over €60

Left **Sign of the Wirtshaus Paulsborn** Right **Enjoying an outdoor meal at Blockhaus Nikolskoe**

🔟 Restaurants & Beer Gardens

Haus Sanssouci
Offering fantastic views over Wannsee, this idyllic cottage-style restaurant serves mostly German food, but it has lobster nights and other specials too. There are also three guest rooms. 🕿 *Am Großen Wannsee 60 • 11:30am–11pm Tue–Sun • (030) 805 30 34 • €€–€€€*

Forsthaus Paulsborn
This rustic restaurant next to Jagdschloss Grunewald is based in an old hunting lodge. 🕿 *Hütten-weg 90 • summer: 11am–11pm Tue–Sun; winter: 11am–6pm Tue–Sun • (030) 818 19 10 • €€€*

Wirtshaus Schildhorn
Nouvelle cuisine in Grune-wald. In summer you can enjoy your *bratwurst* outside, in a pic-turesque spot right on the shore-line at Wannsee. 🕿 *Havelchaussee/ Straße am Schildhorn 4a • summer: 11am–midnight daily; winter: 11am–10pm Sat & Sun • (030) 30 88 35 00 • €€*

Blockhaus Nikolskoe
Traditional German fare is served in this historic log cabin, built as a Russian *dacha*. 🕿 *Nikolskoer Weg 15 • from 10am daily • (030) 805 29 14 • no credit cards • €€*

Wirtshaus zur Pfaueninsel
A small venue, serving rustic German food in the open air. This is an ideal place for refreshments before a visit to Pfaueninsel. 🕿 *Pfaueninselchaussee 100 • summer: 10am–8pm daily; winter: 10am–6pm daily • (030) 805 22 25 • €€*

Alter Krug Dahlem
Large beer garden with a lengthy menu, offering excellent wines and desserts. 🕿 *Königin-Luise-Str. 52 • 10am–midnight daily • (030) 832 70 00 • €€–€€€*

Luise
One of Berlin's nicest beer gardens, on the Free University campus, Luise's is crowded even at lunchtime and always boasts a good atmosphere. The delicious salads and sandwiches here are particularly worth trying. 🕿 *Königin-Luise-Str. 40 • 10am–1am daily • (030) 84 18 88 11 • €€*

Grunewaldturm-Restaurant
A great place for mushroom and game dishes, with views of Wannsee. 🕿 *Havelchaussee 61 • 11am–7pm Mon–Fri, 9:30am–7pm Sat & Sun • (030) 300 07 30 • €€*

Goldener Greif in Schloss Klein-Glienicke
This restaurant offers sophisticat-ed cuisine and surroundings; light fish dishes and salads in summer, game and roasts in winter. 🕿 *Königstr. 36 • Mar–Jan: noon–late Wed–Sun • (030) 805 40 00 • €€€*

Diekmann im Chalet Suisse
Swiss hospitality and a cosy atmosphere in Grunewald. Local and exquisite Swiss cooking features strongly on the menu. 🕿 *Clayallee 99 • noon–midnight daily • (030) 832 63 62 • €€€*

Following pages **Inside the Cupola of the Reichstag**

Left **Haus der Kulturen der Welt** Centre **In Tiergarten** Right **Shell-Haus**

Tiergarten & Federal District

IN 1999, BERLIN'S GREEN *centre became the government district. Around Tiergarten, Berlin's largest and most popular park, stand the Reichstag, the Bundeskanzleramt and Schloss Bellevue, seat of the President of the Federal Republic of Germany. Tiergarten itself is a great place for strolling and cycling, and it also boasts the Neuer See, the Spree River and Berlin's Zoo. In summer, its lawns are used for soccer games and barbecue parties.*

The renovated Reichstag

Sights

1. Reichstag
2. Kulturforum
3. Großer Tiergarten
4. Siegessäule
5. Diplomatenviertel
6. Hamburger Bahnhof
7. Sowjetisches Ehrenmal
8. Gedenkstätte Deutscher Widerstand
9. Hansa-Viertel
10. Villa von der Heydt

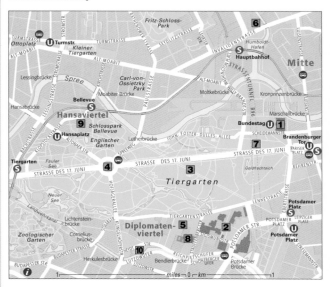

1 Reichstag

More than any other Berlin landmark, the Reichstag – seat of the German parliament – has come to symbolize German history *(see pp10–11)*.

2 Kulturforum

This unique complex of buildings features the best museums and concert halls in western Berlin *(see pp32–5)*.

3 Großer Tiergarten

The Großer Tiergarten is Berlin's largest park, straddling an area of 200 hectares (494 acres) between the eastern and western halves of the town. Formerly the Elector's hunting grounds, it was redesigned in the 1830s as a park by Peter Joseph Lenné. At the end of the 19th century, the Siegesallee was established in the east of the park, more than 500 m (1640 ft) in length, lined by the statues of monarchs and politicians. After World War II, the starving and freezing population chopped down nearly all the trees for firewood and dug up the lawns to grow food. Thanks to reforestation work since the 1950s, Tiergarten today has become Berlin's favourite green space and the lungs of the city. ◈ *Tiergarten • Map M5/6*

4 Siegessäule

In the middle of Tiergarten stands the 62-m (203-ft) high Victory Column, erected to commemorate Prussian victory against Denmark in the war of 1864. After victory over Austria in 1866 and France 1871, the structure was crowned by a 35-ton gilded statue of the goddess Victoria. There are excellent views from the viewing platform *(see p39)*. ◈ *Großer Stern • Map M6 • Closed for renovation until 2011 • Admission charge*

Statue on Siegessäule

5 Diplomatenviertel

In the late 19th century, an embassy district sprang up. Its extent is still marked today by two pompous Fascist buildings (Italian and Japanese embassies of 1938 and 1943 respectively). Most structures were destroyed during World War II, and until the reunification of Germany the diplomatic buildings were left to decay. Since 1999, new life has been breathed into the diplomats' quarter and, thanks to its adventurous architecture, it has been transformed into one of the most interesting parts of Berlin. Especially worth seeing are the Austrian and Indian embassies on Tiergartenstraße as well as, on Klingelhöferstraße, the embassies of the Nordic countries *(see p41)* and of Mexico. ◈ *Between Stauffenbergstr. and Lichtensteinallee as well as along Tiergartenstr. • Map E4*

Left **Roof of the Japanese Embassy** Right **The Austrian Embassy**

Peter Joseph Lenné

Lenné (1789–1866), regarded as Germany's most important landscape architect, was born into a family of gardeners in Bonn. He studied in Paris and joined the Royal Gardens in Potsdam as an apprentice in 1816. There he met Schinkel and, together, these two men set out to design the parks of Berlin and Potsdam in the harmonious style of the time.

Main entrance Bendlerblock

6 Hamburger Bahnhof

The former Hamburg railway station, now the "Museum of the Present Day", holds a cross-section of contemporary paintings and the latest multi-media works of art and installations. One of the highlights is the private collection of Erich Marx, including works by Beuys and others. Apart from well-known artists such as Andy Warhol, Jeff Koons and Robert Rauschenberg, it also shows works by Anselm Kiefer and Sandro Chiao. ◉ *Invalidenstr. 50–51 • Map F2 • 10am–6pm Tue–Fri, 11am–8pm Sat, 11am–6pm Sun • Admission charge*

7 Sowjetisches Ehrenmal

The giant Soviet Memorial near Brandenburg Gate was officially opened on 7 November 1945, the anniversary of the Russian October Revolution. It is flanked by two tanks, supposedly the first ones to reach Berlin. The memorial commemorates 300,000 Red Army soldiers who died during World War II in the struggle to liberate Berlin. The large column was constructed from marble blocks from Hitler's Reich Chancellery, which had just been torn down. The column itself, designed by Nicolai

Sergijevski, is crowned by the huge bronze statue by Lev Kerbel. Behind the memorial, 2,500 Russian soldiers are buried. ◉ *Straße des 17. Juni • Map K2*

8 Gedenkstätte Deutscher Widerstand

The 1930s complex, which is today known as Bendlerblock, lies behind the former Prussian Ministry of War. During World War II it served as army headquarters. It was here that a group of officers planned the assassination of Adolf Hitler. When the attempt failed on 20 July 1944, Claus Schenk Count von Stauffenberg and the others involved were arrested in the Bendlerblock, and many of them were shot in the courtyard during the night.

Sowjetisches Ehrenmal

A memorial, created by Richard Scheibe in 1953, commemorates these events. On the upper floor is a small exhibition documenting the German resistance against the Nazi regime. Today, the Bendlerblock has been incorporated into the Berlin branch of the Federal Ministry of Defence. ◉ *Stauffenbergstr. 13–14 • Map E4 • 9am–6pm Mon–Wed & Fri, 9am–8pm Thu, 10am–6pm Sat & Sun • (030) 26 99 50 00*

Lortzing Memorial in Tiergarten

9 Hansa-Viertel

The Hansa estate west of Schloss Bellvue was built for the "Interbau" trade fair in 1957. World War II bombs had flattened Tiergarten, and 36 residential complexes were erected in the park, designed by distinguished architects from around the world, including Walter Gropius (Händel-allee 3–9), Alvar Aalto (Klopstock-str. 30–32) and Oscar Niemeyer (Altonaer Str. 4–14). ⊗ *Tiergarten, Hanseatenweg • Map D3*

10 Villa von der Heydt

The late-Neo-Classical Villa von der Heydt is one of the few surviving examples of the architectural villa style typical of Tiergarten. It was built in 1860–61, according to plans by Hermann Ende and G.A. Linke, for one of the most elegant residential areas in Berlin at the time. Since 1980, the Prussian Heritage Foundation has had its headquarters here. ⊗ *Von-der-Heydt-Str. 18 • Map E4*

Villa von der Heydt

A Day Out

Morning

Start your tour of Tiergarten at the **Reichstag** *(see pp10–11)*. Explore the government district from here starting with the Bundeskanzleramt (the Federal Chancellor's Office, diagonally opposite). Stop at **Restaurant Käfer** *(see p101)* in the Reichstag for breakfast. Via John-Foster-Dulles-Allee you will pass the Carillon and the Haus der Kulturen der Welt on the way to **Großer Tiergarten** *(see p97)*. Continue along one of the paths into the park, directly opposite the old Kongresshalle, until you reach Straße des 17. Juni. If you turn right here, you will be heading directly towards **Siegessäule** *(see p97)*. From there continue along Fasanerieallee in a southwesterly direction until you get to the **Café am Neuen See** *(see p101)*, where you could have lunch.

Afternoon

A stroll through the **Diplomats' Quarter** *(see p97)*: from Neuer See, it is only a few steps along Lichtensteinallee and Thomas-Dehler-Straße in an easterly direction until you get to Klingelhöferstraße with its Scandinavian embassies. On Tiergartenstraße you will pass, among others, the embassies of Japan, Italy, India and Austria. From here you could continue south along Klingelhöferstraße, making a small detour for refreshments at **Café Einstein** *(see p101)*. Continue along Lützowufer until you reach the **Kulturforum** *(see pp32–5)* via Potsdamer Brücke. A good place for an evening meal would be **Vox** *(see p74)*.

Left **On Neuer See** Centre **The Löwenbrücke** Right **Estonian Embassy; Greek Embassy ruins**

Hidden Treasures

1 Neuer See
Shimmering in a mysterious emerald green, the largest lake in Tiergarten is perfect for rowing. Afterwards you can recover in the Café am Neuen See. ◈ *S-Bahn station Tiergarten • Map M5*

2 Löwenbrücke
The Lion Bridge, which leads across a small stream near Neuer See, is "suspended" from the sculptures of four lions. This idyllic spot is a favourite meeting point for gays in Berlin. ◈ *Großer Weg • Map M5*

3 Lortzing-Denkmal
There are 70 statues of philosophers, poets and statesmen in Tiergarten. The statue of the composer Lortzing, at one end of Neuer See, is one of the most beautiful. ◈ *Östlicher Großer Weg • Map M5*

4 Houseboats
Docked on the banks of the Spree are some of the remaining few houseboats in Berlin – an idyllic haven in the middle of the city. ◈ *Straße des 17. Juni, Tiergarten-ufer • Map M3*

5 Carillon
The *carillon*, officially dedicated in 1987, is the largest of its kind in Europe. The 68 bells are rung every day at noon and 6pm in the 42-m (138-ft) high black tower. ◈ *John-Foster-Dulles-Allee (Haus der Kulturen der Welt) • Map E3 • Open-air concerts: 3pm Sun May–Sep*

6 Englischer Garten
The landscaped English-style garden near Schloss Bellevue is ideal for strolling. ◈ *An der Klopstockstr. • Map M5*

7 Estonian Embassy
The old Estonian Embassy, in a quiet side street next to the ruined Greek Embassy, is characteristic of the diplomats' quarter. ◈ *Hildebrandtstr. 5 • Map E4*

8 Locks
The two canal locks behind the zoo, taking visitors across the dammed Landwehrkanal, are popular resting places. ◈ *At the Zoo, S-Bahn station Tiergarten • Map M5*

9 Gaslights in Tiergarten
With 80 historic gaslights along the paths, an evening stroll in Tiergarten is very romantic. ◈ *At S-Bahn station Tiergarten • Map M5*

10 Landwehrkanal
The sloping, grass-covered banks of Landwehrkanal are ideal spots to chill out. ◈ *Corneliusstr. • Map M/N5/6*

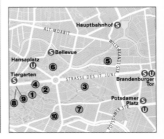

Price Categories

For a three-course meal for one with half a bottle of wine (or equivalent meal), taxes and charges included

€	under €20
€€	€20–30
€€€	€30–45
€€€€	€45–60
€€€€€	over €60

Left **In the Café am Neuen See** Right **Café Einstein**

🔟 Restaurants & Cafés

1 Café am Neuen See
On the shore of the lake, this is a restaurant, café and beer garden. The "Italian breakfast" is delicious. ⌖ *Tiergarten, Neuer See, Lichtensteinallee 2 • Map M5 • Mar–Oct: 10am–11pm daily; Nov–Feb: 10am–8pm Sat & Sun • (030) 254 49 30 • €€*

2 Schleusenkrug
This small café, right next to a lock, has a rustic beer garden and is very popular with students. ⌖ *Tiergarten-Schleuse • Map M5 • 10am–1am daily (to 7pm winter) • (030) 313 99 09 • no credit cards • €*

3 Café Einstein
Based in the villa belonging to the film star Henny Porten, this is the ultimate in Viennese style. ⌖ *Kurfürstenstr. 58 • Map E5 • 8am–1am daily • (030) 261 50 96 • €€€*

4 Käfer im Reichstag
An ambitious restaurant, better known for its view than its food. ⌖ *Platz der Republik • Map K2 • 9am–midnight • (030) 226 29 90 • €€€€*

5 Lochner
This fine dining, gourmet restaurant serves no-nonsense, top-quality German cuisine. ⌖ *Lützowplatz 5 • Map E4 • from 6pm Tue–Sun • (030) 23 00 52 20 • €€€€*

6 Lutter & Wegner Potsdamer Platz
This tiny outlet of the Lutter & Wegner restaurant *(see p75)* offers great Berlin and Austrian-French dishes in the historic setting of the 1920s Grand Hotel Esplanade. ⌖ *Bellevuestr. 1 • Map F4 • 9am–2am • (030) 26 39 03 72 • €€€*

7 Billy Wilder's
A small, popular American-style bistro named after the great film director. ⌖ *Potsdamer Str. 2 • Map F4 • from noon daily • (030) 26 55 48 60 • €€*

8 Brasserie Desbrosses
An appealing, historic French restaurant. Its seafood is particularly good. ⌖ *Potsdamer Platz 3 • Map F4 • 6:30am–11pm daily • (030) 337 77 63 40 • €€€€*

9 Paris-Moskau
A classic restaurant serving seasonal dishes with an emphasis on game and seafood. ⌖ *Alt-Moabit 141 • Map J1 • noon–3pm Mon–Fri, from 6pm daily • (030) 394 20 81 • €€€*

10 Alte Pumpe
There is always a good atmosphere in this traditional Berlin restaurant. ⌖ *Lützowstr. 42 • Map E5 • noon–10pm Mon–Sat, 10am–4pm Sun • (030) 26 48 42 65 • €€*

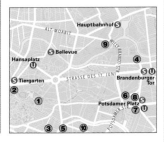

Note: All restaurants accept credit cards and offer vegetarian dishes unless stated otherwise.

Left **Martin-Gropius-Bau** Centre **Above a door in Schöneberg** Right **Shield, Jüdisches Museum**

Kreuzberg & Schöneberg

KREUZBERG IS POSSIBLY *Berlin's most notorious district, and it definitely qualifies as its most colourful area.* Here, in historic tenement blocks that are slowly but surely being renovated, Turkish families live next door to drop-outs and alternatives, artists and students. Social tensions, still characteristic of Kreuzberg today, make this a varied and interesting district – but at the same time a problematic one. The neighbouring district of Schöneberg is markedly quieter; this part of town is not as experimental as Kreuzberg, neither is it as elegant as Charlottenburg – here Berlin is simply enjoyed by its inhabitants. Winterfeldtplatz is surrounded by many inviting pubs, and in the area around Nollendorfplatz entire roads have been taken over and transformed by Berlin's gay scene, with their shops, bars and night clubs.

Statue on Mehringplatz

 Sights

1. Deutsches Technikmuseum
2. Jüdisches Museum
3. Checkpoint Charlie
4. Topographie des Terrors
5. Anhalter Bahnhof
6. Oranienstraße
7. Nollendorfplatz
8. Viktoriapark
9. Martin-Gropius-Bau
10. Riehmers Hofgarten

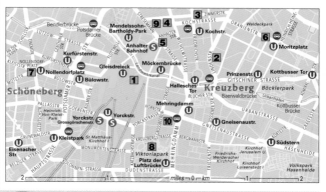

Deutsches Technikmuseum

The history of technology and crafts is the theme of this fascinating museum, located in the grounds of a former station. Visitors can learn about developments in aviation and admire 40 planes, including a Junkers Ju 52 and a "raisin bomber", the type of plane used for the Berlin airlift. Old ships and steam locomotives bring back the days of the Industrial Revolution. ◈ *Trebbiner Str. 9 • Map F5 • 9am–5:30pm Tue–Fri, 10am–6pm Sat & Sun • (030) 90 25 40 • Admission charge (free for children after 3pm)*

Jüdisches Museum

The Jewish Museum is not only unique architecturally, but it is also one of Berlin's most fascinating museums. Its collections present an overview of almost 1,000 years of German-Jewish cultural history; a special exhibition is devoted to everyday Jewish life in Berlin from the end of the 19th century *(see p46)*. ◈ *Lindenstr. 9–14 • Map G5 • 10am–10pm Mon, 10am–8pm Tue–Sun • (030) 25 99 33 00 • Admission charge*

Checkpoint Charlie

The Haus am Checkpoint Charlie, next to the former crossing point for the Alllied forces, has an exhibition on the history of the Berlin Wall and the various means people used in trying to

The old sign at Checkpoint Charlie

escape from East to West Berlin, ranging from a hot-air balloon to a car with a false floor. Only a replica of the control hut remains of the former border. ◈ *Friedrichstr. 43–45 • Map G4 • 9am–10pm daily • (030) 253 72 50 • Admission charge*

Topographie des Terrors

After 1934, three terrifying Nazi institutions had their headquarters in this area: the security service (Sicherheitsdienst, SD) was based at Wilhelmstraße 102 in the Prinz-Albrecht-Palais; the school of arts and crafts at Prinz-Albrecht-Straße 8 was occupied by the Gestapo; while Heinrich Himmler, head of the SS, resided next door at No. 9, at the Hotel Prinz Albrecht. After World War II, all the buildings were bulldozed except for the cellars where, in 1933–45, prisoners had been interrogated and tortured. There is also a documentation centre. ◈ *Stresemannstr. 110, entrance Niederkirchner Str. 8 • Map F4 • May–Sep: 10am–8pm daily; Oct–Apr: 10am–6pm daily • (030) 25 48 67 03*

Left **Inside Deutsches Technikmuseum** Right **Exhibition of Nazi crimes at Topographie des Terrors**

Left **Plaque on Nollendorfplatz** Centre **Façade of the Metropol** Right **Ruins of Anhalter Bahnhof**

Anhalter Bahnhof

Only pitiful fragments remain of the railway station that was once the largest in Europe. The giant structure was erected in 1880 by Franz Schwechten as a showcase station: official visitors to the Empire were meant to be impressed by the splendour and glory of the German capital as soon as they reached the railway station. In 1943 the station was badly damaged by bombs and in 1960 it was pulled down. The waste ground behind the façade was meant to become a park; today the Tempodrom is based here, hosting concerts and cabaret shows.
⊗ *Askanischer Platz 6–7 • Map F5*

Oranienstraße

Oranienstraße is the heart of Kreuzberg. It is the wildest, most colourful and most unusual street of the district, where alternative shops and pubs jostle for space with doner kebab takeaways and Turkish greengrocers. All aspects of life and politics in Kreuzberg are centred around this road. ⊗ *Between Lindenstr. and Skalitzer Str. • Map H5*

Flower stall on Winterfeldtmarkt

Nollendorfplatz

Nollendorfplatz and neighbouring Winterfeldtplatz are right in the centre of Schöneberg. The former square has always been a focal point for the gay scene in Berlin, and a plaque at U-Bahn station Nollendorfplatz commemorates approximately 5,000 homosexuals killed in concentration camps by the Nazis. Today, gay life is concentrated more in the surrounding streets. Before World War II, Nollendorfplatz was also a centre of entertainment. The Metropol-Theater, today a discotheque, then boasted Erwin Piscator as its innovative director. And next door lived the writer Christopher Isherwood, whose novel formed the basis of the famous musical "Cabaret". ⊗ *Map E5*

Turkish Berlin

In the 1960s, thousands of Turkish *gastarbeiter* ("guest workers") came to Berlin in response to a shortage of labour. Today the Turkish community numbers around 190,000 and it is mainly their children who leave their mark on life in the city. There are few "guest workers" left; most Turkish Berliners own their own shops and consider themselves to be true Berliners. The rate of naturalization is still fairly low, and many German Berliners have no contact with everyday life in the Turkish community. At 40 per cent, the rate of unemployment among young Turkish Berliners is depressingly high.

Tempodrom: **www.tempodrom.de**

Memorial by Schinkel in Viktoriapark

8 Viktoriapark

This rambling park was set up as a recreational space for workers in Kreuzberg in 1888–94 to plans by Hermann Mächtig. It has an artificial waterfall, and the Neo-Gothic Schinkel memorial at the top of Kreuzberg, 66 m (216 ft) high, commemorates Prussian victory in the Wars of Liberation against Napoleon. ⊗ *Kreuzbergstr.* • Map F6

9 Martin-Gropius-Bau

The richly ornamented former museum of arts and crafts is one of Berlin's most attractive exhibition centres *(see pp46–7)*. ⊗ *Niederkirchnerstr. 7* • Map F4 • *changing exhibitions and opening times, but usually 10am–8pm Wed–Mon* • *(030) 25 48 60* • *Admission charge*

10 Riehmers Hofgarten

Over 20 buildings make up this elegant estate, built as officers' quarters in the Gründerzeit (after the founding of the German Empire in 1871). Restored in the 1970s, there is also a pleasant hotel with restaurant. ⊗ *Yorckstr. 83–86* • Map F6

Riehmers Hofgarten

A Day in Kreuzberg

Morning

🕐 Start from the ruins of **Anhalter Bahnhof**, which you can reach by S-Bahn. From here continue along Stresemannstraße in a northwesterly direction to the **Martin-Gropius-Bau**. While away a few hours in this impressive building, then take a break in the museum café. Afterwards, a visit to the neighbouring **Topographie des Terrors** exhibition *(see p103)* will bring you face to face with the dark Nazi past of this area. Walk along Niederkirchnerstraße, past an original section of the Berlin Wall, to Wilhelmstraße. Take a left into Zimmerstrasse and visit some of the many contemporary art galleries lining the street. Continue to Friedrichstrasse to visit **Checkpoint Charlie** and the Wall Museum at the former border *(see p103)*.

Afternoon

You can buy a tasty lunch at **Sale e Tabacchi** *(see p109)* in Kochstraße. Continue along Kochstraße in an easterly direction and you will get to the heart of Kreuzberg. Make a detour south on Lindenstraße to the **Jüdisches Museum** *(see p103)* or carry on into **Oranienstraße**. Take the U-Bahn U6 from U-Bahn station Hallesches Tor to Platz der Luftbrücke. The **Viktoriapark** nearby is a good place for a rest, while shopaholics prefer a stroll up and down Bergmannstraße. At the end, turn north into Baerwaldstraße and continue to Carl-Herz-Ufer, where you will be able to round off the day with a delicious evening meal at the **Altes Zollhaus** *(see p109)*.

The website **www.kreuzberg24.net** *has useful information on local amenities.*

Left **Rathaus Schöneberg** Centre **Oberbaumbrücke** Right **On Mariannenplatz**

TOP 10 Best of the Rest

1 Rathaus Schöneberg
It was from this Town Hall, on 26 June 1963, that the US President John F Kennedy made his famous speech, declaring "I am a Berliner" and expressing his commitment to the freedom of West Berlin. ◈ *John-F-Kennedy-Platz*

2 Mehringplatz
Once Kreuzberg's prettiest square, Mehringplatz was destroyed in World War II and is today surrounded by modern residential buildings. ◈ *Map G5*

3 Flughafen Tempelhof
Tempelhof, built in 1939 by Ernst Sagebiel and then Germany's biggest airport, survives as the largest Fascist structure in Europe. After years of debate the airport closed in 2008. Future uses for it include a park, a convention centre and a venue for fashion shows and trade fairs. ◈ *Platz der Luftbrücke • Map G6*

4 Mariannenplatz
This square is dominated by the Gothic-style artists' house Bethanien. A former hospital, it is today used as studio space by experimental artists. ◈ *Map H5*

5 Oberbaumbrücke
Pedestrians and cyclists can cross to the other side of the Spree River from Kreuzberg to Friedrichshain on this red-brick bridge, one of Berlin's loveliest, which was erected in 1894–6. ◈ *Warschauer/Skalitzer Str.*

6 Altes Mosse-Palais
One of Berlin's most important publishing houses was based in this Art Nouveau corner house in the former newspaper district. ◈ *Kochstr. • Map G4*

7 Friedhöfe Hallesches Tor
Numerous celebrities lie buried in the four cemeteries, including the composer Felix Mendelssohn Bartholdy. Also the writer E T A Hoffmann, whose work inspired Offenbach to write *The Tales of Hoffmann*. ◈ *Mehringdamm • Map G5*

8 Gasometer Schöneberg
Once a massive gas holder, this Schöneberg landmark was decommissioned in the 1990s and turned into a viewing platform. ◈ *Torgauer Str. 12–15 • Map E6*

9 Kottbusser Tor
Kreuzberg in the raw: social misery tucked away in between new buildings in the Turkish heart of the district. ◈ *Map H5*

10 Kammergericht
In 1947–90, the magnificent supreme court, built in 1909–13, was used as Allied Control Council. ◈ *Potsdamer Str. 186 • Map E6*

Left **A stall in Winterfeldtmarkt** Centre **Marheineke-Markthalle** Right **At Grober Unfug Comics**

🔟 Shops & Markets

1 Winterfeldtmarkt
At Berlin's largest and most wonderful market you can buy fresh fruit and vegetables as well as other goods from around the world, such as clothes and New-Age items. ✆ *Winterfeldtplatz • Map E5 • 8am–4pm Sat, 8am–1pm Wed*

2 Türkenmarkt am Maybachufer
No other market in Berlin is quite as exotic. This is where Berliners and Turks alike buy their unleavened bread and fresh goat's cheese. ✆ *Maybachufer • Map H5 • noon–6:30pm Tue & Fri*

3 Molotow
Funky and trendy fashion from Berlin designers – perhaps not to everyone's taste, but guaranteed to cause a stir. ✆ *Gneisenaustr. 112 • Map G6 • (030) 693 08 18*

4 Oranienplatz and Oranienstraße
Kreuzberg's main square and unofficial high street specialize in all things alternative. ✆ *Oranienstr./ corner Oranienplatz • Map G5*

5 MaaßenZehn
Designer jeans or trendy belts – all with minor faults – at heavily reduced prices. ✆ *Maaßenstr. 10 • Map E5 • (030) 215 54 56*

6 Depot 2
This small boutique sells the latest streetwear and hip hop fashion of a local label. ✆ *Oranienstr. 9 • Map H5 • (030) 611 46 55*

7 High-Lite
Worried about standing out in the alternative crowd in Kreuzberg? This is the place to get your shades, body piercings and other essentials. ✆ *Bergmannstr. 99 • Map F/G6 • (030) 691 27 44*

8 Ararat
One of the best-stocked and trendiest stationery shops in Berlin, Ararat has many designer items for sale. ✆ *Bergmannstr. 99a • Map F/G6 • (030) 693 50 80*

9 Marheineke-Markthalle
This is one of the last remaining market-halls in Berlin. Modernised in 2007, it boasts colourful fruit and vegetable stores and a wide range of organic produce. ✆ *Marheinekeplatz • Map G6 • 8am–8pm Mon–Fri, 8am–6pm Sat*

10 Grober Unfug Comics
This store sells comic books of all periods and in various languages – its name means "complete rubbish". ✆ *Zossener Str. 33 • Map G6 • (030) 69 40 14 90*

Left **The bar at Mister Hu** Centre **Vox Bar** Right **Riverside at Ankerklause**

🔟 Pubs, Bars & Discos

1 Ankerklause
An unrefined but hugely popular late-night place for students and artists. 🔊 *Kottbusser Damm 104 • Map H5 • (030) 693 56 49*

2 Yorckschlösschen
A pub-restaurant with a great Old Berlin feel. Live jazz concerts at the weekend. 🔊 *Yorckstr. 15 • Map F6 • (030) 215 80 70*

3 Mister Hu
Thanks to its magnificent cocktails this is one of the most popular bars in the district. 🔊 *Goltzstr. 39 • Map E5 • (030) 217 21 11*

4 Van Loon
Enjoy a snack surrounded by nautical artifacts on this old barge moored in Urbanhafen. In summer you can sit on the green banks to drink your beer.
🔊 *Carl-Herz-Ufer 5–7 • Map G5 • (030) 692 62 93*

5 Vox Bar at Hyatt
A smart yet casual hotel bar with live jazz in the evening. Superbly smooth service, delicious cocktails and the city's largest whisky selection. 🔊 *Grand Hyatt Hotel, Marlene-Dietrich-Platz 2 • Map F4 • (030) 25 53 17 72*

6 Rauschgold
This is an extremely popular bar, best late at night and very crowded at weekends. Karaoke, themed nights and a mixed crowd. 🔊 *Mehringdamm 62 • Map F6 • (030) 78 95 26 68*

7 Golgatha
A popular venue for students, this classic beer garden on the Kreuzberg also attracts an older clientele, bopping to funk on the small and intimate dancefloor. 🔊 *Dudenstr. 48–64 (Viktoriapark) • Map F6 • (030) 785 24 53*

8 SO 36
A Kreuzberg classic, the SO 36 is an über-alternative and very lively urban dance club and event venue. The crowd is a good mix of straight and gay. 🔊 *Oranienstraße 190 • Map H5 • (030) 61 40 13 06*

9 Würgeengel
The drinks at the "Angel of Death" are not, in fact, lethal, but the bar staff and most of the clientele are straight out of a Buñuel film. 🔊 *Dresdener Str. 122 • Map H5 • (030) 615 55 60*

10 Max & Moritz
Traditional Berlin tavern with touches of Art Nouveau, that fronts as a tango salon on Sundays. Lessons start at 7:30pm; club starts at 8:30pm. 🔊 *Oranienstraße 162 • Map H5 • (030) 69 51 59 11*

Price Categories

For a three-course	€	under €20
meal for one with half	€€	€20–30
a bottle of wine (or	€€€	€30–45
equivalent meal), taxes	€€€€	€45–60
and charges included	€€€€€	over €60

Left **Gorgonzola Club** Right **The sign outside Sale e Tabacchi**

🔟 Restaurants & Cafés

Altes Zollhaus
1 International and German cuisine, served in a former border control point on the banks of the Landwehrkanal. Try the house speciality: *Brandenburger Landente aus dem Rohr* – a roast duck dish, or dishes with wild mushrooms, when in season. ◈ *Carl-Herz-Ufer 30 • Map G5 • from 6pm Tue–Sat • (030) 692 33 00 • €€€*

Entrecôte
2 Ever since Madonna enjoyed a meal here the usually low-key Entrecôte has become the talk of the town. ◈ *Schützenstraße 5 • Map G4 • noon–midnight Mon–Fri, 6pm–midnight Sat, 6–11pm Sun • (030) 20 16 54 96 • €€€*

Osteria No. 1
3 The Italian local par excellence: noisy and expensive, but serving unique pizzas and excellent pasta dishes. Later, try the wine bar next door. ◈ *Kreuzbergstr. 71 • Map F6 • (030) 786 91 62 • €€*

Hasir
4 One branch of the Turkish-Arabic fast food chain, serving falafels and other delicacies until late. ◈ *Maaßenstr. 10 • Map E5 • (030) 215 60 60 • no credit cards • €*

Sale e Tabacchi
5 Italian restaurant with elegant interior, popular with the media crowd. In summer, reserve a table in the central courtyard. ◈ *Rudi-Dutschke-Str. 23 • Map G4 • 10am–2am daily • (030) 252 11 55 • €€€*

Defne
6 An intimate restaurant serving modern Turkish food. ◈ *Planufer. 92c • Map H5 • from 4pm daily • (030) 81 79 71 11 • no credit cards • €€*

Le Cochon Bourgeois
7 Top-quality French cooking at moderate prices, attracting a Bohemian local crowd and others. ◈ *Fichtestr. 24 • Map H6 • from 6pm Tue–Sat • (030) 693 01 01 • €€*

Merhaba
8 One of the best Turkish restaurants in Berlin, dishing up great lamb kebabs and other Turkish specialities. ◈ *Wissmannstr. 32 • Map H6 • 10am–midnight daily • (030) 692 17 13 • €€*

Hartmanns Restaurant
9 A fine addition to Berlin's gourmet scene, serving traditional German cuisine with a twist. ◈ *Fichtestraße 31 • Map H6 • 6pm–midnight Mon–Sat • (030) 61 20 10 03 • €€€*

Gorgonzola Club
10 This cosy Italian restaurant produces straightforward classics. It is located right next to the Würgeengel bar *(see p108).* ◈ *Dresdener Str. 121 • Map H5 • from 6pm daily • (030) 615 64 73 • €€*

Following pages: **Gendarmenmarkt at night**

109

Left **Portal of Kronprinzenpalais** Centre **Opernpalais** Right **Inside the Komische Oper**

Central Berlin: Unter den Linden

MOST VISITORS TO BERLIN *regard the magnificent boulevard of Unter den Linden as the heart of the small historic Mitte district. Many of Berlin's sights are concentrated along the grand avenue and around Bebelplatz, creating an impressive picture of Prussian and German history from the early 18th century until the present day. South of Unter den Linden is Gendarmenmarkt, one of Europe's most attractive squares. Many varied and elegant restaurants and cafés are located around this Neo-Classical square. Not far away, chic Friedrichstraße is lined with luxury shops and department stores as well as modern offices and apartments.*

Sculpture on Schlossbrücke

🔟 Sights

1. Brandenburger Tor
2. Deutsche Guggenheim
3. Forum Fridericianum
4. Gendarmenmarkt
5. Museumsinsel
6. Friedrichstraße
7. Holocaust-Denkmal
8. Wilhelmstraße
9. Schlossplatz
10. Museum für Kommunikation

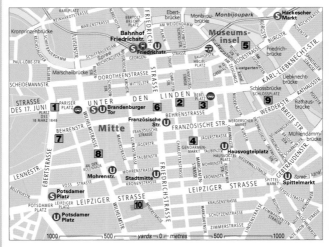

Around Town – Central Berlin: Unter den Linden

Share your travel recommendations on traveldk.com

1 Brandenburger Tor

Berlin's best-known landmark on Pariser Platz leads through to Unter den Linden *(see pp8–9)*. ◎ *Pariser Platz • Map K3*

2 Deutsche Guggenheim

This branch of the American Guggenheim museum, together with the Deutsche Bank branch Unter den Linden, shows changing exhibitions of modern art of the highest standard from the US. Deutsche Guggenheim has thus managed to become one of the most successful and popular art venues in the city, with an emphasis placed on installations. In 2008, Anish Kapoor's *Memory* was a particular highlight. Treasures from the Deutsche Bank archives are also shown here. Pop into the small museum shop and refresh yourself with a coffee from the museum café *(see p49)*. ◎ *Unter den Linden 13–15 • Map K4 • 10am–8pm Fri–Wed, 10am–10pm Thu • (030) 202 09 30 • Admission charge, free on Mon*

3 Forum Fridericianum

The historic structures of this architectural complex in Unter den Linden are among the finest attractions in Berlin. From 1740, Frederick the Great commissioned the prestigious Early-Neo-Classical buildings for the area around today's

Altes Palais at Forum Fridericianum

Bebelplatz, and personally influenced their design: Deutsche Staatsoper, the first free-standing opera house in Europe; Catholic St Hedwigs-kathedrale, Alte Bibliothek and Prinz-Heinrich-Palais, later the Humboldt University. Bebelplatz itself is particularly interesting. A memorial set into the ground reminds of its dark past – in 1933, it was the venue for the Nazi book burning. Frederick's successors commissioned Altes Palais and a memorial statue of "the old Fritz", surrounded by "his" buildings. Christian Daniel Rauch created the 13.5-m (44-ft) high equestrian bronze figure in 1840. It portrays Frederick the Great wearing his trademark tricorn hat and coronation mantle and carrying a walking stick. The statue has always turned its back to the east – but wags claim that the East German government mistakenly set up the figure the wrong way around. ◎ *Unter den Linden and Bebelplatz • Map K4*

Deutsche Guggenheim, Unter den Linden

Frederick as Architect

Forum Fridericianum was not only Frederick the Great's memorial to himself, it also ensured that Unter den Linden became one of the greatest boulevards in Europe. The king, who favoured a strict Neo-Classical style, drew up the plans for the Staatsoper and other buildings himself, and Knobelsdorff executed his ideas.

➤ *For more on Unter den Linden* see pp12–15

Left **Inside the Konzerthaus** Centre **Deutscher Dom** Right **Front view of Altes Museum**

Gendarmenmarkt

This square, whose strict layout is reminiscent of an Italian Renaissance *piazza*, is probably the most beautiful in Berlin. To the left and right of Schauspielhaus – today's Konzerthaus – stand the twin towers of Deutscher and Französischer Dom (German and French cathedrals), dating back to the late 18th century. Gendarmenmarkt, named after a regiment of *gens d'armes* stationed nearby, was built at the end of the 17th century, as a market square. The Schauspielhaus (theatre) on the north side of the square, built by Schinkel in 1818–21, was used as a theatre until 1945. Damaged in World War II, it was reopened as Konzerthaus (concert hall) in 1984. A statue of the playwright Friedrich Schiller stands in front of the building. Französischer Dom, to its right, is a prestigious Late-Baroque building; concealed behind it is the French Friedrichstadtkirche, a church serving Berlin's Huguenot community. The Deutscher Dom opposite, built in 1708 on the south side of the square for the Reformed Protestant Church, did not receive its first tower until 1785. Today it has an exhibition on democracy in Germany. ◈ *Mitte • Map L4*

Figure of Athena in Pergamonmuseum

Museumsinsel

Museum Island, a UNESCO World Heritage Site, is one of the most important complexes of museums in the world, holding major arts collections and imposing full-scale ancient structures. Based here are the Pergamonmuseum, the Alte Nationalgalerie (the old national gallery), Bode-Museum and Altes and Neues Museum. The Neues Museum houses the famous Ägyptisches Museum *(see pp20–23 and 46)*. ◈ *Pergamonmuseum, Bodestr. 1–3 • Map J5 • 10am–6pm daily, till 10pm Thu • (030) 20 90 55 77* ◈ *Alte Nationalgalerie • Bodestr. 1–3 • Map J5 • 10am–6pm Tue–Sun, until 10pm Thu • (030) 20 90 58 01 • Admission charge*

The Huguenots in Berlin

In 1685, the Great Elector issued the famous Edict of Potsdam, granting asylum in Berlin to around 20,000 Huguenots, who were persecuted in their native France because of their Protestant faith. Skilled academics and craftsmen, they moulded the social and cultural life of the city and enriched Berlin with the French art of living. Today, still, the French community worships in the Friedrichstadtkirche on Gendarmenmarkt.

Antique vase in the Pergamonmuseum

Quartier 206 in Friedrichstraße

6 Friedrichstraße

Friedrichstraße has risen to some of the glamour and vibrancy it possessed before World War II. Today, Berlin's Fifth Avenue once again boasts elegant shops and upmarket restaurants and cafés. Especially worth visiting are the three Quartiers 205, 206 and 207 (the latter designed by architect Jean Nouvel) within the Friedrichstadtpassagen, containing the Galeries Lafayette store and Department Store Quartier 206 among others *(see p119)*. At the northern end of the street is the famous Dussmann store (books, music, events), S-Bahn station Friedrichstraße and the former entertainment district, with the Friedrichstadtpalast and Admiralspalast *(see p118)*.
Ⓢ Mitte • Map J–L4

7 Holocaust-Denkmal

This memorial, officially called "Memorial to the Killed Jews of Europe", serves as Germany's national Holocaust memorial. After years of debate, US star architect Peter Eisenman completed the memorial in 2005. It is comprised of a large field with dark grey steles of varying heights up to 2 m (6 ft) high, which symbolize the six million Jews and others murdered by the Nazis in their concentration camps between 1933 and 1945. Underneath the memorial there is an information centre which explains the causes and history of the genocide.
Ⓢ Ebertstr. • Map L3

A Day of Culture

Morning

⏰ Unter den Linden begins at **Pariser Platz** in front of **Brandenburger Tor** *(see pp8–9)*. Stroll eastwards along the wide avenue, past Hotel Adlon Berlin. Then turn right into **Wilhelmstraße** *(see p116)*, the former political nerve centre. On the right-hand side you will pass the new building of the British Embassy. In Behrenstraße you can see the **Holocaust-Denkmal**. Turn left into Französische Straße, which will take you to **Friedrichstraße**. Here you can shop at the **Galeries Lafayette** *(see p119)* or in the **Department Store Quartier 206** *(see p119)*.

After your shopping expedition, you may wish to recover over a snack lunch in the gourmet food department, which is situated in the basement of Galeries Lafayette.

Afternoon

Before you continue your exploration of Friedrichstraße, make a detour to **Gendarmenmarkt** with its Konzerthaus as well as Deutscher and Französischer Dom. From here return to **Friedrichstraße** and its modern buildings. Walk down the street to Leipziger Straße. Turn left into Leipziger Straße, and on the left you will see the giant structure of the former Ministry of Aviation. Today the Federal Ministry of Finance is based here. From here you can retrace your steps to Unter den Linden or return to Gendarmenmarkt. An evening meal at the Italian restaurant **Malatesta** *(see p121)* is highly recommended.

Left **The former Ministry of Aviation, Wilhelmstraße** Centre **Hotel Adlon** Right **Stadtschloss**

Nazi Architecture

One of few surviving examples of the monumental architectural style favoured by Fascists is the former Reichsluftfahrtministerium (Ministry of Aviation), commissioned by Hermann Göring in 1935–6 from Ernst Sagebiel. At the time, the monotonous sandstone building was the world's largest and most modern office block, strengthened by steel girders against aerial attack. After reunification, the Treuhandanstalt was based here; today it houses the Federal Ministry of Finance.

Wilhelmstraße

In imperial Berlin, the centre of the German Empire's governmental power was based in Wilhelmstraße. Around 100 years later, nothing remains of the prestigious historic buildings which represented the equivalent of No. 10 Downing Street in London or Quai d'Orsay in Paris. All political decisions were made at Wilhelmstraße: both Chancellor (No. 77) and President (No. 73) of the German Reich lived here in old town houses. Their gardens became known as "ministerial gardens". Adolf Hitler had the street systematically developed into the nerve centre of Nazi power. The Neue Reichskanzlei (the Chancellor's office) was built in 1937–9 to plans by Albert Speer, at the

British Embassy, Wilhelmstraße

corner of Vossstraße and Wilhelmstraße. It was blown up in 1945. Behind the Reichskanzlei was the so-called "Führerbunker" where Adolf Hitler committed suicide on 30 April 1945 (today it is a car park). Of the historic buildings, only the former Reichsluftfahrtministerium (Ministry of Aviation) remains. Today, Wilhelmstraße is lined by modern residential and office buildings; the British Embassy, built in 2000 by Michael Wilford, creates a link with the international importance of this street. Between Unter den Linden and Leipziger Str. • Map K/L3

Schlossplatz

Today Schlossplatz seems deserted, but once the Stadtschloss (town residence) of the Hohenzollerns stood here. It was blown up by the East German government in 1950–51, and today just a few historic fragments of the original can be seen. Remains include the façade of the doorway where Karl Liebknecht supposedly proclaimed the Socialist Republic in 1918. The portal has been incorporated into the former Staatsratsgebäude on the south side of the square. On its eastern side, Schlossplatz used to be bordered by the Palast der Republik (palace of the republic), the former seat of the East German parliament demolished in 2008.

Development of the Humboldt-Forum cultural centre will be complete in 2015. It will have a façade reminiscent of the old Hohen-zollern Palace, a library and the non-European collections of the Dahlem Museums *(see p89)*. A temporary "White Cube" building will show modern art exhibits until then. ◎ *Mitte • Map G3, K5*

Portal of the Staatsratsgebäude

10 Museum für Kommunikation

The world's largest Post Office Museum was opened as early as 1872. Its excellent displays document the history of communication from the Middle Ages via the first postage stamps to today's satellite technology. Particularly worth seeing are a blue and a red Mauritius stamp, one of the first telephone installations (dating back to the year 1863) and three talking robots who interact with the visitors. Children – young and old – always enjoy the Computergalerie, where they can learn and gain new insights while playing. ◎ *Leipziger Str. 16 • Map L4 • 9am–5pm Tue–Fri, 10am–6pm Sat & Sun • (030) 20 29 40 • Admission charge*

Museum für Kommunikation at night

A Day of Culture

Morning

🕐 Start your stroll on Unter den Linden, at the corner of Friedrichstraße. Once this spot was one of Berlin's liveliest street junctions, and there is still plenty to see today. For breakfast or refreshments, pop into **Café Einstein** *(see p120)*. Afterwards continue eastwards along the boulevard; you will pass numerous fascinating buildings, for example, on the right, the Deutsche Bank with the Kunst-museum **Deutsche Guggenheim** *(see p113)*. From here you can already see the equestrian statue of Frederick the Great, which marks the centre of **Forum Fridericianum** *(see p113)*. This area as well as Bebelplatz are right in the centre of Old Berlin, with Staatsoper, St Hedwigskathedrale, Altes Palais and Humboldt-Universität. You could have lunch in one of the restaurants based in the **Opernpalais**.

Afternoon

In the afternoon continue your stroll along Unter den Linden and, if you like, make a detour to the north to **Museumsinsel** *(see p114)*. Afterwards, if you still feel energetic enough, you could visit **Berliner Dom** *(see p44)*. Opposite the cathedral you will see **Schlossplatz**, with its floating "White Cube" art museum. You could round off your day of sightseeing in Mitte with a delicious evening meal at **Dressler Unter den Linden** *(see p121)*. To get there, just retrace your steps and return along Unter den Linden in a westerly direction.

Left **DDR Museum** Centre **Komische Oper** Right **Admiralspalast**

Best of the Rest

DDR Museum
1 This museum of everyday life in East Germany recreates socialist interiors and displays examples of East German design, including a Trabant car one can sit in. ◎ Karl-Liebknecht-Str. 1 • Map K5 • (030) 847 12 37 31

The Kennedys
2 A museum dedicated to the Kennedy family, including hundreds of photographs and many items of memorabilia. ◎ Pariser Platz 4a • Map K3 • (030) 20 65 35 70 • www.thekennedys.de

WMF-Haus
3 The former headquarters of the porcelain and cutlery manufacturer WMF has remarkable façades, decorated with beautiful mosaics. ◎ Leipziger Str., corner Mauerstr. • Map L3

Alte Kommandantur
4 Designed by Schinkel, this impressive classicist building houses the Berlin offices of media company Bertelsmann. ◎ Unter den Linden 1 • Map K5

Maxim-Gorki-Theater
5 The renowned theatre was once Berlin's Singakademie, or singing school. Paganini and Liszt, among others, performed here. ◎ Am Festungsgraben 2 • (030) 20 22 11 29 • Map K5

S-Bahnhof Friedrichstraße
6 Remodelled several times, this has always been one of Berlin's most famous stations. In 1961–89, it was the principal crossing point between East and West. ◎ Friedrichstr. • Map J4

Admiralspalast
7 Berlin's most legendary venue, dating from the 1920s, stages musicals and comedy shows. ◎ Friedrichstr. 101 • Map J4 • www.admiralspalast.de

Palais am Festungsgraben
8 The Baroque palace of 1753 has maintained its original elegant interior. ◎ Am Festungsgraben 1 • Map K5 • (030) 208 40 00

Komische Oper
9 One of Germany's most magnificent opera houses, dating from 1892, is concealed behind a modern façade. All performances are in German. ◎ Behrenstr. 55–57 • Map K3 • (030) 47 99 74 00

Dalí Museum
10 A rotating exhibition of some 400 works by the 20th-century surrealist, including drawings, paintings and sculptures. ◎ Leipziger Platz 7 • Map L3 • (030) 206 735 860 • www.dalimuseum.de

Left **Outside Berlin Story** Centre **Fashion at Galeries Lafayette** Right **In Quartier 206**

🔟 Shops

Galeries Lafayette
Located within Quartier 207, this is the only German branch of the luxury French store. Here you will find elegant fashion and gourmet foods on the lower level. ⊗ *Friedrichstr. 76–78 • Map L4 • 10am–8pm Mon–Sat • (030) 20 94 80*

Quartier 206
This is where stylish Berliners come to shop for up-to-the-minute and top-of-the-range designer clothes. Shops include Gucci, DKNY and the Department Store Quartier 206. ⊗ *Friedrichstr. 71 • Map L4*

Quartier 205
Q205 has high-end stores such as Leysieffer chocolatier and Annette Görtz modedesign, but it is not quite as exclusive as the attached Q206. A large foodcourt is downstairs. ⊗ *Friedrichstr. 67–70 • Map L4 • 10am–8pm Mon–Sat*

Jack Wolfskin
Stock up on apparel, equipment and footwear before setting out on any outdoor activities at this large branch of Germany's famous outfitter. ⊗ *Behrenstr. 23/corner of Friedrichstr. • Map K4 • (030) 20 64 80 70*

Fassbender & Rausch
Giant chocolate sculptures of the Reichstag and Brandenburger Tor adorn the windows and tempt visitors into this shop, a chocaholic's paradise. ⊗ *Charlottenstr. 60 • Map L4 • (030) 20 45 84 40*

Berlin Story
Almost anything you've ever wanted to read about Berlin, as well as photographs and souvenirs, is available here. ⊗ *Unter den Linden 26 • Map K4 • (030) 20 45 38 42*

Kulturkaufhaus Dussmann
A mecca for culture-junkies, this multi-media store offers good books, computer games and a large section of classical music on CD. The store is also open in the evening. ⊗ *Friedrichstr. 90 • Map K4 • (030) 202 50*

Ritter Sport
The chocolate-maker's flagship store has fun merchandise and a museum, which explains how chocolate is created. ⊗ *Französische Str. 24 • Map K4 • (030) 20 09 50 80*

Escada
Stylish design for women, boasting a fantastic selection of luxurious materials. ⊗ *Friedrichstr. 176–179 • Map L4 • (030) 238 64 43*

Bucherer
A luxury outlet selling quality watches and jewellery. ⊗ *Friedrichstr. 176–179 • Map L4 • (030) 204 10 49*

Left **Café LebensArt** Centre **Opera Court** Right **Brauerei Lemke in an S-Bahn arch**

🔟 Pubs & Bars

Newton-Bar
One of the trendiest bars in town. Sink into the deep leather armchairs and sip your cocktails, surrounded by Helmut Newton's photographs. ◈ *Charlottenstr. 57 • Map L4 • 10am–3am daily • (030) 202 95 40*

Opera Court
Afternoon teas, coffee and cake are served daily at the historic Opera Court, with its original glazed ceiling, in the luxurious Hotel de Rome *(see p179).* ◈ *Hotel de Rome, Behrenstr. 37 • Map G3 • (030) 460 60 90*

Operntreff
Completely furnished in leather, this small but elegant bar in the historic Opernpalais is an ideal stopping-off point for night owls looking for a place to go after an evening at the opera. ◈ *Unter den Linden 5 • Map K3 • 8am–midnight daily • (030) 20 26 83*

Theodor Tucher
A nice restaurant/bistro next to the Brandenburg Gate. Hosts readings and art events. ◈ *Pariser Platz 6a • Map F4 & K3 • 9am–1am daily • (030) 22 48 94 63 • €€*

LebensArt
A café rather than a pub or bar, offering breakfast and afternoon cakes, this is one of the few places open at night on Unter den Linden. ◈ *Unter den Linden 69a • Map K4 • 9am–8pm daily • (030) 44 72 19 30*

Café Einstein
This small and cosy branch of the Café serves excellent wines and Austrian specialities. ◈ *Unter den Linden 42 • Map F4 & K4 • 7am–10pm daily • (030) 204 36 32*

Ständige Vertretung
The name harks back to the permanent West German representation in East Berlin, but the drinks are bang up to date. ◈ *Schiffbauerdamm 8 • Map J3 • 11am–1am daily • (030) 282 39 65*

Label 205 im Q205
An elegant underground lobby bar with cool drinks and piano music. ◈ *Quartier 205, Friedrichstr. 68 • Map L4 • 9am–10pm daily • (030) 20 94 45 45*

Brauhaus Lemke
Atmospheric pub under the S-Bahn arches; courtyard. ◈ *Dircksenstr. S-Bahn arch No. 143 • Map J5 • 11am–midnight daily • (030) 30 87 89 89*

Windhorst
Trendy jazz bar – classy, elegant, good. ◈ *Dorotheenstr. 65 • Map K3 • from 6pm Mon–Fri, from 9pm Sat • (030) 20 45 00 70*

Price Categories

For a three-course
meal for one with half   € under €20
a bottle of wine (or   €€ €20–30
equivalent meal), taxes   €€€ €30–45
and charges included   €€€€ €45–60
                                              €€€€€ over €60

Left **Outside Dressler Unter den Linden** Right **San Nicci**

Restaurants & Cafés

Margaux
A stylish yet affordable gourmet restaurant, the Margaux serves sophisticated French-German nouvelle cuisine. ❧ *Unter den Linden 78 • Map K3 • 7–10:30pm Mon–Sat • (030) 22 65 26 11 • €€€€€*

San Nicci
This glitzy Italian restaurant at the Admiralspalast *(see p56)* is all about stars, fashion and excellent food. ❧ *Friedrichstraße 101 • Map F3 & J4 • 11:30am–midnight daily • (030) 306 454 980 • €€€*

Grill Royal
If you like great steaks, you can choose your cut at this flashy steakhouse. ❧ *Friedrichstraße 105b • Map F3 & J4 • 6pm–midnight daily • (030) 28 87 92 88 • €€€*

Tadschikische Teestube
A well-kept secret specializing in traditional Russian-Asian tea ceremonies as well as providing authentic snacks to nibble. ❧ *Am Festungsgraben 1 • Map G3 & K4 • 5pm–midnight Mon–Fri, 3pm–midnight Sat & Sun • (030) 204 11 12 • €*

Dressler Unter den Linden
In season, this French brasserie is an excellent place to come for oysters. At other times, the inexpensive three-course set menu is recommended. ❧ *Unter den Linden 39 • Map K3 • 8am–1am daily • (030) 204 44 22 • €€€*

Lorenz Adlon
A first-class French-German restaurant offering a formal, rather stiff atmosphere. ❧ *Unter den Linden 77 • Map F3 & K3 • 7–10:30pm Tue–Sat • (030) 22 61 19 60 • €€€€*

Guy
A romantic courtyard wine bar and restaurant serving gourmet food. ❧ *Jägerstraße 59–60 • Map G4 & K4 • noon–3pm, 6pm–1am Mon–Fri, 6pm–1am Sat • (030) 20 94 26 00 • €€€*

Malatesta
Gourmet Italian food served in stylish, minimalist surroundings. ❧ *Charlottenstr. 59 • Map L4 • noon–midnight daily • (030) 20 94 50 71 • €€€*

Refugium
A cosy cellar restaurant next to the French cathedral. International and German dishes. ❧ *Gendarmenmarkt 5 • Map L4 • noon–11pm daily (winter: from 5pm Mon–Fri) • (030) 229 16 61 • €€€*

Aigner
Original Viennese restaurant serving typically Austrian food. ❧ *Französische Str. 25 • Map K4 • noon–1am daily • (030) 203 75 18 50 • €€€*

Note: *All restaurants accept credit cards and offer vegetarian dishes unless stated otherwise.*

Left **Hackesche Höfe** Centre **Tacheles, Oranienburger Straße** Right **In the Hackesche Höfe**

Central Berlin: Scheunenviertel

THE SCHEUNENVIERTEL, *literally the "barn quarter", Berlin's former Jewish quarter, has experienced a unique revival in recent decades. Originally, the thriving Jewish community lived in neighbouring Spandauer Vorstadt, beyond the city limits, while the Scheunenviertel was better known as a red-light district. The Nazis, however, applied the name of "Scheunenviertel" to both areas, in order to tarnish the Jews. After World War II the district was much neglected and gradually fell into decay. Today, many of the historic merchants' yards and narrow side streets have been restored, reviving the Scheunenviertel's unique and lively character. Many pubs and restaurants, galleries and shops are now based here and the area has become very fashionable with locals and visitors alike, especially at night. The tragic history of its former inhabitants, however, remains unforgotten.*

Neue Synagoge

TOP 10 Sights

1. Oranienburger Straße
2. Neue Synagoge
3. Hackesche Höfe
4. Sophienstraße
5. Tacheles
6. Museum für Naturkunde
7. Dorotheenstädtischer Friedhof
8. Brecht-Weigel-Gedenkstätte
9. Gedenkstätte Große Hamburger Straße
10. Postfuhramt

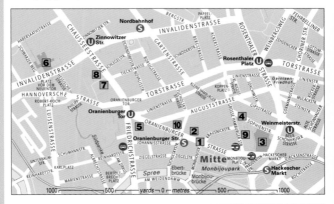

Oranienburger Straße

Like no other street, Oranienburger Straße, in the centre of the old Scheunenviertel, symbolizes the rise and fall of Jewish culture in Berlin. Traces of its Jewish past are visible all along the street, such as the Neue Synagoge and several Jewish cafés and restaurants (see p129). Some 18th- and 19th-century buildings bear witness to the street's former splendour – the Postfuhramt (see p125), for example, or the house at No. 71–72, built in 1789 by Christian Friedrich Becherer for the Grand Lodge of the Freemasons of Germany. ✆ Mitte, between Friedrichstr. and Rosenthaler Str. • Map J4/5

Neue Synagoge

The New Synagogue, built in 1859–66, was once the largest in Europe. In 1938, it managed to survive "Reichskristallnacht" thanks to the vigilance of a brave guard, but it was damaged by bombs during World War II. Behind the Moorish façades are a prayer room and the Centrum Judaicum. ✆ Oranienburger Str. 28–30 • Map J4/5 • 10am–6pm Sun–Thu, 10am–2pm Fri • (030) 8802 8300 00 • Free admission

Hackesche Höfe

Berlin's largest and most attractive group of restored commercial buildings, Hackesche Höfe extends between Oranienburger and Rosenthaler Straße and up to Sophienstraße in the east. The complex of buildings, comprised of nine interconnecting courtyards, was designed around the turn of the 20th century by Kurt Berndt and August Endell, two leading exponents of Art Nouveau. The first courtyard especially features elements that are typical of this style: geometric patterns are laid out in vibrant colours on glazed tiles, covering the entire building from the foundations to the guttering. What had lain in ruin after 1945 has been carefully restored and now forms one of the most popular nightlife centres in the city. Restaurants and cafés (see pp128–9), the Varieté Chamäleon (see p56), galleries and small shops have all settled in this area. ✆ Rosenthaler Str. 40–41 • Map I5

Sophienstraße

Narrow Sophienstraße has been beautifully restored and now looks exactly as it did in the late 18th century. A number of shops and arts and crafts workshops are now based in the modest buildings and courtyards. Close by stands Sophienkirche, the first Protestant parish church, founded by Queen Sophie Luise in 1712. Next to the Baroque church is a small cemetery with some 18th-century tombs. ✆ Große Hamburger Str. 29 • Map I5

The old Sophienkirche

Left **Bertolt Brecht's study** Right **Memorial on Große Hamburger Straße**

5 Tacheles

The ruins of the former Wilhelm-Einkaufspassagen, one of Berlin's most elegant shopping centres dating back to the turn of the 20th century, have been transformed by artists into an alternative arts centre. It now houses workshops and cafés and offers a regular programme of events. ◎ *Oranienburger Str. 54–56a • Map F3 • (030) 282 61 85*

6 Museum für Naturkunde

The Museum of Natural History – one of the largest of its kind – has the world's largest dinosaur skeleton: a brachiosaurus found in Tanzania. Also displayed are fossils, meteorites and minerals *(see also p47)*. ◎ *Invalidenstr. 43 • Map F2 • 9:30am–6pm Tue–Fri; 10am–6pm Sat & Sun • (030) 20 93 85 91 • Admission charge*

7 Dorotheenstädtischer Friedhof

Many celebrities have found their final resting place in this charming cemetery, dating back to 1762. To the left of the entrance are the graves of Heinrich Mann (1871–1950) and Bertolt Brecht (1898–1956); further along are the pillar-like tombstones of philosophers Johann Gottlieb Fichte (1762–1814) and Georg Wilhelm Friedrich Hegel (1770–1831). On Birkenallee (left off the main path) you can see the graves of master builder Karl Friedrich Schinkel (1781–1841)

and architects Friedrich August Stüler (1800–65) and Johann Gottfried Schadow (1764–1850). ◎ *Chausseestr. 126 • Map F2 • summer: 8am–8pm daily; winter: 8am–4pm daily*

Schinkel, Dorotheen-städtischer Friedhof

8 Brecht-Weigel-Gedenkstätte

Bertolt Brecht, one of the 20th century's greatest playwrights, lived here with his wife, Helene Weigel, from 1953–6. Original furnishings are on display alongside documents and photographs. ◎ *Chausseestr. 125 • Map F2 • 10–11:30am Wed & Fri; 10am–noon & 5–6:30pm Thu; 10am–3:30pm Sat; 11am–6pm Sun • (030) 200 571 844 • Admission charge*

Jewish Berlin

In the 19th century, Berlin had a population of 200,000 Jews, the largest such community in Germany. Apart from wealthier Jews in the west of the city, it also attracted many impoverished Jews from Poland and Russia who settled in Spandauer Vorstadt. One part of the district, the criminal red-light district, was also known as Scheunenviertel. Nazi propaganda used the name to denote the entire Spandauer Vorstadt, in order to tarnish the Jews by association. Today, the Jewish quarter is still known under its "wrong" name as "Scheunenviertel", although very few Jews live here now. Only some 5,000 Jewish Berliners managed to survive between 1933–45 in hide-outs.

9 Gedenkstätte Große Hamburger Straße

Before 1939, this was an important Jewish street, with several Jewish schools, the oldest Jewish cemetery in Berlin and an old people's home. The latter achieved tragic fame during the Nazi period – the SS used it as a detention centre for Berlin Jews before transporting them to the concentration camps. A monument commemorates thousands of Jews who were sent to their death from here. To the left of the home is a Jewish school, on the site of an earlier school founded in 1778 by the Enlightenment philosopher Moses Mendelssohn (1729–86). To the right of the monument is the Jewish cemetery, where some 12,000 Berlin Jews were buried between 1672 and 1827. In 1943, the Nazis almost completely destroyed the cemetery. Only a few Baroque tombs, or *masebas*, survived; these are now embedded into the small original cemetery wall. The place presumed to be Moses Mendelssohn's tomb is marked by a monument. ◈ *Große Hamburger Str. • Map J5*

10 Postfuhramt

The richly ornamented Postfuhramt (post office transport department) dates from the 19th century. It is now an exhibition hall for alternative photography and art shows, and a centre for performance art. It also houses the C/O Berlin gallery. ◈ *Oranienburger Str. 35 • Map J4*

Frieze on the Postfuhramt façade

A Day in Scheunenviertel

Morning

🕐 Take the S-Bahn to Friedrichstraße and explore this road, Berlin's former entertainment district. Walk north along the street up to Reinhardtstraße, and turn left here towards Bertolt-Brecht-Platz. Continue south to Albrechtstraße to the **Berliner Ensemble** *(see p126)*. Once you have admired the theatre where the great playwright used to work, you could make a detour to visit his home, **Brecht-Weigel-Gedenkstätte** in Chausseestraße. The best way to get there is on foot – walk along Chausseestraße. If you remain in Friedrichstraße and turn right behind Friedrichstadtpalast you will get to **Oranienburger Straße** *(see p123)*, you will get to the heart of the fashionable Scheunenviertel. At the corner of the street rises the arts centre **Tacheles**, and a few steps to the east the shiny golden dome of the **Neue Synagoge** will come into view *(see pp45 and 123)*.

Afternoon

Before exploring the Scheunenviertel district, you should take some refreshments; not far from the Synagogue is **Keyser Soze** *(see p129)*. Walk along Tucholskystraße, then turn right into Auguststraße. Here you will find some of the most attractive courtyards, for example **Kunsthof** at the corner of Gartenstraße. Return along Auguststraße to **Gedenkstätte Große Hamburger Straße** and the **Hackesche Höfe** *(see p123)* to shop and for an evening meal.

Left **Inside Sophienkirche** Centre **The Berliner Ensemble** Right **The Deutsches Theater**

ᵀ⁰ᴾ10 Best of the Rest

1 Charité
Many important physicians, such as Rudolf Virchow and Robert Koch, worked and taught at this world-famous hospital, founded in 1710. A Museum of Pathology has some 23,000 remarkable exhibits on display. Ⓢ *Schumannstr. 20–21 • Map J3 • Medizinhistorisches Museum 10am–5pm Tue, Thu, Fri, Sun, 10am–7pm Wed & Sat • (030) 450 53 61 29*

2 Alte and Neue Schönhauser Straße
Alte Schönhauser Straße is one of the oldest streets in Spandauer Vorstadt. The lively road is still characterized by a colourful jumble of traditional and new fashion shops. Ⓢ *Hackescher Markt • Map J5*

3 Deutsches Theater
Once Max Reinhardt's place of work, the theatre – widely considered the best German-language theatre – shows mainly German classics, often in new interpretations. Ⓢ *Schumannstr. 13a • Map J3 • (030) 28 44 12 25*

4 Berliner Ensemble
This theatre, established in 1891–2 by Heinrich Seeling, was the main venue for Bertolt Brecht's plays. Ⓢ *Bertolt-Brecht-Platz 1 • Map J3 • (030) 28 40 81 55*

5 Hochbunker
One of the last surviving World War II bunkers. Ⓢ *Albrechtstr. corner of Reinhardtstr. • Map J3*

6 Monbijoupark
A small park, in which once stood the little Monbijou palace. It is now an attractive green space for a rest. Ⓢ *Oranienburger Str./Spree • Map J5*

7 Auguststraße
The area round this road is one of the closest to the original old Scheunenviertel, featuring old interior courtyards and brimming with art galleries. Ⓢ *Between Oranienburger and Rosenthaler Str. • Map G2*

8 Koppenplatz
In this small square, a monument of a table and upturned chair recall the expulsion of the Jews. Ⓢ *Near Auguststr. • Map G2*

9 Sophienkirche
This parish church, built in 1712, has managed to preserve its traditional Old Berlin charm. Be sure to see the Baroque pulpit. Ⓢ *Große Hamburger Str. 29 • Map G2*

10 Tucholskystraße
This narrow street is typical of the transformation of Scheunenviertel – trendy shops next to decaying façades. Ⓢ *Map J4*

Left **Heckmann-Höfe** Centre **Sophienhöfe** Right **The alternative Kunstwerke gallery**

🔟 Old Courtyards

1 Sophie-Gips-Höfe
Famous for the Hoffman art collection, which is based here, this former sewing machine factory is a popular meeting place for locals. ◈ *Sophienstr. 21–22 • Map G3*

2 Sophienhöfe
The 19th-century red-brick artisans' workshops have been transformed into artists' studios. ◈ *Sophienstr. 17–18 • Map G3*

3 Heckmann-Höfe
These lavishly restored yards, the most elegant in Berlin, attract visitors today with a restaurant and fashionable clothes shops. ◈ *Between Rosenthaler and Tucholskystr. 34 • Map J4*

4 Kunstwerke
Large-scale installations by the resident artists are regularly on display at the alternative gallery space; one of Carsten Höller's slides is a permanent feature. The courtyard also has a café in the conservatory. ◈ *Auguststr. 69 • Map G2*

5 Rosenthaler Straße 37
This narrow unrestored alleyway and courtyard gives a good impression of how the entire area once looked. Just enter via the archway – you will be able to stroll around and drink a beer at the tables on the left. Until 1933, a Jewish school for the blind was based in these buildings. ◈ *Rosenthaler Str. 37 • Map G2*

6 Schulhof
Time seems to have stood still around 1900 in this courtyard, today part of the district's Kulturamt (cultural office). ◈ *Auguststr. 21 • Map G2*

7 Hof Joachimstraße
The extensive courtyard of the former Postfuhramt permits a glimpse of the original façade of the building. ◈ *Joachimstr. 11 • Map G2*

8 Auguststraße 83
A café and an art gallery are now based in the yard of a former sewing machine factory. ◈ *Auguststr. 83/Linienstr. 147 • Map G2*

9 Kunsthof
A courtyard full of nooks and crannies, which is today occupied by a number of workshops, offices and cafés. Take a look at the richly ornamented staircases. ◈ *Oranienburger Str. 27 • Map J4/5*

10 Sophienstr. 22 and 22a
Two small inner courtyards, partially planted, are surrounded by yellow and red brick walls. ◈ *Sophienstr. 22–22a • Map G3*

Left **The O & G club** Centre **Drinks at Yosoy** Right **The Reingold bar**

🔟 Pubs, Bars & Discos

1 Riva
This elegant and trendy bar is named after an Italian soccer player. ✆ *Dircksenstr., Arch 142 • Map J5 • 6pm–4am daily • (030) 24 72 26 88*

2 Bellini Lounge
Head this way for some of the most authentic tropical cocktails mixed north of the equator. ✆ *Oranienburger Str. 42 • Map J4 • 6pm–3am daily • (030) 97 00 56 18*

3 Betty F
A trashy gay and straight pub that pays an ironic homage to former US First Lady Betty Ford. Great cocktails. ✆ *Mulackstraße 13 • Map H2 • from 9pm daily • (0172) 252 197 395*

4 Reingold
A relaxed, fashionable bar with a 1920s atmosphere. Perfect for a nightcap after dinner in Mitte. ✆ *Novalistraße 11 • Map G2 • from 7pm Tue–Sat • (030) 28 38 76 76*

5 O & G
In a former socialist fruit store, O & G's DJs create a flirtatious atmosphere for young Mitte lovers. ✆ *Oranienburger Str. 48–49 • Map J5 • from 6pm daily • (030) 25 76 26 28*

6 B-flat
Live jazz and occasionally dance are on offer at this small venue. ✆ *Rosenthaler Str. 13 • Map J5 • from 8pm daily • (030) 283 31 23*

7 Delicious Doughnuts
An old favourite among the hip new clubs of the district, promising to take you "back to the roots". Hot funk and soul rhythms are played. ✆ *Rosenthaler Str. 9 • Map J5 • from 10pm daily • (030) 28 09 92 74*

8 Oxymoron
This small bar, club and restaurant in Hackesche Höfe, featuring chintz decoration, serves light German and international meals. ✆ *Rosenthaler Str. 40–41 • Map J5 • from 10am daily • (030) 28 39 18 86*

9 Yosoy
This attractively furnished Spanish restaurant serves tasty tapas, good wines and exciting cocktails – which is why it is crowded till late into the night. ✆ *Rosenthaler Str. 37 • Map J5 • from 11am daily • (030) 28 39 12 13*

10 Kaffee Burger
This pub and music venue is a favourite with East Berlin hipsters thanks to its quirky record release parties, readings and film screenings. ✆ *Torstr. 58–60 • Map G2 • from 9pm Mon–Sat, from 7pm Sun • (030) 28 04 64 95*

Price Categories

For a three-course meal for one with half a bottle of wine (or equivalent meal), taxes and charges included

€ under €20
€€ €20–30
€€€ €30–45
€€€€ €45–60
€€€€€ over €60

Left **Alpenstück** Right **Pan Asia**

🔟 Restaurants & Cafés

1 Pan Asia
Asian dishes, many with seared fish and vegetables – not too spicy – in minimalist 1960s surroundings. ✪ *Rosenthaler Str. 38 • Map J5 • noon–midnight daily • (030) 27 90 88 11 • €€*

2 Keyser Soze
Unpretentious restaurant serving breakfast until 6pm and hearty German snacks throughout the day. ✪ *Tucholskystr. 33 • Map J4 • 8am–3am daily • (030) 28 59 94 89 • €€*

3 Monsieur Vuong
This tiny Vietnamese snack joint provides delicious Asian dishes. Always crowded, no reservations. ✪ *Alte Schönhauser Straße 46 • Map G3 & J5 • noon–midnight daily • (030) 99 29 69 24 • €*

4 Maxwell
Gourmet restaurant in a New York-style loft; unfussy fusion food. ✪ *Bergstr. 22 • Map G2 • 6–11:30pm daily • (030) 280 71 21 • €€€*

5 Beth-Café
Small Jewish café of the Adass-Jisroel community, serving Jewish snacks. ✪ *Tucholskystr. 40 • Map J4 • 11am–8pm Sun–Thu, 11am–5pm Fri • (030) 281 31 35 • no credit cards • €*

6 Hackescher Hof
The best restaurant in Hackesche Höfe serves traditional German fare. ✪ *Rosenthaler Str. 40–41 • Map J5 • 7am–3am Mon–Fri, 9am–3am Sat & Sun • (030) 283 52 93 • €€€*

7 Nola's am Weinberg
The Swiss cuisine served here is surprisingly inspired. Try one of their delicious fondues. ✪ *Veteranenstraße 9 • Map G2 • 10am–1am Mon–Sun • (030) 440 40 766 • €€*

8 Alpenstück
The best of the homely restaurants serving traditional, hearty fare from Southern Germany and Austria in a cosy setting, decorated in an Alpine style. ✪ *Gartenstraße 9 • Map G2 • 6pm–1am daily • (030) 217 516 46 • €€*

9 Kamala
This hidden gem on touristy Oranienburger Strasse offers Thai cuisine and an impressive wine list. No kitschy thrills and good value for money. ✪ *Oranienburger Str. 69 • Map J5 • noon–11:30pm daily • (030) 283 27 97 • €*

10 Barist
A mixture of French, Italian and Austrian dishes are on offer here. There is always a good atmosphere under the S-Bahn arches; live jazz at weekends. ✪ *Am Zwirngraben 13–14 • Map G2 • 10am–2am daily • (030) 24 72 26 13 • €€*

Note: All restaurants accept credit cards and offer vegetarian dishes unless stated otherwise.

129

Left **Altar painting in Marienkirche** Centre **Frieze on the Münze** Right **Knoblauch-Haus**

Central Berlin: Around Alexanderplatz

THE AREA AROUND ALEXANDERPLATZ *is one of the oldest parts of the city; it was here that the twin towns of Cölln and Berlin merged to become one town in the 13th century. Berlin's oldest coherent quarter, the 18th-century Nikolaiviertel and its medieval Nikolaikirche, the city's oldest church, lie in the shadow of the TV tower, the pride of the "capital" of former East Germany. On the occasion of Berlin's 750th anniversary, in 1987, the East German government had the Nikolaiviertel restored. Very few of the original buildings are preserved, however; most houses were rebuilt from scratch. Only a few paces away from the alleyways of Nikolaiviertel extends Alexanderplatz, referred to by locals simply as "Alex". Before World War II, Alex defined the heartbeat of the city; after the ravages of war, it seemed vast and a little forlorn. Although the giant square is now livelier again, especially in summer, a chilly easterly wind still blows between the houses. The vibrancy of the square, as described by Alfred Döblin in his novel* Berlin Alexanderplatz, *is only slowly returning to the area. Much building and reconstruction work is planned for Alex in the coming years.*

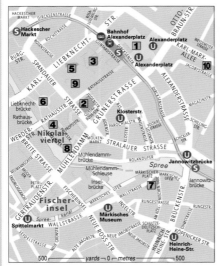

Berliner Rathaus

🔟 Sights

1. Alexanderplatz
2. Berliner Rathaus
3. Berliner Fernsehturm
4. Nikolaiviertel
5. Marienkirche
6. Marx-Engels-Forum
7. Märkisches Museum
8. Ephraim-Palais
9. Neptune Fountain
10. Karl-Marx-Allee and Frankfurter Allee

1 Alexanderplatz

The vast, largely desolate square in the centre of East Berlin, called "Alex" by Berliners, was one of the most vibrant places in Berlin before World War II – and no doubt it will be again some day. Alfred Döblin beautifully

Heraldic animal at the Rathaus

captured the rhythm of the city in his world-famous novel *Berlin Alexanderplatz*. Not much remains today of the once frenzied atmosphere, although there is plenty of hustle and bustle around the Galeria Kaufhof department store *(see p135)*.

Originally, Alex was a cattle and wool market. Not many of the prewar buildings survived – only Berolinahaus and Alexanderhaus, next to the historic S-Bahn station Alexanderplatz, remain, both dating back to 1929. The square was almost completely laid to waste in World War II, and most of the surrounding soulless tower blocks were built in the 1960s. There are now plans to build skyscrapers on Alexanderplatz. ⊗ *Mitte • Map J6*

2 Berliner Rathaus

Berlin's proud town hall is the office of the Governing Mayor and is the political centre of power in Greater Berlin. The Rathaus was built in 1861–9, according to plans by Hermann Friedrich Waesemann on the site of an older town hall. It was designed to demonstrate the power and the glory of Berlin, and the architect took his inspiration for the new governmental building from Italian Renaissance *palazzi*.

The building is also known as the "Red Town Hall" – not a reminder of its Socialist past, but a reference to the red bricks from Brandenburg province from which it is built *(see also p38)*. ⊗ *Rathausstr. 15 • Map K6 • 9am–6pm Mon–Fri • (030) 90 26 0*

3 Berliner Fernsehturm

The 368-m (1,207-ft) high TV tower is the tallest building in Berlin, affording views of up to 40 km (25 miles) in good weather. There is a viewing platform at 203 m (666 ft). The Tele-Café above rotates once around its own axis every 30 minutes. The tower, visible from afar, was erected in 1965–9 by the East German government to signify the triumph of East Berlin, their "capital". ⊗ *Panoramastr. 1a • Map J6 • Mar–Oct: 9am–midnight; Nov–Feb: 10am–midnight • (030) 242 33 33 • Admission charge*

Left **Weltzeituhr (world time clock) on "Alex"** Right **Inside the Tele-Café of Fernsehturm**

Left **Nikolaikirche, Nikolaiviertel** Centre **Märkisches Museum** Right **A street in Nikolaiviertel**

4 Nikolaiviertel

Around the medieval Nikolaikirche (see p44), the small Nikolaiviertel with its narrow nooks and crannies, Old Berlin restaurants and souvenir shops is one of the most charming parts of the city. The area extending between the banks of the Spree River and Mühlendamm was razed to the ground in World War II. The East German authorities restored it after the war – unfortunately not always successfully: some houses were covered in prefabricated façades.

Knoblauchhaus was one of few to escape destruction. Dating from 1835, it was the former home of the Knoblauch family (Neue Synagoge was designed by architect Eduard Knoblauch). Today it houses a museum depicting everyday life in Berlin, and includes a fully furnished apartment in the Biedermeier style. ◈ *Mitte, Knoblauchhaus: Poststr. 23 • Map K6 • 10am–6pm Tue, Thu–Sun, 10am–8pm Wed • (030) 240 02 01 71 • Admission charge*

5 Marienkirche

Originally built in 1270, Marienkirche was extensively remodelled in the 15th century. Thanks to its Baroque church tower, designed by Carl Gotthard Langhans in 1790, it is one of Berlin's loveliest churches. Inside, the alabaster pulpit by Andreas Schlüter (1703) and the main altar (1762) are particularly worth seeing. The 15th-century Gothic font and a 22-m (72-ft) long fresco, *Der Totentanz* (The Dance of Death) from 1485 are its two oldest treasures. Once the centre of a densely built-up neighbourhood, the church is now the only reminder of the historic city core. ◈ *Karl-Liebknecht-Str. 8 • Map K6 • Apr–Oct: 10am–9pm daily; Nov–Mar: 10am–6pm daily • (030) 242 44 67*

Marx and Engels

6 Marx-Engels-Forum

Shortly after German reunification in 1989, the motto "Next time it will all be different" was scrawled onto this monument to Karl Marx and Friedrich Engels, the fathers of Socialism. The bronze statues, created by Ludwig Engelhart in 1986, adorn the square. ◈ *Map K5/6*

7 Märkisches Museum

Berlin's municipal museum displays architectural treasures such as doorways and the head of one of the horses from the top of the Brandenburg Gate, plus various items relating to theatre and music in Berlin. ◈ *Am Köllnischen Park 5 • Map L6 • 10am–6pm Tue, Thu–Sun, noon–8pm Wed • (030) 308 62 15 • Admission charge*

Altar in Marienkirche

Ephraim-Palais

Ephraim-Palais

8 The curved Baroque palace, built in 1766 for the wealthy merchant Nathan Veitel Heinrich Ephraim, was once regarded as the city's most beautiful spot. Rebuilt after the old palace was demolished, it is now a museum with exhibitions on Berlin art history. ✎ *Poststr. 16 • Map K6 • 10am–6pm Tue & Thu–Sun, noon–8pm Wed • (030) 24 00 21 21 • Admission charge*

Neptune Fountain

9 The green Neo-Baroque fountain, dating from 1895, depicts the sea god Neptune. He is surrounded by four female figures, symbolizing Germany's Rhine, Weichsel, Oder and Elb Rivers. ✎ *Am Rathaus • Map K6*

Karl-Marx-Allee and Frankfurter Allee

10 This avenue, lined by Soviet-style buildings, was built as a show-piece for Socialism in 1949–55. Known then as "Stalinallee", it provided ultra-modern apart-ments. ✎ *Mitte/Friedrichshain*

Neptune Fountain

A Day around Alexanderplatz

Morning

🕐 Start your day by going to **Alexanderplatz** *(see p131)* where you can watch the crowds in the square and perhaps do a spot of shopping before strolling to **Marienkirche**. Not far from here you can chill out at **Neptune Fountain** and then admire the statues of Marx and Engels in the **Marx-Engels-Forum**. From there it is only a few steps to the **Berliner Rathaus** *(see p131)*. The basement restaurant, or Ratskeller, is an excellent place for an early lunch, or you could stroll to the nearby historic Nikolaiviertel, and enjoy a meal, for example at **Reinhard's** *(see p137)*, which serves rustic fare.

Afternoon

Experience the historic ambience of the **Nikolaiviertel** by exploring on foot, if possible, its narrow alleyways. Nikolaikirche and the Knoblauchhaus are especially worth a visit. From here walk back to Alexanderplatz and – if the weather is nice – take the lift up to the viewing café in the **Berliner Fernsehturm** *(see p131)*. After refreshments you can continue on foot or take the U-Bahn from Alex to Strausberger Platz to admire the products of Socialist architecture in **Frankfurter Allee**. On Grunerstraße you will reach the opposite bank of the Spree River, where you can immerse yourself in Berlin's municipal history at the **Märkisches Museum** just around the corner. In the evening, go for a meal at **Zur Gerichtslaube** *(see p137)*.

Left **Stairs of the Stadtgericht** Centre **Palais Podewil** Right **Ruins of Franziskanerkirche**

Best of the Rest

Stadtgericht
The imposing municipal courts building boasts extravagant stairs in the lobby area, with curved balustrades and elegant columns. ◎ *Littenstr. 13–15 • Map K6 • 8am–6pm Mon–Fri*

Franziskanerkirche
The ruins, remnants of a 13th-century Franciscan abbey, are surrounded by lawns, making this a picturesque spot for a rest in the city centre.
◎ *Klosterstr. 74 • Map K6*

Stadtmauer
A fragment of the 13th–14th-century town wall that once surrounded the twin towns of Berlin and Cölln. ◎ *Waisenstr. • Map K6*

Palais Podewil
The light yellow Baroque palace, built in 1701–4, has been transformed into Podewil, a cultural centre and one of the best places for contemporary music.
◎ *Klosterstr. 68 • Map K6 • 11am–10pm Mon–Sat • (030) 24 74 96*

Parochialkirche
This church, by Johann Arnold Nering and Martin Grünberg, was one of Berlin's most charming Baroque churches, but the magnificent interior was destroyed in World War II, and the bell tower collapsed.

It is now a venue for contemporary music concerts. ◎ *Klosterstr. 67 • Map K6*

Märkisches Ufer
This picturesque riverside promenade gives a good impression of the city in the late 18th century. ◎ *Map L6*

Heiliggeistkapelle
The 13th-century hospital church is a beautiful example of Gothic brick architecture.
◎ *Spandauer Str. 1 • Map K6*

Ribbeckhaus
The only Renaissance house in central Berlin, with a remarkable, lavishly ornamented façade. ◎ *Breite Str. 36 • Map K5*

AquaDom and Sea Life Berlin
Discover a host of species living in rivers, lakes and seas, and see amazing corals and tropical fish at this fascinating centre, which boasts the largest cylindrical aquarium in the world *(see p65)*.

Historic Port
Historic barges and tugboats that once operated on the Spree River are moored here. Boat tours of the harbour can be booked.
◎ *Märkisches Ufer • Map L6 • Apr–Oct: 11am–6pm Tue–Sun • (030) 21 47 32 57*

Left **Galeria Kaufhof façade** Centre **Inside Die Puppenstube** Right **Der Teeladen in Nikolaiviertel**

🔟 Shops & Markets

1 Galeria Kaufhof
The largest department store in East Berlin stocks everything your heart could desire. Its food department entices customers with a range of international gourmet foods. 🗺 *Alexanderplatz 9 • Map I6 • 9:30am–8pm Mon–Wed, 9:30am–10pm Thu–Sat • (030) 24 74 30*

2 Die Puppenstube
Adorable dolls made from porcelain and other materials await, as do mountains of cute fluffy teddy bears. 🗺 *Propststr. 4 • Map K6 • 10am–6:30pm Mon–Sat, 11am–6pm Sun • (030) 242 39 67*

3 Teddy's
An old-fashioned toy store, with probably the best selection of teddy bears in the city. 🗺 *Propststr. 4 • Map K6 • 10am–6pm daily (from 11am Sat & Sun) • (030) 247 82 44*

4 Der Teeladen
A charming specialist tea shop opposite Nikolaikirche, full of delicious scents. 🗺 *Propststr. 3 • Map K6 • 10am–6:30pm Mon–Fri, 10am–4pm Sat • (030) 242 32 55*

5 Good Old Germany
Trendy not tacky souvenirs: retro and modern German classics of design, porcelain, textiles, fashion and delicacies. 🗺 *Spandauer Str. 3 • Map K6 • 10am–9pm daily • (030) 26 36 99 41*

6 U- and S-Bahnhof Alexanderplatz
This bustling area has a selection of shops for daily needs, plus late-opening fast food outlets and German *imbisse* (food stands). 🗺 *Alexanderplatz • Map J6*

7 Alexa
This shopping mall is home to some 180 retail outlets as well as Kindercity, a children's entertainment centre, and LOXX, the world's largest digitally operated model train display. 🗺 *Am Alexanderplatz, Grunerstr. 20 • Map K6 • 10am–9pm Mon–Sat • (030) 269 34 00*

8 Erzgebirgischer Weihnachtsmarkt
A vast array of stalls laden with German handicrafts including traditional wooden nutcrackers. 🗺 *Propststr. 8 • Map K6 • 11am–6pm daily • (030) 241 12 29*

9 die mitte
Visit this large shopping centre for flagship fashion stores Esprit and New Yorker, or multimedia at Saturn. 🗺 *Alexanderplatz • Map J6 • 10am–9pm Mon–Sat • (030) 263 99 70*

10 Münzstrasse
This tiny street, just off Alexanderplatz, is full of original fashion boutiques and designer stores. A real mecca for fashion aficionados. 🗺 *Münzstr. • Map J6*

Left **Brauhaus Georgbräu** Centre **Zur letzten Instanz** Right **Telecafé Fernsehturm**

Zur letzten Instanz
1 Berlin's oldest pub dates back to 1621, and former guests include Napoleon, the German artist Heinrich Zille and former Soviet leader Mikhael Gorbachev. ◈ *Waisenstr. 14–16 • Map K6 • noon–1am Mon–Sat • (030) 242 55 28 • €€*

Brauhaus Georgbräu
2 Attracting Bavarians and tourists alike, this beer garden offers rustic fare and beer from both Berlin and Munich. ◈ *Spreeufer 4 • Map K5/6 • summer: 10am–midnight daily; winter: from noon Mon–Fri • (030) 242 42 44 • €€*

La Siesta
3 This small and friendly coffee shop offers tasty and inexpensive soups and snacks. In the summer, you can enjoy them alfresco, in the square. ◈ *Garnisonkirchplatz 2 • Map J5 • from 8am Mon–Fri • (030) 56 97 31 61 • €*

Zum Nußbaum
4 A charming historic pub in Nikolaiviertel, serving draught beers and *Berliner Weiße* in summer. ◈ *Am Nußbaum 3 • Map K6 • noon–11pm daily • (030) 242 30 95 • €€*

Chefetage
5 This tiny place serves excellent coffee, sandwiches and soups, all cooked fresh from regional ingredients. Service is speedy. ◈ *Inselstraße • Map L6 • 9am–midnight Mon–Fri, 9am–6pm Sat & Sun • (030) 24 72 36 55 • €–€€*

Alt-Berliner Weissbierstube
6 This cosy replica of an old Berlin pub specializes in Berliner Weiße, the city's classic summer beer doctored with shots of syrup. ◈ *Rathausstraße 21 • Map K6 • from 11am daily • (030) 242 44 54 • €*

Café Ephraim's
7 Coffee and cakes plus good views of the Spree River attract locals and tourists. ◈ *Spreeufer 1 • Map K5/6 • noon–10pm daily • (030) 24 72 59 47 • no credit cards • €€*

Telecafé Fernsehturm
8 Enjoy a snack in the skies above Berlin; the café does a full rotation every 30 minutes. ◈ *Panoramastr. 1a • Map J6 • 10am–midnight daily • (030) 242 33 33 • €€*

Zum Fischerkietz
9 Atmospheric pub-restaurant, serving beer and the speciality, *Berliner Weiße*. ◈ *Fischerinsel 5 • Map L6 • 11am–midnight daily • (030) 201 15 16 • €€*

Historische Weinstuben
10 A tiny wine bar/pub serving beer and simple German food in historic surroundings. ◈ *Poststr. 23 • Map K6 • noon–midnight daily • (030) 242 41 07 • €€*

Price Categories

For a three-course
meal for one with half
a bottle of wine (or
equivalent meal), taxes
and charges included

€ under €20
€€ €20–30
€€€ €30–45
€€€€ €45–60
€€€€€ over €60

Left **Restaurant Zur Gerichtslaube** Right **Reinhard's in Nikolaiviertel**

⑩ Restaurants

Reinhard's
One of the most charming restaurants in the Mitte district. Savour the international food, surrounded by photos and paintings of famous contemporaries. ◉ *Poststr. 28 • Map K6 • 9am–midnight daily • (030) 242 52 95 • €€€*

HEat
The ultra-chic fusion restaurant at the SAS Radisson *(see p179)* serving an imaginative blend of Oriental and European tastes. ◉ *Karl-Liebknecht-Str. 3 • Map K5 • 6:30am–11pm daily • (030) 23 82 80 • €€€*

Zur Gerichtslaube
The former court building is a stylish setting for traditional Berlin specialities. ◉ *Poststr. 28 • Map K6 • 11:30am–1am daily • (030) 241 56 98 • €€*

Le Provencal
Baked oysters, scallop soup and other seafood delicacies are served in this cosy family-run French restaurant. ◉ *Spreeufer 3 • Map K6 • noon–midnight • (030) 302 75 67 • €€€*

Zum Paddenwirt
A mecca for fans of traditional Berlin food, including fried herrings and brawn, and a strong beer. ◉ *Nikolaikirchplatz 6 • Map K6 • noon–midnight daily • (030) 242 63 82 • no credit cards • €*

Zillestube
Named after the folksy Berlin painter Heinrich Zille, this tiny pub serves hearty Berlin food and traditional beers, in a rustic setting. ◉ *Propststr. 9 • Map K6 • from 11am daily • (030) 242 52 47 • €€*

Marcellino
The best Italian restaurant in the area, with a terrace and a large inviting garden, offering shade on a hot summer's day. Excellent pasta dishes and specials. ◉ *Poststr. 28 • Map K6 • 11am–1am daily • (030) 242 73 71 • €€*

La Riva
A more upmarket Italian venue in Nikolaiviertel, offering delicious pasta dishes, which can be enjoyed outside in summer, with a view of the Spree River. ◉ *Spreeufer 2 • Map K6 • 11am–11pm daily • (030) 242 51 83 • €€*

Kartoffelhaus No. 1
The menu is dominated by potato dishes and Berlin specialities. ◉ *Poststr. 4/5 • Map K6 • noon–midnight daily • (030) 24 72 09 45 • €€*

Mutter Hoppe
Delicious traditional German food, served in gigantic portions, makes up for the service, which is not always the friendliest. ◉ *Rathausstr. 21 • Map K6 • 11:30am–midnight daily • (030) 241 56 26 • €*

Note: All restaurants accept credit cards and offer vegetarian dishes unless stated otherwise.

Left **The façades of restored houses in Hagenauer Straße** Right **The Jewish Cemetery**

Prenzlauer Berg

BERLIN'S PRENZLAUER BERG DISTRICT *attracts locals and tourists like no other part of town because it has undergone the most dramatic changes in recent decades. Today, the old tenement blocks in the former workers' district of East Berlin have been taken over by cafés, pubs and restaurants, and the nightlife is exciting and vibrant. Even when Berlin was still a divided city, Prenzlauer Berg was an area favoured by artists and an alternative crowd – and it exerts a similar pull today. Several buildings in the quiet side streets have not yet been renovated and give a genuine impression of what Berlin once used to be like. But Prenzlauer Berg is undergoing a transformation. Since the reunification of the city, this quarter has become a popular residential area. Many West Germans, decried as "yuppies" by the locals, settle here, restore the buildings and buy up the apartments. The standard of life in the district has risen noticeably. High-end boutiques, trendy bars, restaurants and cafés are clustered mainly around Kollwitzplatz and Husemannstraße, giving the tree-lined streets an almost Parisian flair. Kastanienallee, the catwalk of Berlin's hip young scene, is dubbed "Casting Allee".*

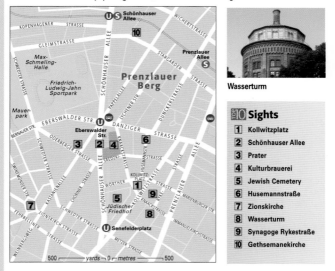

Wasserturm

🔟 Sights

1. Kollwitzplatz
2. Schönhauser Allee
3. Prater
4. Kulturbrauerei
5. Jewish Cemetery
6. Husemannstraße
7. Zionskirche
8. Wasserturm
9. Synagoge Rykestraße
10. Gethsemanekirche

For more information on Prenzlauer Berg, visit **www.tic-berlin.de**

Kollwitz monument in Kollwitzplatz

1 Kollwitzplatz

Once a quiet square, Kollwitzplatz is today the noisy and turbulent heart of the district. All around the green square, locals congregate in numerous cafés, pubs, bars and restaurants; in summer especially, the fun carries on till late at night. From the appearance of the lavishly restored façades it is hard to tell that Kollwitzplatz was once one of Berlin's poorest areas. The impoverished past of the district and its 19th-century tenement blocks is today only recalled by the name of the square. The artist Käthe Kollwitz (1867–1945) *(see p51)* once lived and worked at Kollwitzplatz 25 (now destroyed) and spent much of her life in the district, where she highlighted the poverty of the local workers in her sculptures, drawings and sketches.
◈ *Prenzlauer Berg* • *Map H2*

2 Schönhauser Allee

Schönhauser Allee, 3 km (2 miles) long, is the main artery of the district. In the centre of the dual carriageway is the high-level viaduct of U-Bahn line U 2, painted green. Schönhauser Allee, which runs northeast from Rosa-Luxemburg-Platz to the edge of town, is lined with shops and pubs. A few buildings have not yet been restored and give a good impression of the "old" Prenzlauer Berg – especially the buildings between Senefelderplatz and Danziger Straße. ◈ *Prenzlauer Berg* • *Map H1/2*

3 Prater

The Prater is one of the few remaining entertainment complexes that were once common in Germany's big cities. It was built in 1837 just outside the original city gates, and was first jokingly called "Prater" by Berliners after its world-famous counterpart in Vienna. A concert hall was added in 1857 and by the turn of the century it had become so popular that the nickname stuck. Today, you can enjoy beer and food at the restaurant of the same name *(see p143)*. ◈ *Kastanienallee 7–9* • *Map G2* • *6pm–midnight Mon–Sat, noon–midnight Sun* • *(030) 448 56 88*

4 Kulturbrauerei

The giant building originally housed Berlin's Schultheiss brewery, one of the few remaining breweries that once made Prenzlauer Berg famous. The complex of buildings, parts of which are more than 150 years old, was designed by Franz Schwechten. It was completely restored in 1997–9, and has become a lively and popular meeting point for locals. Restaurants, cafés, pubs, a cinema, small shops and even a theatre have sprung up within the complex of red and yellow brick buildings and now line its numerous interior courtyards. ◈ *Schönhauser Allee 36–39 (entrance: Knaackstr. 97)* • *Map H1* • *(030) 44 31 50*

Kulturbrauerei tower

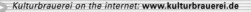

Left **A house in Kollwitzplatz** Centre **At the Prater** Right **In Kollwitzstraße**

Prenzlberg or Prenzlauer Berg?

Many locals today simply say "Prenzlberg" when talking about "their" quarter. But this name is used mainly by West Berliners and West Germans who have recently moved here – the real name is Prenzlauer Berg, just as it is written. The supposed nickname is just a new-fangled term for a district that has become fashionable after the fall of the Wall.

5 Jewish Cemetery

The small Jewish cemetery is one of the most charming cemeteries in the city. The tombstones lie or stand here amid dense scrub and high trees. The cemetery was set up in 1827, when the former Jewish cemetery in Große Hamburger Straße was closed. Two of the famous personalities who have found their final resting places here are the painter Max Liebermann (1847–1935) and the composer Giacomo Meyerbeer (1791–1864). ✪ Schönhauser Allee 23–25 • Map H2

6 Husemann-straße

The East German regime undertook a perfect restoration of this idyllic street for Berlin's 750th anniversary celebrations. A stroll through the leafy roads lined with houses from the

Gründerzeit (the years after the founding of the German Empire in 1871) is one of the nicest ways to experience Prenzlauer Berg. Ancient-looking street lamps and signs, cobbled streets, antiquated shop signs and a few atmospheric pubs take the visitor back to the late 19th century. ✪ Between Wörther and Danziger Str. • Map H1/2

7 Zionskirche

Zionskirche, dating from 1866–73, and the square of the same name form a tranquil oasis in the middle of the lively district. The Protestant church has always been a political centre, too. During the Third Reich, resistance groups against the Nazi regime congregated here and, during the East German period, the alternative "environment library" (an information and documentation centre) was established here. Church and other opposition groups who were active here played a decisive role in the political transformation of East Germany in 1989–90, which eventually led to reunification.

✪ Zionskirchplatz • Map G2 • 8pm–10pm Mon, 11am–7pm Thu, noon–6pm Sun • (030) 449 21 91

Zionskirche

8 Wasserturm

The unofficial symbol of the district is the giant, 30-m (98-ft) high Water Tower in Knaackstraße, built in 1877 as a water reservoir, but shut down in 1914. The engine house in the tower was used as an unofficial prison by the SA in 1933–45 – a period recalled by a commemorative plaque. The tower stands on Windmühlenberg (windmill hill), where some of the windmills that had made Prenzlauer Berg famous in the 19th century once stood. Today the round brick building has been converted into trendy apartments.

Synagoge Rykestraße

The synagogue, built in 1904, is one of the few Jewish places of worship to have survived "Reichs-kristallnacht" on 9 November 1938, the violent destruction of Jewish shop premises by the Nazis. The historic interior of the synagogue was built from red bricks in the shape of a basilica. Today it is part of an apartment block. ✎ *Rykestr. 53 • Map H2 • by prior arrangement • (030) 88 02 83 16*

Gethsemanekirche

Outside this red-brick church, dating back to 1891–3, East German secret police beat up peaceful protesters. It was the starting point for the collapse of the East German regime. ✎ *Stargarder Str. 77 • Map H1 • May–Oct: 5–7pm Wed & Thu (otherwise by prior arrangement) • (030) 445 77 45*

Entrance to Gethsemanekirche

A Day in Prenzlauer Berg

Morning

🕐 Set off from U-Bahn station Senefelderplatz – one of the lively spots in Prenzlauer Berg. From here, explore the old tenement blocks and backyards. Now continue in a westerly direction along Fehrbelliner Straße to **Zionskirchplatz** with its eponymous church. There are numerous cafés on the square, such as **Kapelle**, where you could stop for a capuccino. Continue along Zionskirchstraße, then turn left into Kastanienallee. This is one of the most colourful streets in the quarter. At the end of the street you could pop into **Prater** *(see p143)*; now turn right into Oderberger Straße, one of the best preserved streets of the district. Continue along Sredzkistraße in an easterly direction until you reach **Husemannstraße**. Have a good look around the Old Berlin streets, you may find something interesting to buy.

Afternoon

You could have lunch at one of the many restaurants in **Kollwitz-platz** *(see p139)*: **Gugel-hof** and **Zander** are both worth recommending *(for both see p143)*. Continue along Knaackstraße to the small **Synagoge Ryke-straße**. From here it is only a few paces to the **Wasserturm** in Knaack-straße. Give your feet a rest on the small green space around the tower, before continuing along Belforter and Kollwitz-straße to Schönhauser Allee. You will find perfect tranquillity there in the **Jewish Cemetery**.

Left **Senefelderplatz** Centre **Pfefferberg** Right **ZEISS-Großplanetarium**

Best of the Rest

1 Greifenhagener Straße
Not the most beautiful street of Old Berlin, but one of the best preserved. ◈ Map H1

2 Pfefferberg
This alternative cultural centre hosts concerts, performance art events and festivals. ◈ Schönhauser Allee 176 • Map H2 • (030) 44 38 33 42

3 Senefelderplatz
The wedge-shaped square is dedicated to Alois Senefelder, a pioneer of modern printing techniques. At its centre is a "Café Achteck", a historic public urinal. ◈ Map H2

4 ZEISS-Großplanetarium
A trip to outer space – see stars, planets and galaxies under the silvery dome of the Planetarium. ◈ Prenzlauer Allee 80 • 9am–noon Tue–Thu, 7–9pm Fri; also pm Sat & Sun • (030) 421 84 50

5 Mauerpark
The vast sporting terrain near the former border, comprising Max Schmeling Hall and Jahn Sports Park, was built for the Berlin Olympic bid in 2000. Today it hosts sports and music events, and a Sunday flea market. ◈ Am Falkplatz • Map G1

6 Helmholtzplatz
Apart from the trendy cafés and bars, time seems to have stopped in 1925 in this square. The residential buildings are reminiscent of a social housing programme. ◈ Map H1

7 Prenzlauer Berg Museum
This lively museum charts the history of the district and its poor working-class inhabitants in the 19th century. ◈ Prenzlauer Allee 227–228 • Map H2 • 9am–7pm Mon–Fri • (030) 42 40 10 97

8 Konnopke
This legendary Currywurst-imbiss was opened in 1930 under the U-Bahn steel viaduct. The spicy sausages are among the best in the city. ◈ At the southern exit of U-Bahn Schönhauser Allee • Map H1 • 6am–8pm Mon–Fri, noon–7pm Sat • (030) 442 77 65

9 Oderberger Straße
This leafy street is lined with boutiques and cafés but also has a few historic buildings. The old municipal swimming baths of Prenzlauer Berg are also located on this road, at No. 84. ◈ Map G/H1

10 Thälmannpark
One of few parks in the northeast of the city, dominated by Socialist prefabricated buildings. It has a giant monument to Ernst Thälmann, a communist who was murdered by the Nazis. ◈ Prenzlauer Allee • Map H1

Price Categories

For a three-course	€ under €20
meal for one with half	€€ €20–30
a bottle of wine (for	€€€ €30–45
equivalent meal), taxes	€€€€ €45–60
and charges included	€€€€€ over €60

Left **Gugelhof** Right **Café November**

🔟 Restaurants, Pubs & Bars

1 Oderquelle
This quaint little *Kietz* (neighbourhood) pub serves up basic Berlin and German dishes in an alternative, relaxed setting. ⊗ Oderberger Str. 27 • Map G1 • 6pm–1am daily • (030) 44 00 80 80 • €€

2 Gugelhof
Bill Clinton was once a guest at this restaurant, which attracts clients from all over Berlin. The menu features an original combination of German and French dishes. ⊗ Knaackstr. 37 • Map H1/2 • 4pm–1am Mon–Fri, 10am–1am Sat & Sun • (030) 442 92 29 • €€

3 Zander
A small restaurant, offering imaginative interpretations of local fish specialities. The three-course set menu is one of the best in the district. ⊗ Kollwitzstr. 50 • Map H2 • 6–11pm Tue–Sun • (030) 44 05 76 78 • €€€

4 Weinstein
An amicable, rustic wine bar with a great selection of Austrian and German wines and solid bistro fare. ⊗ Lychener Str. 33 • Map H1 • 5pm–2am daily (from 6pm Sun) • (030) 441 18 42 • €€€

5 Prater
Surprises at the Prater include a beer garden, a rustic restaurant in the courtyard, and free live concerts.
⊗ Kastanienallee 7–9 • Map G2 • 6pm–midnight Mon–Sat, noon–midnight Sun • (030) 448 56 88 • no credit cards • €€

6 Knaack-Club
Almost legendary club, playing rock and indie to an alternative crowd. ⊗ Greifswalder Str. 224 • Map H2 • from 10pm Fri & Sat • (030) 442 70 60 • no credit cards

7 Restauration 1900
This venerable restaurant still pulls in the crowds with its deliciously light German cuisine. ⊗ Husemannstr. 1 • Map H1/2 • 10am–open ended daily • (030) 442 24 94 • €€

8 Pasternak
Go Russian at this Moscow-style venue, with borshch, Russian music and vodka. ⊗ Knaackstr. 22 • Map H1/2 • from 9am Mon–Sat; 10am–1am Sun • (030) 441 33 99 • €€

9 Café November
Popular restaurant and bar on the Prenzlauer Berg hill. ⊗ Husemannstr. 15 • Map H1/2 • 10am–1am Mon–Fri, 9am–2am Sat & Sun • (030) 442 84 25 • €

🔟 Mao Thai
One of the best and friendliest Thai restaurants in town, the Mao Thai serves traditional and artistically presented Southeast Asian food. ⊗ Wörther Straße 30 • Map H2 • noon–midnight daily • (030) 441 92 61 • €€

Note: All restaurants accept credit cards and offer vegetarian dishes unless stated otherwise.

Left **Normannenstraße** Centre **Schloss Friedrichsfelde** Right **Köpenick's coat of arms**

Berlin's Southeast

ERLIN'S EAST AND SOUTH *are remarkably different in character. Friedrichshain, Lichtenberg and Hohenschönhausen in the east are densely
built-up, former working-class areas, while green Treptow and idyllic Köpenick
in the far southeast seem like independent villages. The tenement blocks of
East Berlin were steeped in history during World War II and later under
the East German regime. Historic Köpenick and Großer
Müggelsee, meanwhile, are popular daytrip destinations.*

🔟 Sights

1. Köpenicker Altstadt and Köpenicker Schloss
2. O2 World
3. Gedenkstätte Normannenstraße
4. Deutsch-Russisches Museum
5. East Side Gallery
6. Großer Müggelsee
7. Treptower Park
8. Volkspark Friedrichshain
9. Tierpark Friedrichsfelde
10. Gedenkstätte Hohenschönhausen

Köpenick Town Hall

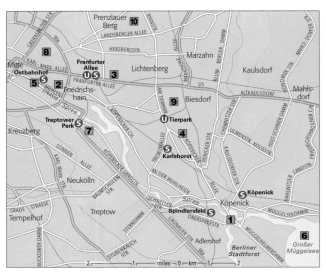

Pool in Köpenicker Altstadt

1 Köpenicker Altstadt and Köpenicker Schloss

The island community of Köpenick has a venerable history: as early as the 9th century, people had settled on Schlossinsel (palace island). The former fishing village stayed independent until 1920. Its coat of arms still features two fish, and the Old Town, on the banks of the Dahme River, has low fishermen's huts from the 18th and 19th centuries. On 16 October 1906, a homeless man named Wilhelm Voigt, dressed as a captain, led a troop of soldiers into the town hall, arrested the mayor and confiscated the municipal coffers. The "Hauptmann von Köpenick" (Captain of Köpenick) is commemorated by a statue in front of the Rathaus (town hall). The vast structure, dating from 1901–4, is a typical example of Gothic brick architecture from Brandenburg province.

The Köpenick palace, situated on Schlossinsel, in the south of the district, was built in 1677–81 to plans by the Dutch architect Rutger van Langervelt for the future King Frederick I. In the 17th century, the charming Baroque palace was extended by Johann Arnold Nering and others. Today it houses part of the collections of the Kunstgewerbe-

Hauptmann von Köpenick

museum (arts and crafts museum) (*see p47*). Rathaus: Alt-Köpenick 21 • 8am–6pm Mon–Fri, 10am–6pm Sat & Sun • (030) 90 29 70 Schlossinsel • 10am–6pm Tue–Sun • (030) 266 29 51 • Admission charge

2 O2 World

Opened in 2008, O2 World is the city's largest entertainment arena, seating 17,000 people. As well as being home to the Alba Berlin basketball team and the Eisbären Berlin ice-hockey club, it hosts pop concerts and shows of all kinds, including the 2009 MTV Europe Music Awards. Mühlenstr. 12–30/O2-Platz 1 • Ticket hotline (01803) 20 60 70/(030) 20 60 70 80

3 Gedenkstätte Normannenstraße

The former headquarters of the much-feared "Stasi", East Germany's secret police, is now a memorial commemorating the thousands of victims of the East German regime and of Erich Mielke, the minister in charge of the secret police. Visitors can see his offices, the canteen and various pieces of spying equipment, revealing the methods used by the Socialist big-brother regime. Ruschestr. 103, Haus 1 • 11am–6pm Mon–Fri, 2–6pm Sat & Sun • (030) 553 68 54 • Admission charge

4 Deutsch-Russisches Museum

World War II ended here on 8 May 1945, when Germany signed its unconditional surrender. Documents, uniforms and photographs, displayed in the former officers' casino, relate the story of the war. Zwieseler Str. 4 • 10am–6pm Tue–Sun • (030) 50 15 08 10

Left **East Side Gallery** Centre **Inside Köpenicker Schloss** Right **Volkspark Friedrichshain**

East Side Gallery

A fragment of the Berlin Wall, 1.3 km (1,422 yards) long, was left standing next to the Spree River. In 1990, 118 artists from around the world painted colourful images onto the grey concrete wall, making it a unique work of art. Particularly famous is a picture by the Russian artist Dmitri Vrubel, showing Leonid Brezhnev and the East German leader Erich Honecker, exchanging fraternal Socialist kisses. Most murals were restored by the original artists in 2009. ◈ At Mühlenstr./Oberbaum-brücke • Map H4

Memorial in Treptower Park

Großer Müggelsee

Großer Müggelsee, known as Berlin's "bathtub", is the largest of the city's lakes, covering an area of 766 hectares (1,892 acres). Müggelsee is not as popular as Großer Wannsee, its West Berlin counterpart, mainly because it is located so far away from the centre of town, in the southeast corner of the city. The lake is known for the beer gardens on its south side, which can be reached by boat from Friedrichshagen. All around the lake there are excellent paths for walking and cycling. You can also swim in the lake, for example at the beach resort of Rahnsdorf. ◈ Treptow-Köpenick district

Treptower Park

Treptower Park, established in the 19th century as a recreation area for Berlin's working-class communities, is today best known for the giant Sowjetisches Ehrenmal (Soviet Memorial). In April 1945, 5,000 Red Army soldiers, who died during the liberation of Berlin, were buried here. Beyond the mass graves rises a 12-m (39-ft) bronze statue of a Russian soldier, holding a child in one arm and a sword in the other, which he has used to destroy a swastika. ◈ Alt-Treptow

Volkspark Friedrichshain

Berlin's oldest landscaped gardens, the people's park, was designed by Joseph Peter Lenné in 1840. Today it provides an oasis of tranquillity in the middle of the densely built-up district of Friedrichshain. World War II has left its traces here, too. Kleiner and Großer Bunkerberg – two heaps of rubble (the latter nick-named "Mount Rubble") reaching a height of 78 m (256 ft) – were piled up here after the war. Less traumatic is the Märchenbrunnen, a charming Neo-Baroque fairy-tale fountain created by Ludwig Hoffmann. It is decorated with 106 richly ornamented figures from popular fairy tales. ◈ Am Friedrichshain • Map H2

East Side Gallery: **www.eastsidegallery.com**

Aviary in Tierpark Friedrichsfelde

9 Tierpark Friedrichsfelde

Located in the historic parklands around Friedrichsfelde Palace, Europe's largest zoological garden boasts spacious enclosures and is home to several rare species. Particularly worth a visit are the lions and Siberian tigers, which are kept in rocky outdoor enclosures. The park is also known for its successful elephant breeding programme. Friedrichsfelde Palace, erected in 1695, is situated in the middle of this 160-hectare (400-acre) estate.

Am Tierpark 125 • Jan–Mar: 9am–4pm daily; Apr–Sep: 9am–6pm; Oct: 9am–5pm daily; Nov–Dec: 9am–4pm daily • (030) 51 53 10 • Admission charge

10 Gedenkstätte Hohenschönhausen

This former secret police prison for "political" prisoners was in use until 1990. Before 1951, it served as a reception centre for the Red Army. On a guided tour, you can visit the watchtowers and the cells – particularly horrifying are the so-called "submarine cells", rooms without windows used for solitary confinement, where inmates were interrogated and tortured.

Genslerstr. 66 • Guided tours 9am–4pm daily and by prior arrangement • (030) 98 60 82 30 • Admission charge

A Day in Berlin's Green Southeast

Morning

Begin your tour of Berlin's Southeast at Alexanderplatz. Sights in this area are not always near each other, so taking the S-Bahn from here is recommended.

First, take S-Bahn line S3 to Karlshorst, where you can visit the **Deutsch-Russisches Museum** *(see p145)*. From here it is not far to the **Stasi-Museum Normannenstraße** *(see p145)* – return to S-Bahn station Ostkreuz, then take S-Bahn line S4 and U-Bahn line U5 to Magdalenenstraße. After visiting all these museums you could recover outdoors. Take U-Bahn line U5 to **Tierpark Friedrichsfelde**, where you can visit both the zoological garden and Friedrichsfelde Palace.

Afternoon

Spend the afternoon making an excursion to Köpenick. Take S-Bahn line S3 to Köpenick, and enjoy a typically German meal in the **Ratskeller** *(see p149)*, the town hall cellar. Afterwards explore **Köpenick Old Town** *(see p145)*. The centre of the old fishing village is especially worth a visit. There are many cafés near **Köpenicker Schloss** *(see p145)*, where you could stop for a coffee and a piece of cake.

Continue your journey by S-Bahn to Friedrichshagen, the access point for **Großer Müggelsee** *(see p146)*. From here take one of the tourist boats to **Müggelsee-Terrassen**, where you can round off the day with a tasty evening meal at a choice of restaurants.

Around Town – Berlin's Southeast

Left **Arena** Centre **Berghain/Panorama Bar** Right **Cassiopeia**

🔟 Bars & Clubs

1 Berghain/Panorama Bar
Located in a former power station, this techno club has a strict door policy – be prepared to queue. However, a perfect sound system and funky crowds make the wait worthwhile. Cameras not allowed. ◈ *Am Wriezener Bahnhof • from midnight Sat to Sun night • (030) 29 36 02 10*

2 Arena
This sprawling post-industrial riverside complex of concert halls, a club ship *(Hoppetosse)* and a moored swimming pool *(Badeschiff)* is unusual even by Berlin standards. ◈ *Eichenstr. 4 • open most days, but check in advance • (030) 533 20 30*

3 Cassiopeia
Join hippies, punks and freestylers in this underground urban enclave for ungentrified clubbing and live concerts. ◈ *Revaler Str. 99 • from 7pm Wed–Sat • (030) 533 20 30/20 05 67 67*

4 Astro Bar
This retro sci-fi-styled bar has moderately priced cocktails, pin-ball machines and a trashy charm. ◈ *Simon-Dach-Str. 40 • from 6pm daily • (030) 29 66 16 15*

5 CSA
Named after the Czech Airlines office that was based here, CSA is a stylish cocktail bar that serves perfect drinks to pleasant lounge music. ◈ *Karl-Marx-Allee 96 • from 8pm daily • (030) 29 04 47 41*

6 Red Rooster Bar
Attached to the Odyssee hostel, this bar is a low-budget option in Friedrichshain's pricey cocktail-land, complete with great service and comfy leather sofas. ◈ *Grünberger Str. 23 • from 4pm daily • (030) 29 00 33 10*

7 Monster Ronson's Ichiban Karaoke Bar
At this lively bar, karaoke fans practise their craft in soundproof booths fitting up to 16 people, or sing on a stage. Try the brunch on Sundays. ◈ *Warschauer Str. 34 • from 7pm daily • (030) 89 75 13 27*

8 Matrix
Located in basement vaults under the Warschauer Str. train station, Matrix is one of the largest clubs in the city. Popular with a young crowd, it attracts Berlin's best DJs. ◈ *Warschauer Platz 18 • 10pm–7am daily • (030) 29 36 99 90*

9 Club der Visionäre
This casual boathouse bar with attached floats on Landwehr-kanal is a lo-fi, Tom-Sawyeresque venue, at its best in summer. ◈ *Am Flutgraben 1 • 2pm–late Mon–Fri, noon–late Sat • (030) 69 51 89 42*

10 Insel
Once a communist youth club, this miniature castle on a Spree island is now a techno, hip-hop, dance, punk and metal club. Live concerts in summer. ◈ *Alt-Treptow 6 • 7pm–1am Wed, 10pm–late Fri & Sat • (030) 53 60 80 20*

Price Categories

For a three-course	€ under €20
meal for one with half	€€ €20–30
a bottle of wine (or	€€€ €30–45
equivalent meal), taxes	€€€€ €45–60
and charges included	€€€€€ over €60

Left **Restaurant freiheit fünfzehn** Right **The Ratskeller in Köpenick's Old Town**

🔟 Restaurants

1 freiheit fünfzehn
German and French cuisine are served aboard a schooner moored at the pier. There is also occasional cabaret and live music. If you prefer dry land, you can enjoy your meals in the beer garden. 🛇 *Freiheit 15 • 6pm–midnight Tue–Sat, 11am–midnight Sun • (030) 658 87 80 • €€*

2 Ratskeller Köpenick
Traditional Berlin fare is served in the vast vaulted cellars where Wilhelm Voigt once famously took advantage of gullible local civil servants *(see p145).* 🛇 *Alt-Köpenick 21 • 11am–11pm daily • (030) 655 51 78 • €€*

3 Klipper Schiffsrestaurant
This two-masted boat, dating back to 1890, has been turned into a cosy restaurant; the menu features fish and game dishes. 🛇 *Bulgarische Str. • 10am–1am daily • (030) 53 21 64 90 • no credit cards • €€*

4 Schrörs Biergarten
Popular, informal beer garden near the lake, specializing in hearty food from the grill. 🛇 *Josef-Nawrocki-Str. 16 • summer: from 11am daily; winter: 11am–6pm Tue–Sun • (030) 64 09 58 80 • no credit cards • €*

5 Die Spindel
This rustic restaurant serves gourmet cuisine and excellent wines. 🛇 *Bölschestr. 51 • noon–2:30pm and from 6pm Tue–Sun • (030) 645 29 37 • €€€*

6 Eierschale Haus Zenner
One of the classic day-trip destinations: families once used to "bring and brew their own coffee". Today it is a popular outdoor café and beer garden. 🛇 *Alt-Treptow 14–17 • 10am–10pm Mon–Thu & Sun, 10am–4am Fri & Sat • (030) 533 73 70 • no credit cards • €€*

7 Krokodil
Situated in the Old Town, near the river baths in Gartenstraße, this is one of the nicest garden venues, especially in summer. 🛇 *Gartenstr. 46–48 • 5pm–midnight Mon–Sat, 11am–11pm Sun (brunch 11am–3pm) • (030) 65 88 00 94 • €€*

8 Bräustübl
A typical Berlin beer garden and restaurant, belonging to the Berliner Bürger-Brau brewery, which serves game dishes. 🛇 *Müggelseedamm 164 • noon–midnight Wed–Sat, 11am–midnight Sun • (030) 645 57 16 • €€*

9 Lehmofen
Meat and vegetarian dishes, freshly cooked in a clay oven, are the top attractions in this Anatolian restaurant with summer terrace. 🛇 *Freiheit 12 • noon–midnight daily • (030) 655 70 44 • €€*

10 Leander
This romantic bistro with an old-world feel is great at any time of day. The food is creative and cosmopolitan – and a bargain to boot. 🛇 *Jungstr. 29 • from 10am daily • (030) 29 00 48 03 • €€*

Note: All restaurants accept credit cards and offer vegetarian dishes unless stated otherwise.

Left **Inside Schloss Charlottenhof** Centre **Chinesische Haus** Right **Vestibül in Neues Palais**

Potsdam & Sanssouci

POTSDAM IS AN IMPORTANT PART OF EUROPEAN *cultural history – a splendid centre of European Enlightenment, which reached its climax in the 18th century in the architectural and artistic design of Frederick the Great's palace. The palace complex of Sanssouci, with its beautiful, extensive park, is both magnificent and playful and has been designated a World Heritage Centre of Culture by UNESCO. Every year, it enchants millions of visitors from around the world. The town of Potsdam, numbering some 300,000 inhabitants, is the capital of the federal province of Brandenburg. This former garrison town has much to delight its visitors, including small palaces and old churches, idyllic parks and historic immigrant settlements.*

Frederick the Great playing the flute in Sanssouci

🔟 Sights

1. Schloss Sanssouci
2. Neues Palais
3. Schlosspark Sanssouci
4. Schloss Cecilienhof
5. Schloss Charlottenhof
6. Marmorpalais
7. Holländisches Viertel
8. Nikolaikirche
9. Marstall (Filmmuseum)
10. Filmpark Babelsberg

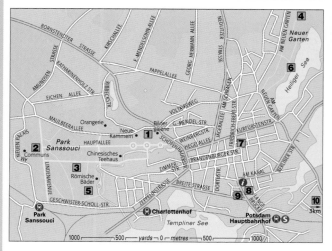

Preceding pages **The stairs leading up to Schloss Sanssouci**

1 Schloss Sanssouci

The Prussian King Frederick the Great wished to live "sans souci", in a palace outside the boundaries of the hated city – the French phrase means "without worries". In 1745, Frederick commissioned his favourite architect Georg Wenzeslaus von Knobelsdorff to plan and construct this magnificent Rococo palace according to his own designs.

The main building with its yellow façade rises proudly above the former terraced vineyards, leading up to the domed building and its elegant marble hall at the centre of the palace complex. In both its design and shape, the marble hall pays homage to the Pantheon in Rome. To its left and right are some very attractive rooms designed by von Knobelsdorff and Johann August Nahl; these include the famous concert room, adorned with paintings by Antoine Pesne, and Frederick's library. In this wing, the monarch liked to play the flute or to philosophize with Voltaire. Valuable paintings by Frederick the Great's favourite painter, the French artist Antoine Watteau, adorn the palace walls.
Ⓢ *Maulbeerallee • Apr–Oct: 10am–6pm Tue–Sun; Nov–Mar: 10am–5pm Tue–Sun; guided tour obligatory • (0331) 969 41 90 • Admission charge*

Vase in Park Sanssouci

2 Neues Palais

To the north of Sanssouci palace park rises the Baroque Neues Palais. One of Germany's most beautiful palaces, it was built in 1763–9 for Frederick the Great according to designs by Johann Gottfried Büring, Jean Laurent Le Geay and Carl von Gontard. The vast two-storey structure comprises 200 rooms, including the Marmorsaal (marble hall), a lavishly furnished ballroom, and the Schlosstheater, where plays are once more performed today. Frederick's private chambers are equally splendid, especially his study furnished in Rococo style, the upper gallery with valuable parquet flooring and the Oberes Vestibül, a room clad entirely in marble. Ⓢ *Am Neuen Palais • Apr–Oct: 10am–6pm Wed–Mon; Nov–Mar: 10am–5pm Wed–Mon; audio guide available • (0331) 969 42 02 • Admission charge*

3 Schlosspark Sanssouci

It is easy to while away an entire day in the extensive palace park, which covers 287 hectares (709 acres) of land. Of the many charming buildings hidden in the lavishly designed landscape garden, the Rococo-style Chinesische Haus, built in 1754–6 by Johann Gottfried Büring, is especially worth seeking out.

Left **Neues Palais** Right **Concert Hall in Schloss Sanssouci**

S-Bahn S7 goes to Potsdam from Berlin. The journey takes about 45 minutes from S station Friedrichstr.

Left **A street in Holländisches Viertel** Centre **Marmorpalais** Right **Marstall (Filmmuseum)**

Originally it served as a tea-house and dining room, and it now houses an exhibition of porcelain pieces from East Asia.

The Römische Bäder (Roman Baths), a group of pavilions next to the lake, are also inspired by historic models. Modelled on an Italian Renaissance villa, they were built between 1829 and 1840 by Friedrich Karl Schinkel as guest and bathing houses.

The Orangerie, constructed in 1851–60 by Friedrich August Stüler, was also originally intended to accommodate the king's guests. Today it houses a small gallery of paintings.

⊗ *Chinesische Haus: Am Grünen Gitter*
• *mid-May–mid-Oct: 10am–6pm Tue–Sun*
• *(0331) 969 42 25*

⊗ *Römische Bäder: Lennéstr.*
• *May–end Oct: 10am–6pm Tue–Sun*
• *(0331) 969 42 25*

⊗ *Orangerie: Am der Orangerie 3–5*
• *May–Oct: 10am–6pm Tue–Sun*
• *(0331) 969 42 80*

The Potsdam Conference

In July and August 1945, the heads of government of the United States (Harry Truman), the USSR (Joseph Stalin) and Great Britain (Winston Churchill) met in Schloss Cecilienhof, in order to seal the future of Germany in a treaty. Vitally important points such as the demilitarization of Germany, the level of reparations to be paid, the punishment of war criminals, the resettlement of Germans from Poland and the new borders of Germany were decided here.

Schloss Cecilienhof

This little palace, built in the style of an English country manor house, entered the history books in 1945, when Germany's fate was sealed by the Potsdam Conference. Built in 1914–17, the palace is a UNESCO World Heritage Site and is now used as a hotel. It also houses a small exhibition documenting the Conference and the palace's furnishings.
⊗ *Im Neuen Garten • Apr–Oct: 10am–6pm Tue–Sun; Nov–Mar: 10am–5pm Tue–Sun • (0331) 969 42 44*

Schloss Charlottenhof

A small Neo-Classical palace in Park Sanssouci, built in 1829 by Schinkel for the heir to the throne, Friedrich Wilhelm IV. Particularly worth seeing is the tent-like Humboldtsaal.
⊗ *Geschwister-Scholl-Str. 34a • May–Oct: 10am–6pm Tue–Sun • (0331) 969 42 28*

Marmorpalais

This small, early Neo-Classical palace at the side of the lake was built in 1791–7 by Carl Gotthard Langhans and others. It features an elegant concert hall as well as contemporary furniture and porcelain. ⊗ *Heiliger See (Neuer Garten) • May–Oct: 10am–6pm Tue–Sun; Nov–Apr: 10am–4pm Sat & Sun • (0331) 969 42 46*

Holländisches Viertel

A pleasant way to explore Potsdam is a walk through the historic Old Town, with its art

Nikolaikirche on Alter Markt

galleries, cafés and restaurants. Built between 1733 and 1742, the area originally served as a settlement for Dutch workers after whom it is now named. The small red-brick buildings are decorated with attractive stucco ornaments. *Friedrich-Ebert-, Kurfürsten-, Hebbel-, Gutenbergstr.*

Nikolaikirche

Potsdam's most attractive church was designed by Schinkel in 1830 in an early Neo-Classical style. Its giant dome is particularly striking. *Am Alten Markt • 9am–5pm Mon–Sat; 11:30am–5pm Sun • (0331) 270 86 02*

Marstall (Filmmuseum)

The small museum, based in the Baroque former stable buildings of the king's town residence, uses old cameras, props and projectors to document the history of German film. *Breite Str. 1a • 10am–6pm Tue–Sun • (0331) 27 18 10*

Filmpark Babelsberg

The Filmpark offers visitors a tour of the legendary UFA-Studios, which were among the world's most important when they operated here in Babelsberg from 1917 to 1945. Exciting U-boat trips, stunt performances and special effects are shown. *Großbeerenstr. • Apr–Oct: 10am–6pm daily • (0331) 721 27 50*

A Day in Potsdam

Morning

Begin your exploration in the **Schlosspark Sanssouci** *(see pp153–4)* as early as possible in order to get ahead of the daily influx of visitors. Start with **Schloss Sanssouci** and **Neues Palais** *(see p153 for both)* then visit Chinesische Haus, Römische Bäder and Orangerie. From the orangery's viewing terrace you will have magnificent views over the entire palace complex. If you are up for it, you could also climb up to Schloss Belvedere on top of the hill. From Schlosspark walk along Voltaireweg to Neuer Garten in the northeast of Potsdam, where you can rest and recover over a tasty lunch at **Schloss Cecilienhof** *(see p157)*.

Afternoon

Start the afternoon with a stroll through Neuer Garten. Visit **Schloss Cecilienhof** and, if you like, stop for a break at Heiliger See. Afterwards walk or drive into the centre of Potsdam, starting with the **Holländisches Viertel** (Dutch quarter) where you could pop into one of the numerous cafés. Then continue on a circular walk, strolling past Peter- und Paul-Kirche, the French church, **Nikolaikirche** and the town hall. Finish your day of sightseeing with a visit to the **Marstall** and the film museums in Potsdam and Babelsberg. Take a look at the palace and the telegraph hill. A delicious evening meal awaits you at **Massimo 18** *(see p157)* to round off your day in Potsdam.

Left **Schloss Babelsberg** Centre **Alexandrowka-Haus** Right **Wasserwerk Sanssouci**

Best of the Rest

1 Alexandrowka

A detour to the Russian colony in Potsdam feels like a journey to Russia itself. Decorated log cabins with picturesque gardens were built here in 1826 for a Russian military choir. Don't miss the museum and the Alexander Newski church. ◈ *Russische Kolonie/Puschkinallee*

2 Wasserwerk Sanssouci

This building, resembling a mosque with minarets, houses the water pumping station for Schlosspark Sanssouci. The ancient pump, dating from 1842, can be inspected in the building. ◈ *Breite Str. • mid-May–mid-Oct: 10am–5pm Sat & Sun • (0331) 969 42 48*

3 Telegrafenberg

If you're prepared to climb telegraph hill, you could visit the elegant Einstein tower at the top. It was designed in 1920 by Erich Mendelsohn for the observation of the sun. ◈ *Albert-Einstein-Str. • Guided tours Einsteinturm: (0331) 29 17 41 • Admission charge*

4 Schloss Babelsberg

Built by Schinkel in 1833–5, this Gothic palace is situated in an idyllic park on the banks of the Havel River. ◈ *Park Babelsberg • 10am–6pm Tue–Sun (Nov–Mar: to 5pm) • (0331) 969 42 50 • Admission charge*

5 Potsdam-Museum

A small museum presenting the history of the town of Potsdam, from prehistoric times to the present day. The museum is based in the historic Hiller-Brandtsche Häuser. ◈ *Benkertstr. 3 • 10am–6pm Tue–Sun • (0331) 289 68 03 • Admission charge*

6 Altes Rathaus

The old town hall, built in 1753, is decorated with sculptures and Potsdam's coat of arms – two gilded Atlas figures, each carrying a globe. ◈ *Am Alten Markt*

7 Luisenplatz

This small square with its plain, restored buildings gives a good idea of Potsdam in the early 19th century. ◈ *Luisenplatz*

8 Französische Kirche

In 1752, Johann Boumann built this elliptical Huguenot church with its giant columned portico, while Schinkel designed the beautiful interior in the 1830s. ◈ *Am Bassinplatz • 2:30–5pm daily • (0331) 29 12 19*

9 St-Peter-und-Paul-Kirche

The Catholic church of saints Peter and Paul, modelled on Haghia Sophia in Istanbul, was built in 1867–70 by Stüler. ◈ *Am Bassinplatz • 10am–6pm daily (winter: to 5pm) • (0331) 230 79 90*

10 Brandenburger Tor

The most attractive of five former town gates was built by Gontard and Unger in 1770 in the Neo-Classical style to celebrate Prussian victory in the Seven Years' War. ◈ *Luisenplatz*

Left **Schloss Cecilienhof serves delicious food**

Price Categories

For a three-course
meal for one with half   **€** under €20
a bottle of wine (or   **€€** €20–30
equivalent meal), taxes   **€€€** €30–45
and charges included   **€€€€** €45–60
                              €€€€€ over €60

📖10 Restaurants & Cafés

Speckers Landhaus
The combination of a Prussian interior, friendly service and light cuisine make Speckers Landhaus one of Potsdam's best restaurants. ◎ *Jägerallee 13 • noon–2pm, 6–11pm Tue–Sat • (0331) 280 43 11 • no credit cards • €€€*

Schloss Cecilienhof
The historic palace is now the home of a luxury hotel. Its restaurant serves solid German food. ◎ *Neuer Garten • noon–11pm daily • (0331) 370 50 • €€€*

Massimo 18
This Italian restaurant focuses on the cuisine of the Lombardy region. It has an old wood interior with terracotta colour walls and a beautiful courtyard. The *enoteca* on the first floor sells Lombardy wines. ◎ *Mittelstr. 18 • noon–midnight Tue–Sun • (0331) 81 71 89 83 • €€€*

Restaurant Juliette
A former manor house is the setting for this French restaurant, one of the most charming in the city. It serves top-quality French classics. ◎ *Jägerstr. 39 • noon–3:30pm, 6pm–midnight Wed–Mon • (0331) 270 17 91 • €€€*

Brau- und Brennhaus
This rustic restaurant, set in the brewery of a historic country manor, Krongut Bornstedt, serves hearty meals with local fish, game, sausages, and local beers. ◎ *Ribbeckstr. 6–7 • noon–10pm daily • (0331) 55 06 50 • €€*

Maison Charlotte
An olde-worlde wine bar in a simple redbrick Dutch house, Maison Charlotte specializes in French country fare and excellent wines. ◎ *Mittelstr. 20 • noon–11pm daily • (0331) 280 54 50 • €€€*

Friedrich-Wilhelm
This classic, Michelin-starred gourmet restaurant is probably the best in Potsdam. Light German dishes exquisitely prepared and presented. ◎ *Im Wildpark 1 • 6pm–late Tue–Sat • (0331) 550 50 • €€€*

Waage
Attractive historic restaurant in a central location. Regional game and fish dishes in unusual variations are particularly worth trying. ◎ *Am Neuen Markt 12 • noon–midnight Tue–Sun • (0331) 817 06 74 • €€*

Café Heider
This lovely café in the middle of Potsdam's Old Town offers a fantastic breakfast selection, which you can enjoy outside on the terrace in summer. ◎ *Friedrich-Ebert-Str. 29 • 8am–1am Mon–Fri, 9am–1am Sat, 10am–1am Sun • (0331) 270 55 96 • €*

La Madeleine
A little bistro, serving all sorts of crêpes, such as sweet with jam or savoury with ham – the ideal spot for a quick snack. ◎ *Lindenstr. 9 • noon–midnight daily • (0331) 270 54 00 • no credit cards • €*

Note: *All restaurants accept credit cards and offer vegetarian dishes unless stated otherwise.*

157

STREETSMART

Planning your Trip
160

Arriving in Berlin
161

Getting Around Berlin
162

Information
& Advice
163

Berlin for
Disabled Visitors
164

Banking &
Communications
165

Security & Health Tips
166

Excursions & Days Out
167

Guided Tours
168

Ways to Escape
the Crowds
169

Shopping
170

Berlin on a Budget
171

Places to Stay
172–179

BERLIN'S TOP 10

Left **In Kurfürstendamm** Right **The Christopher Street Day Parade in June**

TOP 10 Planning your Trip

1 When to Go and Climate
The weather in Berlin is better than its reputation. The continental climate, which characterizes the entire region, guarantees mild and dry weather for the main holiday period from May to September. In spring and autumn it can be cold and wet, and it may be advisable not to travel to Berlin between November and February, when it is often cloudy, and a bitingly cold, easterly wind whistles through the city.

2 What to Wear
In the summer months you'll need only lightweight clothing. In spring and autumn you should definitely pack a rain- and windproof jacket as well as an umbrella. Locals dress informally and more flamboyantly than other German urbanites – anything you like goes. The capital has, however, gone more upmarket and you may feel out of place in many restaurants or theatres without a jacket and tie or evening dress.

3 Money
If you're arriving from abroad, you'll be able to buy euros at all banks and bureaux de change (many are based around Bahnhof Zoo). Credit cards, traveller's cheques and EC-cards are accepted everywhere in the centre of town.

4 Insurance
All travellers are well advised to buy insurance cover for accidents, illness and theft. Cancellation insurance may also be worth taking out.

5 Driving
UK, US, Canadian and Australian driving licences are recognized in Germany. Prior to driving into Berlin, visit www.berlin.de/umweltzone to get a sticker declaring your car fit for the environmental zone.

6 Visa and Customs
All visitors to Berlin need valid passports. If you're staying for 90 days or less, you will not normally need a visa. Ask your German Embassy for details. Non-EU citizens may import 200 cigarettes and one litre of spirits per adult.

7 Electrical Appliances
The electric current is 220 volt; but remember to bring an adaptor with two round pins.

8 Time Difference
Berlin is on Central European time. It is one hour ahead of Greenwich Mean Time, six hours ahead of US Eastern Standard Time and 11 hours behind Australian Eastern Standard Time.

9 Children's Needs
If you are travelling with children, book into child-friendly accommodation and look out for family reductions. It can be fun to explore the city with children, but you are advised to avoid the rush hours on U-Bahn and buses, especially if you are travelling with babies or very young children.

10 Pupils and Students
Many museums, theatres and other cultural establishments offer reductions for pupils and students on production of a valid student card.

Embassies

Australian Embassy
Wallstr. 76–79 • Map
L4 • (030) 880 08 80

British Embassy
Wilhelmstr. 70–71
• Map K3
• 030) 20 45 70

Canadian Embassy
Leipziger Platz 17
• Map L4
• (030) 20 31 20

New Zealand Embassy
Friedrichstr. 60
• Map L4
• (030) 20 62 10

South African Embassy
• Tiergartenstr. 18
• Map L4
• (030) 22 07 30

US Embassy
Pariser Platz 2
• Map K3
• (030) 238 51 74

Left **Hauptbahnhof** Centre **The ICE to Berlin** Right **Three typical road signs**

Arriving in Berlin

1 Flughafen Tegel

Berlin's largest airport is situated 8 km (5 miles) to the northwest of the city centre. Lufthansa, Air Berlin, British Airways, KLM, Air France, Iberia, Alitalia and others all operate direct flights here. Delta and United fly to Berlin from New York. A taxi from the airport to Ku'damm costs around €13 and takes 20–30 minutes. Nearly as fast is the journey by bus – Nos TXL, X09 and 109 (about €2.10) stop everywhere in the centre. Tegel is due to close by October 2011, when the new Brandenburg International Airport at Schönefeld is opened. ✆ Airport information: (01805) 00 01 86

2 Flughafen Schönefeld

Located approximately 20 km (12 miles) southeast of Berlin, this airport is served by low cost, charter and East European airlines. The fastest way into the city is via the Airport Express train, which takes 20 minutes to Alexanderplatz and 30 minutes to Bahnhof Zoo. Express bus SXF1 will take you to S-Bahn Südkreuz in 20 minutes. In 2011 Schönefeld will become Berlin's main airport, Brandenburg International. ✆ Airport information: (01805) 00 01 86

3 Airlines

Lufthansa has an office downtown on Ku'damm, while other airlines like Air Berlin have ticket offices at Tegel airport. ✆ Lufthansa: Kurfürstendamm 45 (Neues Kranzler-Eck) • Map P4 • 10am–7pm Mon–Fri • (030) 206 54 69 ✆ Air Berlin: Flughafen Tegel • (01805) 73 78 00

4 Hauptbahnhof

The city's grand, modern central station is officially called Hauptbahnhof. Located in the government district, it is the arrival and departure destination for all long-distance trains. ✆ Europaplatz 1 • Map E3 • (0800) 150 70 90

5 Zoologischer Garten

The Bahnhof Zoo is an important local transportation hub due to its many S- and U-Bahn lines and bus routes which connect here. ✆ Hardenbergplatz • Map N4 • (030) 297 10 55

6 Bahnhof Lichtenberg and Ostbahnhof

Trains from Southern and Eastern Europe stop at these stations. This is the best place to arrive if your final destination is in the eastern part of the city. ✆ Weitlingstr. 22 • (0800) 150 70 90 ✆ Straße der Pariser Kommune

7 Zentraler Omnibusbahnhof (ZOB)

The coach station near Funkturm in Charlottenburg offers fast and inexpensive coach connections to all German and European cities. ✆ Masurenallee 4–6 • Map A4 • (030) 301 03 80

8 Motorways

If you're travelling to Berlin by car, you will have to get there via Berliner Stadtring, an orbital motorway around the city. From the north you will reach the city motorway on the A111 motorway via Stolpe in the direction of Autobahndreieck Funkturm; from the south you will reach the centre on the A115 – the famous Avus motorway.

9 By Car

The speed limit on the orbital Berliner Ring is mostly 100 km/h (62.5 miles per hour); on the urban motorways in Berlin you are limited to 80–100 km/h (50–62.5 miles per hour). There are frequent radar checks.

10 Climate Zone

As of 2008, all of Berlin's downtown area (inside the S-Bahn ring) has been declared a green zone, which means that only vehicles with an approved environmental badge will be permitted, whether German or foreign. To get more information visit the website www.umweltplakette.de where it is also possible to buy the badge.

Left **S-Bahn** Centre **At a bus stop** Right **Exploring Berlin by Velotaxi**

Getting Around Berlin

U-Bahn
The Berlin U-Bahn, or underground railway, has one of the largest networks in Europe, providing the fastest and most convenient means of getting around the city. There are ten U-Bahn lines each sporting their own colour. The U-Bahn runs from 5am to 1am; at weekends most lines run throughout the night. The station indicated on the platform is the final destination of the train. ◈ *BVG customer service (030) 194 49*

S-Bahn
The S-Bahn or Stadtbahn (city railway) has 15 lines, connecting the centre with the suburbs. They run at 5- to 20-minute intervals. Many lines share tracks so you will need to pay attention to indicator boards. ◈ *Information S-Bahn • Bhf. Alexanderplatz, Friedrichstr., Hauptbahnhof • 6am–10pm Mon–Fri, 7am–10pm Sat & Sun • (030) 29 74 33 33*

Buses
Berlin has a dense network of bus routes. The yellow double-decker buses operate mostly in the centre. Bus lines have three-digit numbers, except for express services, which have a preceding "X". Buses and tram lines starting with an "M" service areas without direct U- or S-Bahn links. On boarding, you have to use the front door

(unless you have a buggy, in which case use the back entrance) and present your ticket, or the money for a new one, to the driver. ◈ *BVG customer service (030) 194 49*

Tickets
Tickets for U- and S-Bahn trains and for buses in Berlin are available at all stations and bus stops as well as from bus drivers. Berlin is divided into three zones: A, B and C. The best value for money is a day ticket at €6.30, which is valid until 3am the following day and covers all three zones. A single journey, costing €2.10, is valid for unlimited travel for two hours. A "Kurzstrecke" (short distance) counts as up to three U- or S-Bahn stations or six bus stops, and costs €1.20. Children under 14 pay a reduced rate; those under six travel free. You have to stamp your ticket in a red machine in the station or in a yellow machine on the bus before starting the journey. ◈ *BVG customer service (030) 194 49*

Trams
Trams – operating mostly in the eastern part of the city – are part of the same network (BVG).

Taxis
There are taxi stands all over Berlin. It is not always easy to hail a passing taxi. The basic starting price is €2.50, and a

further €1.02–1.52 is charged per km (2/3 of a mile). A short-distance tariff also exists: if you hail a taxi in the street, you can travel for up to 2 km (1 mile) for €3. ◈ *Taxi: (030) 26 10 26, 443 322, (030) 21 01 01*

Car Hire
You can hire a car from any of the large operators on production of a valid driving licence, passport and credit card; some only accept customers aged 21 years or over. There are car hire places at all airports and in central Berlin. ◈ *Avis: (01805) 55 77 55; Europcar: (0180) 580 00; Hertz: (01805) 33 35 35; Sixt: (01805) 25 25 25*

Velotaxis
An unusual way to explore Berlin is by velotaxi – a bicycle rickshaw. These can be found in the city centre (Apr–Oct only).

Bicycle Hire
There are many bike-hire places all over the city. ◈ *Bicycle station Dorotheenstr. 30 • Mar–Oct: 10am–7:30pm Mon–Fri (to 6pm Sat, 4pm Sun); Nov–Feb: 10am–7pm Mon–Fri (to 4pm Sat & Sun) • (030) 20 45 45 00*

Berlin on Foot
It can be rewarding but tiring to explore Berlin on foot. A stroll along Ku'damm and Unter den Linden is worthwhile. Take care when crossing the cycle paths, which are marked in red.

Left **Berlin city guides** Centre **A newspaper kiosk** Right **The logo of tourist information offices**

🔟 Information & Advice

1 Berlin Infostores

The municipal tourist information service BTM (Berlin Tourismus Marketing) has offices at Hauptbahnhof, Alexanderplatz, near Brandenburg Gate and in Tegel airport. There you can obtain up-to-date information.
- www.visitberlin.de
- *Brandenburger Tor, southern building* • *10am–7pm daily*
- *Alexa Shopping Centre, Alexanderplatz, Grunerstr. 20* • *10am–8pm Mon–Sat*
- *Hauptbahnhof, Europapl. 1, Level 0, northern entrance* • *8am–10pm daily*
- *Neues Kranzler-Eck, Kurfürstendamm 21* • *10am–8pm Mon–Sat, 10am–6pm Sun*

2 Berlin's State Museums

Detailed up-to-date information on the state museums and all the establishments on Museumsinsel can be obtained from a central phoneline. Here you will also find out about the current programme of events – for example about the "long night of the museums".
- *(030) 26 60 or (030) 266 42 42 42*

3 Sanssouci

The visitors' advice service for the palaces and gardens of Potsdam and Sanssouci supplies accurate information and tips as well as guided tours and more via their own telephone service.
- *(0331) 969 42 02*
- www.spsg.de

4 Potsdam Information

Potsdam has its own tourist information service, offering brochures, guided tours and an accommodation service.
- *Brandenburger Str 3* • *Apr–Oct: 9:30am–6pm Mon–Fri, 9:30am–4pm Sat & Sun; Nov–Mar: 10am–6pm Mon–Fri, 9:30am–2pm Sat & Sun* • *Tel (0331) 27 55 80, Fax (0331) 275 58 29*

5 Where to Stay

The Berlin Tourismus Marketing GmbH (BTM) has a telephone hotline which will help reserve a room (for a fee). Several offices also arrange private accommodation, where visitors book into shared apartments for a period of several days or weeks.
- *Tel (030) 25 00 25, Fax (030) 25 00 24 24. From abroad: 0049 30 25 00 25*

6 What's On

There are two fortnightly city magazines with detailed information on all kinds of events – *tip* and *zitty*. The monthly *Berlin-Programm* with detailed events listings is also worth consulting. For younger readers, the magazines *prinz* and *030* contain information on nightclubs and bars. Daily newspapers such as *Tagesspiegel, Berliner Zeitung* and *Berliner Morgenpost* usually publish listings of cultural events on Wednesdays and Thursdays respectively, while tips and reviews can be found in the papers every day.

7 Radio Stations

For radio news in English, you can tune into the BBC World Service (90.2 MHz) or the multi-lingual SFB 4 Multikulti (106.8 MHz).

8 Television

In addition to the national TV stations, the RBB offers a regional programme; tv berlin, a private TV station, also broadcasts information on what's on. Thanks to cable and satellite you can also easily tune into English programmes.

9 Advice for Foreign Nationals

This Senate Office, which deals with the concerns of foreign nationals who live in Berlin, is also a good point of advice for foreign visitors.
- *Potsdamer Str. 65* • *Map E5* • *9am–1pm Mon, Tue, Thu, plus 3–6pm Thu* • *(030) 90 17 23 72*

10 Advice for Gay Visitors

Advice and information for gay and lesbian visitors is always available at Mann-o-Meter (*see p58*).
- *Bülowstr. 106* • *5–10pm Tue–Sun* • *(030) 216 80 08*
- *For lesbians: Kulmer Str. 20a* • *(030) 215 20 00*

Left **Parking for the disabled** Centre **Adapted bus door** Right **Lift to the U-Bahn station**

TOP 10 Berlin for Disabled Visitors

1 Streets and Pavements

Nearly all pavements in Berlin are sloped at junctions to make them suitable for wheelchair users. However, visitors in wheelchairs will need to watch out for cyclists using the red cycle tracks, often in both directions.

2 U- and S-Bahn

Underground and above-ground trains are accessible to wheelchair users but not all stations are equipped with lifts yet. If you wish to travel by U-Bahn, wait at the head of the platform. After the train has stopped, the driver will put up a ramp to bridge the difference in height between platform and train. If you wish to travel by S-Bahn, speak to the station manager before the arrival of the train; he or she will install the ramp you need to board the train. BVG and S-Bahn transport network maps show all stations accessible to wheelchairs. In Berlin, handicapped passengers are entitled to a free service worker for help when travelling. Call (030) 25 41 44 14 (9am–4pm Mon–Fri) at least 24 hours ahead of your journey. Ⓢ *Berliner Verkehrsbetriebe* • *24 hours* • *(030) 194 49.* Ⓢ *Deutsche Bahn Berlin* • *24 hours* • *(030) 118 61*

3 Buses

All buses displaying a wheelchair symbol are specially equipped for disabled access; most buses in the centre have one door with a ramp that can be lowered down to the pavement. At certain times, however, these buses run only at 20-minute intervals.

4 Cars Services and Guided Tours

Disabled visitors wishing to explore Berlin and Brandenburg province on their own by car, or to share a car with driver with other disabled visitors, can contact several specialist travel agents. Ⓢ *BBV Tours Behindertenfahrdienst, Bizetstr. 51–55* • *(030) 92 70 36 30* Ⓢ *Micky Tours, Rhinstr. 7* • *(030) 515 33 36* Ⓢ *Berlin Erkundungen Gangart Berlin, Potsdamer Chaussee 21A* • *(030) 32 70 37 83*

5 Shopping and Entertainment

Shopping malls Potsdamer-Platz-Arcaden and Alexa Shopping Centre at Alexanderplatz are accessible to wheelchair users. The malls have automatic doors, large elevators and adapted lavatories. At Potsdamer-Platz, all event locations (IMAX, CineStar, Cinemaxx) have disabled access.

6 Public Conveniences

Look for the silver "City Toiletten". They can be found in many central areas of Berlin, and most of them are fully accessible.

7 Mobidat.net

The website www. mobidat.net has an English-language version and gives advice on all matters regarding access, services and events for the disabled visitor, including a database for 20,000 Berlin buildings and their facilities.

8 Landesamt

Berlin's Regional Office for Health and Social Security runs a citizen's advice bureau with a telephone help-line. Ⓢ *Sächsische Str. 28* • *Map B6* • *(030) 902 29 64 64* • *Service for the disabled and senior citizens* • *(030) 859 40 10*

9 Wheelchair Hire

The Regional Office *(see above)* also rents out wheelchairs. Order one in advance by telephone. Alternatively, try the German Red Cross (DRK). Ⓢ *(030) 204 38 47* • *DRK (030) 85 00 54 22* • *Wheelchair repair service (0180) 111 47 47*

10 Sight-impaired Visitors

Berlin's charitable association for the blind and sight-impaired advises on facilities that are available for blind visitors. Ⓢ *Allgemeiner Blinden- und Sehbehindertenverein, Auerbacherstr. 7* • *(030) 89 58 80*

Yellow Berlin barrierefrei *stickers indicate disabled access to a venue*

Left **Historic letter box** Centre **Modern card telephone** Right **Bureau de change**

🔟 Banking & Communications

1 Banks

All the large German banks have branches in the centre of town. Most banks open 9am–6pm Mon–Fri; many open for shorter periods on Fridays and Wednesdays.
◊ *Commerzbank, Europa-Center, Tauentzienstr. 9* • *Map N/P5* • *9am–4pm Mon & Wed, 9am–6pm Tue & Thu, 9am–2pm Fri*
◊ *Deutsche Bank, Friedrichstr. 181* • *Map F4* • *10am–8pm Mon, Tue, Thu–Sat, 10am–6pm Wed*
◊ *Berliner Sparkasse, Rankestr. 33–34* • *Map P4* • *9:30am–7pm Mon–Fri*

2 Changing Money

Money is changed at a *Wechselstube* (bureau de change); you can find these near Bahnhof Zoo, at the airports or at a bank. Make sure you ask about commission and charges, as these vary from place to place. Hotels will also change money, but may charge higher fees.
◊ *Exchange AG, Bayreuther Str. 37* • *Map P5* • *9am–7pm Mon–Fri, 10am–1pm Sat* • *(030) 21 47 62 92*
◊ *Reisebank at Hauptbahnhof Europlatz 1* • *Map E2* • *8am–10pm daily* • *(030) 20 45 37 36.* ◊ *Eurochange at Europa-Center Tauentzienstr. 9–12* • *Map D5* • *9am–8pm Mon–Sat* • *(030) 261 14 84*

3 Credit Cards

You can use a credit card, such as Visa or Euro/MasterCard, to pay at most restaurants,

cafés and shops in Berlin but cards are not accepted everywhere and it is a good idea to carry some cash. American Express and Diner's Club are less commonly accepted. You can also use your credit or EC card (plus PIN number) to withdraw money from a machine. Should you lose your card, it is essential that you inform your bank or provider immediately.
◊ *American Express*
• *(069) 75 76 40 00*
◊ *EC Cards*
• *(01805) 02 10 21*
◊ *Eurocard and MasterCard*
• *(069) 79 33 19 10*
◊ *Diner's Club*
• *(01805) 533 66 95*
◊ *Visa* • *(0180) 361 76 170*

4 Telephones

There are public phones (both enclosed cells and open phones) all over the centre of town. These are almost exclusively card phones. Telephone cards can be bought from post offices, in department stores and at kiosks.

5 Post Offices and Letter Boxes

Post offices are hard to miss – they are painted a bright yellow. As elsewhere in Germany, Berlin letter boxes are yellow. ◊ *Center-Filiale, Joachimstaler Str. 7* • *Map P4* • *9am–8pm daily*
◊ *Bahnhof Friedrichstr., Georgenstr. 12* • *Map K4* • *6am–10pm Mon–Fri, 8am–10pm Sat & Sun*

6 Postage

A standard letter (up to 20 g) to anywhere in the EU costs €0.70; a compact letter (up to 50 g) €1.25; a postcard €0.65. Stamps can be bought at the post office, from card shops and machines.

7 Internet Cafés

Most internet cafés are found in trendy areas such as Prenzlauer Berg, Kreuzberg and Friedrichshain. Dunkin Donuts also has internet access.
◊ *Dunkin Donuts at Sony Center, Potsdamer Str. 2* • *Map L2* • *7am–midnight Mon–Fri, 8am–1am Sat, 8am–midnight Sun*

8 Secretarial Services

If your hotel does not offer secretarial services, you could use an independent service. Details of such services are listed in the "Yellow Pages" of the telephone directory.

9 Travellers' Cheques

Travellers' cheques made out in euros or any other currency can be exchanged at all larger banks or at branches of the issuers. Most banks charge a fee.

10 Important Numbers

Important Deutsche Telekom helpline numbers are as follows: • *national directory enquiries 118 33* • *international directory enquiries 118 34* • *operator (0180) 200 10 33*

Left **Ambulance** Centre **A pharmacy in the centre of Berlin** Right **A police van**

🔟 Security & Health Tips

1 Emergencies
As elsewhere in Germany, the emergency phone numbers are 112 for ambulance and fire brigade, and 110 for the police. These can be dialled free of charge from public phone boxes.

2 Safety
Berlin is a fairly safe city. As in any other metropolis, however, you are advised to follow a few golden rules. Keep an eye on your valuables, such as your wallet or handbag, at all times, especially on U- and S-Bahn trains and on buses. At night, the following areas are best avoided: the area behind the Gedächtnis-Kirche, U-Bahn line U9 north of the Zoo, the districts Lichtenberg (especially the station) and Wedding. Eastern areas can be less safe; black or openly homosexual visitors are also advised not to take the S-Bahn at night east of Alexanderplatz or to Brandenburg.

3 Theft
Ask the hotel to place your documents and valuables in a safe if possible, or carry them close to your body. Even if you are making a short visit, it is worth taking out insurance unless you are already covered by your household insurance. Be sure to inform the police immediately of any theft; you'll usually easily find police officers patrolling the streets in the centre. ◈ *Polizeipräsidium, Platz der Luftbrücke 6 • (030) 46 64 46 64*

4 Lost Property
The Zentrales Fundbüro (central lost-property office) keeps anything that has been lost and found anywhere in Berlin. If you have lost an item on public transport, enquire with the Fundbüro der BVG. The Fundbüro der Deutschen Bahn AG is responsible for all items lost on the S-Bahn or the railways. ◈ *Zentrales Fundbüro, Platz der Luftbrücke 6 • (030) 75 60 31 01* ◈ *Fundbüro der BVG, Potsdamer Str. 182 • (030) 194 49* ◈ *Fundbüro der DB • (01805) 99 05 99*

5 Hospitals
Visitors from EU countries are covered for emergency treatment, but British visitors should obtain form E111 from a post office before leaving home. Non-EU visitors should buy special travel insurance to cover medical emergencies.

6 Chemists
There are numerous *Apotheken* (chemists or pharmacies) in town. After 8pm, an emergency phone line will give you information on where to find the nearest open chemist. ◈ *(030) 31 00 31 • www.apotheke-n.com*

7 Dentists
The dental emergency phone line will refer you to the nearest dentist for treatment. ◈ *(030) 89 00 43 33*

8 Emergency Services
There are several other important numbers for emergencies, which usually operate throughout the night. These will provide telephone advice or inform you of other emergency services if necessary. ◈ *Doctors on call • (030) 89 00 91 00* ◈ *German Red Cross Rescue Service • (030) 197 27* ◈ *Emergency Poison Helpline • (030) 192 40* ◈ *Narcotics Emergencies • (030) 192 37* ◈ *Telephone helpline for emotional problems • 0800 111 0 111 • 0800 111 0 222 (spiritual help)*

9 Smoking
Since 2008, smoking is banned in all public places, including bars, restaurants, and clubs. It is allowed only in designated areas.

10 Women travelling on their own
Berlin is quite safe for women on their own, but avoid parks and dark, quiet streets at night. ◈ *Confidential helpline for women • (030) 615 42 43*

Online list of pharmacies: www.akberlin.de, then select "Notdienst" from the options listed

Left **By S-Bahn to the outer districts** Centre **Travelling on Havel and Spree** Right **In Spreewald**

🔟 Excursions & Days Out

1 Spreewald
The river landscape around the little towns of Lübben and Lübbenau, southwest of Berlin, is a unique and unspoilt area of natural beauty. From here you can explore by boat the old settlements of the Sorbs, a Slavic people. Make sure you also enjoy the specialities of the region – fresh fish and vegetables, but most of all the famous pickled Spreewald gherkins. ✆ *Tourismusverband Spreewald e V, Lindenstr. 1, Raddusch • (035433) 722 99*

2 Sachsenhausen concentration camp
A visit to Sachsenhausen, Germany's first Nazi concentration camp, is a haunting experience. It was opened in 1933 as a "wild camp" for political prisoners. From 1936 to 1945, some 100,000 people were murdered here. Next to the camp is an exhibition. ✆ *Gedenkstätte und Museum Sachsenhausen, Straße der Nationen 22 • mid-Mar–mid-Oct: 8:30am–6pm daily; mid-Oct–mid-Mar: 8:30am–4:30pm daily • (03301) 20 02 00*

3 Schloss Rheinsberg
This small palace is an excellent destination for a day-trip. The palace was made famous by the love story of Kurt Tucholsky. Today it is a museum and can only be visited by guided tour. ✆ *Rheinsberg, Müllerstr. 1 • 10am–5pm Tue–Sun • (033931) 72 60 • Admission charge*

4 Werder
Surrounded by the Havelland fruit orchards, this small village celebrates Baumblütenfest, the blossoming of the fruit trees in April and May. ✆ *Potsdam-Information, Brandenburger Str. 3 • (0331) 27 55 80*

5 Caputh
This picturesque small village near Potsdam, surrounded by numerous lakes, boasts a charming Baroque palace as well as Albert Einstein's summer residence at No 7 Waldstraße. ✆ *Potsdam-Information, Brandenburger Str. 3 • (0331) 27 55 80*

6 Frankfurt/Oder
The other Frankfurt, on the Oder River, about 70 km (43 miles) east of Berlin, is well worth visiting, if only for its superb museum devoted to the playwright Heinrich von Kleist. ✆ *Faberstr. 7 • 10am–6pm Tue–Sun • (0335) 53 11 55 • Admission charge*

7 Bad Saarow
An old spa town and once a celebrity haunt, Bad Saarow's thermal springs and hotel invite you for a relaxing weekend. ✆ *Kur- und Fremden-verkehrs-GmbH, Am Kurpark 1 • (033631) 86 80 (tourist information)*

8 Buckow
The small village of Buckow is the centre of the so-called Märkische Schweiz (the Swiss Mark). A landscape of lakes and hills, which seems almost untouched, it is a good place for walking, swimming and boating. The best area is around Schermützelsee. Also at Buckow, the summer residence of Bertolt Brecht can be visited. ✆ *Umwelt- und Fremden-verkehrsamt Märkische Schweiz, Wriezener Str. 1a • (033433) 575 00*

9 Sacrow
North of Potsdam is the tiny village of Sacrow. It has become a favourite tourist spot because of its dreamy Saviour's Church, on the lake of the same name. ✆ *Potsdam-Information, Brandenburger Str. 3 • (0331) 27 55 80*

10 Königs Wusterhausen
A beautiful landscape of lakes stretches all around Königs Wusterhausen, 27 km (17 miles) southeast of Berlin. There are numerous romantic villages such as Grünau and Zeuthen, and one of its most attractive spots is the village of Teupitz, on Teupitz lake. The Schlosshotel is an ideal place to relax. ✆ *Kultur- und Tourismusverband Dahmeland, Am Bahnhof, Königs Wusterhausen • (03375) 252 00*

Left **A historic double-decker bus** Centre **Sightseeing by bus** Right **Visiting the city by velotaxi**

☑10 Guided Tours

1 Sightseeing by Double-Decker Bus

Nothing is more fun than a sightseeing tour of the city on the double-decker nostalgia bus, which is open-top in summer. Buses depart from Café Kranzler on Ku'damm or can be boarded at the main sights. ⬡ *Berlin City Tour • (030) 68 30 26 41* ⬡ *Top Tour • (030) 25 62 55 56*

2 Buses 100 and 200

The cheapest and fastest way to see the city is a journey on buses Nos 100 or 200. These double-deckers go from Bahnhof Zoo and Alexanderplatz right into Prenzlauer Berg, passing all the important sights between West and East *en route*. A city tour for only €2.10.

3 Segway Tours and Bike Tours

One centrally located operator offering both Segway and bike tours of the city is Fat Tire Bike Tours. ⬡ *(030) 24 04 79 91 • www.fattirebike toursberlin.com*

4 Sightseeing Bus Tours

Traditional sightseeing tours by bus, many of them hop-on/hop-off, can be boarded all over the city and are good for getting a quick overview. These bus tours usually last between two and four hours, and take in all the major sights. There are special tours to Potsdam. Departure

points: ⬡ *Berolina Berlin-Service, Kurfürstendamm 220 • (030) 88 56 80 30* ⬡ *Severin & Kühn, Kurfürstendamm 216 u. Alexanderplatz • (030) 880 41 90*

5 Art Tours

Several agencies cut a swathe through Berlin's artistic jungle. Small, professionally conducted tours lead visitors through selected galleries and museums, to fashion designers or to the city's most exciting architectural treasures. The tours are available in various languages. ⬡ *art:berlin, Oranienburger Str. 32 • (030) 28 09 63 90 • www.artberlin-online.de* ⬡ *GoArt, Invalidenstr. 50 • (030) 30 87 36 26 • www.goart-berlin.de*

6 Boat Tours

Berlin's waterways – Havel and Spree Rivers, Landwehrkanal and the lakes Wannsee and Müggelsee – can all be explored by boat. Many tours allow you to take in Berlin's historic sights between Charlottenburg and the centre from the water. Tours last two or three hours, and there are piers at Schloss Charlottenburg, next to the Haus der Kulturen der Welt in Tiergarten, next to the bridge Schlossbrücke as well as in Treptow. ⬡ *Stern- und Kreis-Schifffahrt, Puschkinallee 15 • (030) 536 36 00* ⬡ *Reederei Riedel • (030) 693 46 46 • www.reederei-riedel.de*

7 Berlin from the Air

Several enterprises offer sightseeing trips over Berlin and Brandenburg province in helicopter and in historic planes. ⬡ *Air Service Berlin, Schönefeld Airport, Terminal C • (030) 60 91 37 30 • www.air-service-berlin.de* ⬡ *Sky Travel 24, Strausberg Airport • (0800) 759 87 28 • www.skytravel24.de* ⬡ *Rundflug, Strausberg Airport • (03341) 30 53 64 • www.rundflug-berlin brandenburg.de*

8 Walking Tours

Berlin Walks is a small agency running themed English-language walks, departing daily from the taxi rank outside Zoologischer Garten and Hackescher Markt. Insider Tour also offers walking tours as well as bike tours and pub crawls. ⬡ *Berlin Walks • 10am daily (Apr–Oct: also 1:30pm) and by prior arrangement • (030) 301 91 94 • www.berlinwalks.com* ⬡ *Insider Tour • (030) 692 31 49 • www.insidertour.com*

9 Velotaxis

An inexpensive, and personalized way to see the town is by velotaxi (*see p162*).

10 Berlin Underground

A very special sort of tour are these guided walks through the spooky underbelly of Berlin, making your way through bunkers and ancient tunnels. ⬡ *(030) 49 91 05 17*

Useful websites: www.sightseeing.de and www.berliner stadtrundfahrten.de

Left **Relax in Potsdam's Sanssouci Park** Right **Exploring Berlin on foot**

🔟 Ways to Escape the Crowds

1 Rush Hours
If you're driving around Berlin, try to avoid the main rush hours – between 7am and 9am in the morning, and between 4:30pm and 7pm in the evening. Buses, U- and S-Bahn, too, are very crowded at these times.

2 Lunchtime
At restaurants, cafés and snack bars in the centre, you will often have to stand in line or wait to be seated if you arrive between 12:30pm and 2pm. Most venues in Berlin, though, will continue to serve the same dishes. So, if you wish to enjoy your meal in peace and quiet, set off after 1:30pm.

3 Evenings Out
Popular restaurants, particularly those around Savignyplatz, Gendarmenmarkt and Kollwitzplatz are often booked up between 7pm and 8pm, especially in summer, even during the week. You are therefore best advised to reserve a table in advance, or to arrive a little later, after about 9pm.

4 Early Risers
Many of the popular sights get very crowded, especially from Thursdays to Sundays. It's a good idea to arrive early, and to start your visit as soon as a place opens – especially the Reichstag.

5 Weekends
Most tourists come to Berlin for weekends, and so Ku'damm and Friedrichstraße are completely overrun by visitors on a Saturday morning. In the evening, many events, especially concerts by the Berlin Philharmonic Orchestra and performances in the best theatres, will be sold out. If possible arrange for your visit to start on a Sunday and take in the first few days of the week.

6 Holidays
High season for Berlin visitors is the period from May to July. From the end of July or the beginning of the school holidays, however, the town gets noticeably quieter, as many locals go on holiday too. You'll easily find parking spaces and many restaurants are much emptier than usual – especially in August. The only disadvantage is that theatres and concert halls close then for a summer break.

7 Berlin Parks
If, after a couple of days, you're tired of the hustle and bustle of the big city, go to one of the parks to chill out – Viktoriapark in Kreuzberg, Jungfernheide in Charlottenburg and the area around Tegeler See are picturesque places where you can relax in peace and quiet.

8 Sunday Morning
Even the central areas in Berlin are often completely deserted early on Sunday mornings – the ideal time for a quiet stroll or bike ride down Kurfürstendamm or Unter den Linden. Most cafés and museums open at 10am, so you won't miss out on either cultural discoveries or refreshment.

9 Reservations
Whether you wish to visit the theatre, the opera, the Philharmonie concert hall, a multiplex cinema or a special event, it is almost always worth trying to book tickets as early as possible by phone or at one of the agencies – you'll rarely be lucky enough to buy tickets for the most popular events on the day.

10 Nights
Berlin is a city that never sleeps – it is "open" 24 hours a day. If you don't have to stick to particular times, for your evening meal, for example, make the most of your freedom – in most restaurants you can still enjoy a good meal after 11pm. The same is true of pubs and bars – many close at 3am or 4am, or not at all. Nightclubs and discos don't get going until midnight or later, even during the week. And some museums stay open late, until 10pm, on Thursdays.

Left **In the Europa-Center** Centre **Inside Galeries Lafayette** Right **A stand selling souvenirs**

TOP 10 Shopping

1 Shopping Streets
Kurfürstendamm, Tauentzienstraße and Friedrichstraße are the main three shopping streets in Berlin. You'll find inexpensive shops around Tauentzienstraße and Alexanderplatz. The Galeries Lafayette department store as well as the west side of Ku'damm are upmarket. A good mix of shops can be found in the arcades at Potsdamer Platz, Schlossstraße in the south of Berlin and the Gesundbrunnen-center in the north.

2 Opening Hours
Normally, shops are open between 10am and 8pm on Mondays to Saturdays. Smaller shops, however, close at 2 or 4pm on Saturdays, except in the four weeks before Christmas when they stay open until 6pm. Following a liberalizing of the law affecting opening hours, larger shops often stay open until 10pm at weekends. During special events (for example during the IFA International Broadcasting Exhibition or the Berlinale Film Festival) special opening hours may be in force.

3 How to Pay
Most shops in the city centre accept credit cards such as Visa, MasterCard and American Express, less commonly Diners Club. Almost all shops take Maestro cards.

4 Consumer Protection
If you feel that you are not being treated fairly or if a product you have bought proves to be faulty (and an exchange is refused), you can contact the consumer protection association. ✆ *Verbraucherzentrale Berlin, Hardenbergpl. 2, 3rd floor • 9am–1pm Mon, 9am–4:30pm Tue & Fri, 9am–8pm Wed & Thu • (030) 21 48 50*

5 Sales
End-of-season sales take place at the end of January and the end of July. But you'll be able to find bargains throughout the year in the department stores and shops, often laid out on special stands right next to the main entrance.

6 Fashion
The best fashion and designer stores, selling coveted labels such as Gucci, Versace, Jil Sander, DKNY or Prada, can be found on the west side of Ku'damm and in Friedrichstraße. Kaufhaus des Westens sells a good large range of ladies' and gentlemen's fashions *(see p60)*.

7 Music
Apart from large multi-media and CD-store chains such as Saturn, MediaMarkt, Promarkt and Kaufhof, you will find a vast selection of CDs at Kulturkaufhaus Dussmann *(see p119)*, as well

as in the department store Kaufhaus des Westens or KaDeWe *(see p60)*.

8 Gifts and Souvenirs
If you're looking for gifts and souvenirs to take home, try the Europa-Center *(see p24)* and the KaDeWe *(see p60)*. There are also souvenir shops in Unter den Linden (near Pariser Platz), on Potsdamer Platz as well as at Checkpoint Charlie.

9 Art and Antiques
Most antiques shops are clustered south of Nollendorfplatz *(see p104)* and in the smaller streets off Kurfürstendamm. However, the flea and art fair on the Straße des 17 Juni *(see p60)* and the antiques shops in the S-Bahn arches between Friedrichstraße and Museuminsel are often much better value and offer a wider range of goods and antiques.

10 Around Berlin
In Potsdam as in other small towns, there are many places to shop for arts and crafts items or clothes. A good place for bargain hunters is the B5 Designer Outlet, situated on the national road with the same number. Here many fashionable items are sold at heavily discounted prices. ✆ *B5, exit Demex Park/B5 Centre • 10am–7pm Mon–Thu, 10am–8pm Fri & Sat*

Left **Theatre ticket office** Right **Enjoy Berlin's parks for free**

🔟 Berlin on a Budget

1 Accommodation

For low-cost accommodation you can check into inexpensive youth hostels, hostels run by the YMCA, or a backpacker hostel. Or try a Mitwohnzentrale, an agency arranging shared accommodation in private homes at a low cost *(see also p163)*.

2 Restaurants

As in Britain, Indian and Turkish restaurants are often particularly good value. Another cheap alternative are Turkish doner kebab snack bars and German curry sausage stands – these often also sell other snacks at low prices.

3 Museums

Berlin's municipal museums, especially those on Museumsinsel, can all be visited on a three-day ticket costing €19. Admission is free four hours before closing on Thursdays.

4 WelcomeCard

The BVG Welcome-Card offers the best and cheapest way of visiting exhibitions and museums in Berlin and using public transport throughout the city. The WelcomeCard costs from €22 for one adult and up to three children under the age of 14 (children under 6 travel free). It provides two, three or five days of free travel on all buses and trains of the Berlin-Brandenburg public transport network operating anywhere within the A, B and C fare zones, as well as up to 50 per cent reductions for many tourist attractions.

5 Reduced Tickets

Theatres and the opera house sell reduced tickets at the door on the day of the performance, mainly for pupils and students who can show a valid student card. Alternatively, tickets can be bought cheaply in advance by anyone from ticketing agencies such as Hekticket. 🕾 *Hekticket (030) 230 99 30*

6 Street Artists

Berlin has always been a good place for street artists, especially on Breitscheidplatz and along Ku'damm. There is a legendary mime artist, dressed as a clown, who mimics passers-by outside the cafés on the eastern side of Ku'damm. In summer, in Charlottenburg and Prenzlauer Berg, you can often listen to street musicians and singers directly at your table or outside the restaurant or café.

7 Day of the Open Door

Since Berlin is Germany's political and cultural capital, many public and private institutions regularly offer the chance to take a look behind the scenes, free of charge. A visit to one of the federal ministries is particularly interesting. Daily newspapers will list these events. Every year in summer, "Schaustelle Berlin" (a pun on "Baustelle", meaning building site) conducts guided tours to Berlin's major building sites and other projects *(see also www.berlin.de)*.

8 Free Concerts

Churches and smaller concert halls in the outer districts often put on classical concerts for a low admission fee or even free of charge. The city magazines and daily newspapers list such events in the appropriate columns. All Berlin daily newspapers also give away free tickets for current exhibitions and events. Look at the Berlin pages in the papers for what is currently on offer.

9 Markets

Berlin's weekly flea markets always have a vast range of special offers for sale, besides which they'll offer you the opportunity to try out your haggling skills *(see also pp60–61)*.

10 Parks

Admission to all of Berlin's parks and green spaces is free. You can enjoy their sports facilities, and often also open-air concerts, without having to fork out for a ticket *(see also pp68–9)*.

For shops & markets around town see pp85, 107, 119

Streetsmart

Left **Hotel–Pension Funk** Centre **A suite in die fabrik** Right **Arte Luise Kunsthotel**

🔟 Modest Hotels & Hostels

1 die fabrik
This hotel, its name meaning "the factory", is a guesthouse cum youth hostel. An alternative youth and arts centre in the middle of deepest Kreuzberg, it attracts backpackers from around the world, hoping to meet locals and others. ⊗ Schlesische Str. 18 • (030) 611 71 16 • www.diefabrik. com • no credit cards • €

2 Arte Luise Kunsthotel
The 30 rooms in this small hotel were all individually and imaginatively designed by different local artists, with themes ranging from loud pop art to classic Modernism. The hotel is in a central location, close to lively Scheunenviertel and Unter den Linden. ⊗ Luisenstr. 19 • Map J/K3 • (030) 28 44 80 • www. luise-berlin.com • €€€

3 Myer's Hotel
A family-run hotel in the centre of Prenzlauer Berg, ideal for families or young couples. The rooms are simply decorated yet modern, and the hotel is located in an historic part of town. The service is attentive and the atmosphere relaxed. ⊗ Metzer Str. 26 • Map H2 • (030) 44 01 40 • €€€

4 Hotel Johann
This small hotel with friendly staff offers moderately priced comfort. It is located in a quiet street close to the Jewish Museum and near an open-air swimming pool complex. ⊗ Johanniterstr. 8 • Map G5 • (030) 225 07 40 • www. hotel-johann-berlin.de • €€€

5 Hotel-Pension Dittberner
This is Berlin's best guesthouse close to Ku'damm. There are several rooms in an old building connected by endless corridors – great atmosphere. ⊗ Wielandstr. 26 • Map P2 • (030) 881 64 85 • www. hotel-dittberner.de • €€€

6 Hotel–Pension Funk
Slightly antiquated, venerable guesthouse close to Ku'damm, based in the apartment of the silent-film star Asta Nielsen. The rates are unbeatable, while furnishings and service are personal and friendly. There are only 15 rooms however, so it is advisable to book in advance. ⊗ Fasanenstr. 69 • Map N/P4 • (030) 882 71 93 • www.hotel-pension funk.de • €€

7 Pension Kreuzberg
Clean and friendly, this hotel-guesthouse in Kreuzberg boasts an excellent atmosphere – but unfortunately no en-suite bathrooms. The landlady takes great care of her guests and is happy to pass on her personal tips for nightlife and culture in Berlin. ⊗ Großbeerenstr. 64 • Map F5/6 • (030) 251 13 62 • www.pension-kreuzberg.de • no credit cards • €–€€

8 Hotel Transit
Housed on two floors of a former industrial building, this international youth hostel is located in a lively area close to the town centre. It has large rooms, sleeping up to six people. ⊗ Hagelberger Str. 53–4 • Map F6 • (030) 789 04 70 • www.hotel-transit.de • €€

9 Ostel
Located in Berlin's trendy Mitte district, Ostel is designed to look like a communist-era hotel. There is a choice of rooms including doubles with shared or private bathrooms, rooms with double- or triple-decker bunk beds and apartments that can sleep up to six people. ⊗ Wriezener Karree 5 • Map H4 • (030) 25 76 86 60 • www.ostel.eu • €€

10 EastSeven Berlin Hostel
Located in a lively Prenzlauer Berg neighbourhood brimming with bars and cafés, this friendly hostel is also within walking distance of the Museumsinsel and Alexanderplatz. It offers amenities such as a garden and free Wi-Fi access. ⊗ Schwedterstr. 7 • Map H6 • (030) 93 62 22 40 • www.eastseven.de • €–€€

Note: Unless otherwise stated, all hotels accept credit cards, and have en-suite bathrooms.

Left **A small room in Bleibtreu-Hotel** Right **Courtyard of Hackescher Markt hotel**

Medium-Priced Hotels

1 Bleibtreu-Hotel
Here, you'll fancy yourself in Tuscany – the hotel's stylish interior courtyard and bright, tastefully furnished rooms are an oasis of tranquillity in the bustle of the western half of the city. The international clientele is equally stylish. The hotel has its own restaurant, pool, sauna, massage and much more on offer, and there are shops right outside. ✎ *Bleibtreustr. 31 • Map P3 • (030) 88 47 40 • www.bleibtreu.com • €€€€*

2 Hackescher Markt
A charming hotel in an unbeatable location right opposite Hackesche Höfe – few places in this price range can compete. Large, bright rooms with elegant furnishings, friendly service, an excellent restaurant and many pleasant extras, such as an attractive patio, guarantee a pleasant stay. ✎ *Große Präsidentenstr. 8 • Map J5 • (030) 28 00 30 • www.loock-hotels.com • €€€€*

3 Alsterhof
A quiet classic, this hotel boasts attentive staff, rustic rooms and its own small beer garden in summer, all in an excellent location near the KaDeWe. Ask about special weekend rates. Non-smoking rooms available. ✎ *Augsburger Str. 5 • Map P5 • (030) 21 24 20 • www.alsterhof.de • €€€*

4 Hotel am Scheunenviertel
Well-run establishment with an intimate atmosphere (there are only 18 rooms), popular with tourists on cultural visits. Rooms and lobby have been kept deliberately plain, which creates a slightly spartan impression, but all needs are catered for. ✎ *Oranienburger Str. 38 • Map J4/5 • (030) 282 21 25 • €€€*

5 Hotel-Pension Augusta
This small hotel is a little old-fashioned, and some rooms could do with refurbishing, but that's more than made up for by its surplus of old Berlin charm, central location and low prices. ✎ *Fasanenstr. 22 • Map P4 • (030) 883 50 28 • www.hotel-augusta.de • €€€*

6 Hotel am Zoo
A trendy hotel in a uniquely central location, on Ku'damm. The rooms are all surprisingly large, and the windows have been sound-proofed. ✎ *Kurfürstendamm 25 • Map P4 • (030) 88 43 70 • www.hotelzoo.de • €€€*

7 Hotel-Pension Kastanienhof
A charming hotel in a building dating back to the turn of the 20th century. The rooms are basic but well equipped (with safe, minibar and hairdryer). An ideal base for exploring Prenzlauer Berg. ✎ *Kastanienallee 65 • Map G2 • (030) 44 30 50 • www.kastanienhof.biz • €€€*

8 Riehmers Hofgarten
In Riehmers Hofgarten you can live the life of a Prussian officer. Old Kreuzberg apartments, with sombre rooms and elegant bathrooms, are the perfect setting for a 19th-century lifestyle. The hotel, part of a large complex of 19th-century Gothic red-brick buildings, is certainly remarkable. There is also a restaurant. ✎ *Yorckstr. 83 • Map F6 • (030) 78 09 88 00 • www.riehmershofgarten.de • €€*

9 Hotel Berliner Hof
You can find a more attractive room in other hotels, but you'll be hard pushed to find one at such a low price and in such a central location, on Tauentzienstraße, opposite the KaDeWe department store. ✎ *Tauentzienstr. 8 • Map P5 • (030) 25 49 50 • www.berliner-hof.com • €€€*

10 SORAT Hotel Ambassador Berlin
A medium-priced hotel near KaDeWe, offering a full office service with quiet rooms, good views and a nice breakfast area. ✎ *Bayreuther Str. 42–43 • Map P5 • (030) 21 90 20 • www.sorat-hotels.com • €€€*

Left **In the art'otel berlin** Centre **Lobby and bar in Hecker's Hotel** Right **Ku'Damm 101 Hotel**

10 Designer Hotels

1 art'otel berlin-mitte
Berlin's best designer hotel emphasizes every detail, and everything here has been styled, from the furniture to the soap in your bathroom. The walls of the historic building are decorated with paintings by Georg Baselitz. The hotel is centrally located, close to Nikolai-viertel. ⊗ Wallstr. 70–73 • Map L6 • (030) 24 06 20 • www.artotels.com • €€€

2 Ku'damm 101
This minimalist hotel caters to an art-oriented, mostly European clientele, who like the simple but comfortable rooms with large bathrooms, the stylish, modern interior and the great view from the breakfast room. Prices are highly competitive and the location on the more elegant part of Ku'damm is farther away from the main action. ⊗ Kurfürstendamm 101 • Map G1 • (030) 520 05 50 • www.kudamm101.com • €€€

3 Brandenburger Hof
One of the few hotels in Berlin to be influenced by the Bauhaus, the Branden-burger Hof has free-swinging leather seats and ball-shaped lamps, forming an exciting contrast to the historic building. ⊗ Eislebener Str. 14 • Map P4 • (030) 21 40 50 • www.brandenburger-hof.com • €€€€

4 DeragHotel Großer Kurfürst
If you prefer modern designs, this hotel is not for you – the rooms here are all classically styled. The Großer Kurfürst has successfully incorporated modern facilities into a somewhat dated building. It also features many useful extras, such as free public transport and bicycle hire. ⊗ Neue Roßstr. 11–12 • Map L6 • (030) 24 60 00 • www.deraghotels.de • €€€€

5 Hecker's Hotel
The plain façade of this modern business hotel, centrally situated in a side street just off Ku'damm, belies the much more sophisticated interior – you'll be greeted by modern art, cool minimalism, clever lighting and first-class service. ⊗ Grolmanstr. 35 • Map N3 • (030) 889 00 • www.heckers-hotel.com • €€€

6 Lux Eleven
This stylish, modern apartment hotel is a designer's dream come true. Old townhouses have been converted into mostly white, sleek rooms with all the gadgets of a business hotel. The Luchs restaurant and bar, with its understated elegance, adds to the up-market flair of the hotel. ⊗ Rosa-Luxemburg-Str. 9–13 • Map H2 • (030) 936 28 00 • www.lux-eleven.com • €€€

7 Park Plaza Wallstreet
The design here is based on the theme of New York's Wall Street, with accents such as dollar-bill carpets, murals of stock-brokers and business maxims on the walls. A pleasant hotel in a central location. ⊗ Wallstr. 23–24 • Map L6 • (030) 847 11 70 • www.parkplaza.com/berlinde_wallstrasse • €€€

8 Maritim proArte Hotel Berlin
Predominantly styled in tones of green and blue, this modern business hotel boasts almost 300 modern paintings, which decorate the rooms. ⊗ Friedrichstr. 151 • Map K/L4 • (030) 203 35 • www.maritim.de • €€€€

9 art'otel Kurfürstendamm
Works of art hang, stand and lie everywhere inside and outside this hotel, especially works by Wolf Vostell, and the interior is boldly designed in ultra-modern vibrant colours. ⊗ Joachimsthaler Str. 28–29 • Map P4 • (030) 88 44 70 • www.artotels.com • €€€

10 Hotel Q
Stylish and discreet, this is a favourite among Hollywood stars. Its rooms are designed as "living landscapes" with furniture integrated into the walls. ⊗ Knesebeckstr. 33–34 • Map C5 • (030) 810 06 60 • www.loock-hotels.com • €€€

Note: Unless otherwise stated, all hotels accept credit cards, and have en-suite bathrooms.

Price Categories

Price for a standard double room per night, with breakfast, taxes and other charges included

€ under €60
€€ €60–100
€€€ €100–150
€€€€ €150–200
€€€€€ over €200

Left **Dining at the Hilton Berlin** Right **The lobby of Estrel Residence Congress Hotel**

TOP 10 Hotels for Business Travellers

1 Hilton Berlin
Top executives favour this luxury hotel because of its central location, the views across Gendarmenmarkt, an excellent breakfast and specially designed executive rooms. A full secretarial service is included. ◉ *Mohrenstr. 30 • Map L4 • (030) 202 30 • www. hilton.de • €€€€*

2 NH Berlin Heinrich Heine
This hotel is the best choice if your business requires a longer stay in town. Close to Nikolaiviertel, the apartments are equipped with desks and kitchens; and staff are specially trained to cater for the needs of business travellers. ◉ *Heinrich-Heine-Platz 11 • Map H4 • (030) 27 80 40 • www.nh-hotels.com • €€€*

3 Estrel Residence Congress Hotel
With more than 1,000 rooms, this hotel is Europe's largest, offering a three- to four-star service at moderate prices. Its numerous conference rooms and the latest technological equipment make it the perfect venue for conferences or international business meetings. Yet the hotel is equally ready to cater for the needs of the individual business traveller. ◉ *Sonnenallee 225 • (030) 68 310 • www.estrel.com • €€€*

4 Crowne Plaza Berlin City Centre
Part of an American hotel chain, the Crowne Plaza offers attentive service, tasteful rooms and all the creature comforts that business travellers expect, plus a central location, in the western part of the city. ◉ *Nürnberger Str. 65 • Map P5 • (030) 21 00 70 • www.cp-berlin.com • €€€*

5 Holiday Inn Garden Court
It may seem a little impersonal, but the Holiday Inn's excellent location makes it popular with business travellers from the US. It doesn't have a restaurant. ◉ *Bleibtreustr. 25 • Map P3 • (030) 88 09 30 • www. holidayinnberlin.de • €€€*

6 Mandala Suites
A central boarding house with suites of 40–100 square metres (430–1,076 square feet), elegantly equipped as offices and offering a secretarial service. ◉ *Friedrichstr. 185–190 • Map K/L4 • (030) 20 29 20 • www.themandala.de • €€€€*

7 Leonardo Airport Hotel Berlin Schönefeld
Conveniently situated near Schönefeld airport, this hotel is ideal for brief business trips. A good night's rest is guaranteed, and the service is efficient and friendly. ◉ *Schwalbenweg 18 • (030) 67 90 20 • www. leonardo-hotels.com • €€*

8 Grand City Excelsior Hotel Berlin
Prestigious member of Berlin's Blue-Band-Hotels, the Excelsior is characterized more by sober efficiency than by friendliness but hits the mark with moderate prices, excellent location and a vast range of business services. ◉ *Hardenbergstr. 14 • Map N4 • (030) 315 50 • www.grand city-hotel-berlin-excelsior.de • €€€*

9 NH Jolly Berlin Friedrichstrasse
This luxury hotel is in a building on Friedrichstrasse that opened in 2002. Apart from its East Berlin location, the hotel's main attractions are the spacious rooms, large lobby and inviting bar, all furnished with only the best materials. ◉ *Friedrichstr. 96 • Map F3/K4 • (030) 206 26 60 • www.nh-hotels.de • €€€*

10 Pullman Berlin Schweizerhof
One of Berlin's luxury hotels, the Schweizerhof features beautifully clean lines, precious woods and a large, well-designed fitness area – all in the centre of the western part of the city. ◉ *Budapester Str. 25 • Map N5 • (030) 269 60 • www.sofitel.com • €€€€*

See also pp72–3.

Left **Schlossparkhotel** Centre **Pool in Hotel zur Bleiche** Right **Relexa Schlosshotel Cecilienhof**

🔟 Hotels in Green Surroundings

1 Relexa Schloss-hotel Cecilienhof

Potsdam's best hotel, the Relexa is based in an historic building in the middle of Neuer Garten (see p154). At night, peace descends as the day trippers leave. ⓢ *Am Neuen Garten Potsdam • (0331) 370 50 • www.relexa-hotels.de • €€€€*

2 Landhaus Schlachtensee

This villa, near Schlachten-see and Krumme Lanke, now a small boarding house, oozes the charm of bygone days in rural Berlin. The furnishings in its 20 rooms are a little old-fashioned, but the service is very person-able. ⓢ *Bogotastr. 9 • (030) 809 94 70 • www.hotel-landhaus-schlachtensee.de • €€–€€€*

3 Schlossparkhotel

Only a few minutes from the western part of the city, this is the only hotel near Schloss Char-lottenburg, right next to Schlosspark. Attached to it is a health and fitness centre – the facilities and the service are surpris-ingly good for such a small place: the hotel has only 40 rooms. ⓢ *Heubner-weg 2a • Map A/B3 • (030) 326 90 30 • www.schloss parkhotel.de • €€€–€€€€*

4 Hotel Seehof am Lietzensee

A well-run hotel, centrally located in Charlottenburg, not far from Messege-lände (exhibition grounds), in a picturesque spot on Lietzensee. Apart from a beautiful indoor pool, the hotel also has a delightful sun terrace. ⓢ *Lietzensee-ufer 11 • Map A4 • (030) 32 00 20 • www.hotel-seehof-berlin.de • €€€*

5 Hotel Müggelsee Berlin

A comfortable hotel on Müggelsee, combining near-unspoilt nature and closeness to the city. There is a skittle alley, a fitness club, tennis courts, sauna and billiards, as well as boat and bicycle hire and an extensive programme of leisure events. ⓢ *Müggel-heimer Damm 145 • (030) 65 88 20 • www.hotel-mueggelsee-berlin.de • €€€*

6 Haus La Garde

This tiny guesthouse with only four rooms is hidden in a romantic, non-smoking villa on the Schlachtensee. If lakes aren't your thing, you can chill out in the villa's gardens. ⓢ *Bergengrünstr. 16 • (030) 801 30 09 • www.haus-la-garde.de • €€*

7 Spreeidyll-Hotel am Yachthafen

A small family-run house on the Müggelspree, not far from a bathing beach and a boat-hire booth – the ideal place to relax and forget all about the hustle and bustle of the big city, which is, however, only a few kilo-metres to the northwest.

Come here to chill out. ⓢ *Müggelseedamm 70 • (030) 645 38 52 • www.spree-idyll.de • €€*

8 Forsthaus Paulsborn

Located in Grunewaldsee, in the southwestern Grunewald forest, this hotel is housed in a beautiful old building. There is a restaurant and great terrace as well as riding stables nearby. ⓢ *Hüttenweg 90 • (030) 818 19 10 • www.forsthaus-paulsborn.de • €€€*

9 Penta Hotel Berlin-Köpenick

The slightly sterile and impersonal atmosphere of this hotel is more than made up for by its loca-tion. It is right in the centre of the southeast-ern district of Köpenick, on the banks of the Dahme River – and both Müggelsee and Schöne-feld Airport are only a few minutes' drive away by car or S-Bahn. ⓢ *Grünauer Str. 1 • (030) 65 47 90 • www.pentahotels.com/en/berlin-koepenick • €€*

10 Hotel zur Bleiche

This country-house hotel, located in the middle of the Spreewald lake district, has great facilities including pool, steam rooms, saunas and a great restaurant – a veritable paradise for health and fitness fans. ⓢ *Bleichestr. 16, Burg • (035603) 620 • www.hotel-zur-bleiche.de • €€€€*

Note: *Unless otherwise stated, all hotels accept credit cards, and have en-suite bathrooms.*

Price Categories

Price for a standard double room per night, with breakfast, taxes and other charges included	
€	under €60
€€	€60–100
€€€	€100–150
€€€€	€150–200
€€€€€	over €200

Left **The Backpacker Hostel** Right **At BaxPax, you'll sleep in a VW Beetle**

TOP10 Budget Hotels & Hostels

1 BaxPax Kreuzberg
Much better than a youth hostel yet much cheaper than a guesthouse, BaxPax offers an unusual place to rest your head. You'll be sleeping in beds in decommissioned VW beetles, at under €20 per night. Plus you'll meet young, friendly people from around the world (great for making friends). This dive is in deepest Kreuzberg, and not suitable for those over 30. ✆ *Skalitzerstr. 104 • Map H5 • (030) 69 51 83 22 • www.baxpax.de • €*

2 Jugendgästehaus der DSJ
This vast youth guesthouse is situated in an excellent spot, in the heart of Kreuzberg, and close to the Jüdisches Museum. The showers are shared, but a bed in a multi-bedded room is not expensive. The hostel is favoured by a young and international crowd. ✆ *Franz-Künstler-Str. 10 • Map G5 • (030) 615 10 07 • no credit cards • €*

3 Jugendherberge Berlin-International
One of Berlin's largest youth hostels offers slightly antiquated but comfortable multi-bedded rooms. The staff are very friendly for a hostel in a large city, but the hostel is often overrun by noisy hordes of school kids. ✆ *Kluckstr. 3 • Map E5 • (030) 264 95 20 • €*

4 Generator Hostel
Popular with groups and budget travellers, this is Berlin's largest modern hostel, with a bar and club attached. It may be a little far from the action and a bit noisy, but it's definitely value for money. ✆ *Storkower Str. 160 • (030) 417 24 00 • www.generatorhostels.com • €*

5 Jugendherberge am Wannsee
One of Berlin's oldest youth hostels, popular with groups of students and pupils and not the best place for visitors seeking peace and quiet. The picturesque location on Wannsee makes up for communal showers and dormitories, particularly in summer. ✆ *Badeweg 1 • (030) 803 20 34 • €*

6 Bed & Breakfast
Bed and Breakfast Ring arranges shared accommodation in private homes all over town, at low prices. You'll normally have your own room with one or two beds or an apartment to yourself. Quality varies considerably, but the rooms are mostly priced at under €25 per person. ✆ *www.bandb-ring.de • no credit cards • €*

7 Gaybed Bed and Breakfast
A private gay- and lesbian-friendly guesthouse offering basic rooms and many insider tips on culture and nightlife. The only disadvantage is its location in Moabit – not Berlin's most attractive area. ✆ *Perlebergerstr. • Map D/E2 • (030) 81 85 19 88 • www.gaybed.de • €*

8 Backpacker Hostel Berlin (BaxPax Mitte)
A typically charming Berlin guesthouse, in the most attractive part of Mitte. You can even have your breakfast served in the room. ✆ *Chausseestr. 102 • Map F2 • (030) 28 39 09 65 • www.backpacker.de • €*

9 The Circus Hotel
This hostel, near Alexanderplatz, offers great value accommodation close to many of the city's sights. Dorm beds, single, double and triple rooms are available as well as a rooftop apartment with views over Berlin. There is free Wi-Fi in all rooms and a garden courtyard, restaurant and bike and scooter rental. ✆ *Weinbergsweg 1a • Map G2 • (030) 20 00 39 39 • www.circus-berlin.de • €€*

10 Hotel Christophorus-Haus
This hotel is a little more expensive than others in the same category, but the accommodation in green surroundings is perfect for families travelling by car. The hotel is run by the Protestant church. ✆ *Johannesstift, Schönwalder Allee 26 • (030) 33 60 60 • www.vch.de • €€*

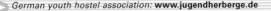

Left **In Villa Kastania** Centre **Spa area in Alexander-Plaza** Right **Propeller Island City Lodge**

TOP 10 Hotels & Guesthouses with Charm

1 Hotel Residenz Berlin

Although this hotel is part of a US chain, it is based in one of the most beautiful old-Berlin town houses near Ku'damm, and guests enjoy the intimate, characterful atmosphere. The late 19th century rooms are tastefully furnished, and the restaurant has outdoor seating in summer. ◎ *Meinekestr. 9 • Map P4 • (030) 88 44 30 • www. hotel-residenz.com • €€€*

2 Ellington Hotel Berlin

This distinctive hotel is an oasis of modern design set within 1920s Bauhaus architecture close to busy Tauentzien and Kurfürstendamm. An affordable, stylish downtown alternative for a young, international clientele. ◎ *Nürnberger Str. 50–55 • Map E2 • (030) 68 31 50 • www. ellingtonhotel.de • €€€€*

3 Alexander-Plaza

Based in an historic building from the late 19th century, this hotel perfectly combines old and new features. The elegant rooms are decorated with plaster ceiling mouldings and equipped with timelessly sophisticated furnishings. This is a very pleasant hotel, both to look at and to stay in. ◎ *Rosenstr. 1 • Map J5 • (030) 24 00 10 • www.hotel-alexander-plaza. de • €€€*

4 DeragResidenz-hotel Henriette

A stylish hotel with classic decoration – oak-panelled walls and thick carpets and curtains adorn the rooms, which are arranged around an inner courtyard. Few hotels in town are better than this, and the service is very friendly. ◎ *Neue Roßstr. 13 • Map L6 • (030) 24 60 09 00 • www.deraghotels. de • €€€*

5 Hotel Gendarm

This small hotel on Gendarmenmarkt is based in a venerable town residence. After a refurbishment in 2009, the designer-appointed rooms exude sophisti-cation and elegance. The hotel also boasts a sauna, pool and fitness facilities. ◎ *Charlottenstr. 61 • Map L4 • (030) 206 06 60 • www.hotel-gendarm-berlin.de • €€€€*

6 acksel Haus

Stylish apartment rooms in a small, slightly alternative guesthouse, based in an old tenement block. The "acksel Haus" is located near Kollwitzplatz, a popular area with young people. ◎ *Belforter Str. 21 • Map H2 • (030) 44 33 76 33 • www.ackselhaus.de • no credit cards • €€€*

7 Art Nouveau Hotel

This old-fashioned guest-house is based in a beautiful Art-Nouveau building. The rooms are furnished in a discreet modern style, and the hotel is typical of Berlin's older buildings. ◎ *Leibnitzstr. 59 • Map P2 • (030) 327 74 40 • www.hotelartnouveau.de • €€€–€€€€*

8 Artist Riverside Hotel Berlin-Mitte

A small hotel promising big things, and in terms of its furnishings at least it keeps these promises. Overlooking the River Spree, the hotel features a sophisticated interior and excellent service, and it is popular with Americans. ◎ *Friedrichstr. 106 • Map K/L4 • (030) 28 49 00 • www.great-hotel. com • €€–€€€*

9 Villa Kastania

Villa Kastania offers service of a high standard and beautiful rooms – some with kitchens. There is also a pool and wellness centre. Situated in Charlotten-burg, close to the Funkturm. ◎ *Kastanien-allee 20 • (030) 300 00 20 • www.villakastania.com • €€*

10 Propeller Island City Lodge

If you're staying at this lodge, you will share it with the artist Lars Stroschen, who designed the rooms himself. ◎ *Albrecht-Achilles Str. 58 • (030) 891 90 16 • www. propeller-island.com • no credit cards • €€€*

Note: *Unless otherwise stated, all hotels accept credit cards, and have en-suite bathrooms.*

Price Categories

Price for a standard	€	under €60
double room per	€€	€60–100
night, with breakfast,	€€€	€100–150
taxes and other	€€€€	€150–200
charges included	€€€€€	over €200

Left **The Sofitel Berlin Gendarmenmarkt** Right **A suite in Hotel Palace**

TOP10 Luxury Hotels

1 Hotel Palace

The expensively restored hotel on the second floor of the Europa-Center is a real find – all the rooms are exquisitely designed, two of the suites (Zackenbarsch and Panda) were styled by the director himself. The hotel staff are unobtrusive and very helpful. ✆ *Budapester Str. 45 • Map N/P5 • (030) 250 20 • www.palace.de • €€€€*

2 Sofitel Berlin Gendarmenmarkt

Relatively inexpensive and the smallest of the first-class hotels (70 rooms, 21 suites), the Sofitel is probably also one of the most attractive, with excellent views of Gendarmenmarkt. ✆ *Charlottenstr. 50–52 • Map L4 • (030) 203 750 • www.sofitel.com • €€€€*

3 Hotel Intercontinental Berlin

Luxury hotel in Tiergarten, nicely situated with great views over the central park, this hotel is popular with business travellers. Although the building itself is not particularly attractive, the rooms are furnished in a timelessly elegant style. Its three restaurants offer first-class food, and the bars, pool and fitness area are also excellent. ✆ *Budapester Str. 2 • Map N5/6 • (030) 260 20 • www.berlin.intercontinental.com • €€€€*

4 Westin Grand Hotel

Luxury accommodation in an historic spot, at the corner of Friedrichstraße and Unter den Linden, offering large, elegant rooms and US-style service. The lobby and the grand stairs are breathtaking. There's also a café and a bar. ✆ *Friedrichstr. 158–164 • Map K4 • (030) 202 70 • aktuelles.westin.de/berlin • €€€€€*

5 Grand Hotel Esplanade

Glitzy and modern, with furnishings somewhere between functional sobriety and Bauhaus-style. Service is excellent and first class facilities include a state of the art fitness centre and the popular Harry's New York Bar. ✆ *Lützowufer 15 • Map N6 • (030) 25 47 80 • www.esplanade.de • €€€€*

6 Swissôtel Berlin

One of Berlin's luxury hotels, the Swissôtel is located at the busy corner of Ku'damm and Joachimsthaler Straße. Great views of the city, especially at night. ✆ *Augsburger Str. 44 • Map P4 • (030) 22 01 00 • www.berlin.swissotel.com • €€€€*

7 The Mandala Hotel Potsdamer Platz

This apartment hotel, in a great spot in Potsdamer Platz, has suites of 35–100 sq m (375–1,100 sq ft) with kitchen, stereo, fitness area, sauna, daily papers and anything else you could possibly wish for. ✆ *Potsdamer Str. 3 • Map K3 • (030) 590 05 00 00 • www.themandala.com • €€€€*

8 Kempinski Hotel Bristol Berlin

A magnificent, cosmopolitan blend of elegance and modern amenities – this hotel, one of Berlin's most famous – has it all. Its international reputation has attracted many famous guests, from Castro to Tina Turner. ✆ *Kurfürstendamm 27 • Map P4 • (030) 88 43 40 • www.kempinskiberlin.de • €€€€*

9 Hotel de Rome

Right off Bebelplatz near the State Opera, just steps away from Unter den Linden. The interior is a vision of Post-Modern ideas, while the Italian restaurant, the Opera café and the spa area live up to the expectations of a hotel geared towards the international jet set. ✆ *Behrenstr. 37 • Map G3 • (030) 460 60 90 • www.hotelderome.com • €€€€€*

10 SAS Radisson Blue

A modern luxury hotel with a huge aquarium in the lobby. It has stylish, bright rooms with great views of Berliner Dom and Alexanderplatz. It has Asian and fusion cuisine restaurants. ✆ *Karl-Liebknecht-Str. 3 • Map K5 • (030) 23 82 80 • €€€€*

General Index

A

Aalto, Alvar 99
Admiralspalast 57, 118
Advice 146
Ägyptisches Museum 46
Aigner 121
Airlines 161
Airports
Schönefeld 161
Tegel 161
Akademie der Künste 9
Aleppozimmer 21
Alexa 135
Alexanderplatz 130–31
Alexandrowka 156
Alliiertenmuseum 90
Alpenstück 129
Alt-Berliner Weissbierstube 136
Alt-Luxemburg 87
Alte Bibliothek 113
Alte Kommandantur 118
Alte Nationalgalerie 114
Alte Pumpe 101
Alte Schönhauser Straße 126
Alter Krug Dahlem 93
Alter Markt 145
Altes Museum 39, 114
Altes Palais 113
Altes Rathaus (Potsdam) 156
Altes Schloss 28
Altes Zollhaus 109
Ambulance 166
Ana e Bruno 87
Anhalter Bahnhof 104
Ankerklause 108
Appelt, Dieter 11
AquaDom and Sea Life Berlin
65, 134
Ararat 107
Architecture
Historic Buildings 38–9
Kurfürstendamm 25
Modern Buildings 40–41
Museumsinsel 23
Nazi Period 68, 116
Potsdamer Platz 19
Stalinism 118, 133
Arena 148
Argentinische Allee 90
Arriving in Berlin 161
Art Galleries 48–9
see also Museums
Aspria 69
Assassination Attempt
(20 July 1944) 98
Assyrischer Palast 20

Astro Bar 148
Athena, Goddess 21, 22
Auguststraße 126, 127
Auguststraße No. 21 Court 127
Auguststraße No. 83 Court 127
Austeria 87

B

B-flat 128
Babelsberg 155, 156
Bad Saarow 167
Banks 165
Bao-Bao (Panda) 36
Bar am Lützowplatz 52
Bar jeder Vernunft 56–7
Barenboim, Daniel 56
Barist 129
Bars 54–5
Berlin's Southeast 148
Central Berlin: Scheunenviertel
128
Central Berlin: Unter den
Linden 120
Prenzlauer Berg 143
Bauhaus-Archiv 49
Bebelplatz 13, 113
Becherer, Christian Friedrich 123
Beer Gardens 136
Behnisch, Günter 9
Bellini Lounge 128
Belvedere 29
Bendlerblock 98
Berghain/Panorama Bar 148
Berlin Highlights 6–7
Berlin Infostores 163
Berlin on a Budget 171
Berlin Story 119
Berlin Wall 11, 14, 19, 43, 103, 146
Berlin, Alexanderplatz 131
Berlin's Southeast 144–9
Berliner Antik- und Flohmarkt 61
Berliner Börse 81
Berliner Dom 44
Berliner Ensemble 126
Berliner Fernsehturm 131
Berliner Festspiele 62
Berliner Filmfestspiele 62
Berliner Kaffeerösterei 86
Berliner Rathaus 38, 131
Berliner Verkehrsbetriebe (BVG)
162, 164, 166, 168
Berlinische Galerie 49
Berndt, Kurt 39, 123
Beth-Café 129
Betty F 128
Beuys, Joseph 98

Bicycle Hire 162
Billy Wilder's 101
Blockhaus Nikolskoe 92, 93
Bocca di Bacco 74
Bode-Museum 114
Book Burning 13, 113
Borchardt 74
Botanischer Garten 70–71
Botschaftsviertel 97
Boumann, Johann 156
Brandenburg Province 131
Brandenburger Hof 73
Brandenburger Tor 6, 8–9, 38, 113
Brandenburger Tor (Potsdam) 156
Brauhaus Lemke 120
Brauhaus Georgbräu 137
Brasserie Desbrosses 101
Bräustübl 149
Brecht, Bertolt 50, 124, 126
Brecht-Weigel-Gedenkstätte 50, 124
Breitscheidplatz 24
Breschnew, Leonid 146
Bröhan-Museum 49
Bücherbogen 85
Bucherer 119
Buckow 167
Bundeskanzleramt 40
Büring, Johann Gottfried 153
Buses 162, 164
Disabled Visitors 164
Guided Tours 168
Tickets 162
Busse, August 35
Butter Lindner 85

C

Cabaret (Musical) 104
Café Aedes 86
Café am Neuen See 101
Café Balzac 86
Café Berio 59
Café Einstein 101
Café Einstein Unter den Linden
120
Café Ephraim's 136
Café Filmbühne am Steinplatz 86
Café Hardenberg 86
Café Heider 157
Café Josty 16, 51
Café Kleine Orangerie 86
Café Krone 91
Café Leysieffer 86
Café M 53
Café Savigny 86
Café Wintergarten im Literatur-
haus 86

Cafés
  Alexanderplatz 136
  Central Berlin: Around Potsdam & Sanssouci 157
  Charlottenburg & Spandau 86
  Prenzlauer Berg 143
Caputh 167
Car Hire 162
Carillon 100
Carmerstraße 80
Cassiopeia 148
Cecilienhof
  see Palaces
Cemeteries
  Dorotheenstädtischer 124
  Große Hamburger Straße 125
  Hallesches Tor 106
  Jüdischer Friedhof 125, 140
  Schönhauser Allee 140
Central Berlin (Mitte)
  Alexanderplatz 130–31
  Gendarmenmarkt 114
  Scheunenviertel 122–9
  Unter den Linden 112–21
Centrum Judaicum 123
Chamäleon-Varieté 56
Charité 51, 126
Charlottenburg & Spandau 78–87
Charlottenburger Rathaus 82
Chausseestraße 124
Checkpoint Charlie 47, 103, 108
Chefetage 136
Children's Attractions 64–5, 160
Chinesisches Haus (Sanssouci) 153
Chipperfield, David 23
Christi-Auferstehungskirche 45
Christo 11
Christopher Street Day 58, 62, 160
Churches 44–5
  Berliner Dom 44
  Christi-Auferstehungskirche 45
  Deutscher Dom 114
  Franziskanerkirche 134
  Französische Kirche 156
  Französischer Dom 45, 114
  Friedrichstadtkirche 114
  Friedrichswerdersche Kirche 45
  Heiliggeistkapelle 134
  Kaiser-Wilhelm-Gedächtnis-Kirche 7, 26–7, 45
  Marienkirche 44, 132
  Nikolaikirche (Mitte) 44, 132
  Nikolaikirche (Potsdam) 155
  Nikolaikirche (Spandau) 79
  Parochialkirche 134
  St-Annen-Kirche 92
  St-Hedwigskathedrale 12, 44, 113

Churches (cont.)
  St-Matthäuskirche 33
  St-Peter-und-Paul-Kirche 92, 156
  Sophienkirche 123, 126
  Zionskirche 140
Cinemas
  Cinemaxx 17
  Kulturbrauerei 139
Cinemaxx 17
Clärchens Ballhaus 55
Club der Visionäre 148
Cochon Bourgeois 128
Concentration Camps 125, 140, 167
Connection 59
Cookies 55
Corbusier-Haus 84
Courtyards 39, 123
Coventry-Kreuz 27
Cranach, Lucas the Elder 14
Credit Cards 160, 170
Crime 166
CSA 148
Currency 170
Cycling 68

D
Dahlem 65, 88–9
Dahlem Museums 46, 89
Dahlem Villas 90
Daimler 17
Dali Museum 118
Danziger Straße 139
Das Speisezimmer 75
Days Out 167
DDR Museum 118
Defne 109
Delicious Doughnuts 128
Department Store 206 60, 119
Department Stores 170
  Department Store Quartier 206 60, 119
  Galeries Lafayette 60, 119
  Kaufhaus des Westens 60, 170
  Kaufhof Galleria 119, 131, 135
  Stilwerk 60–61
Depot 2 107
DeRag Hotel Großer Kurfürst 73
Deutsch-Russisches Museum 145
Deutsche Guggenheim 49, 113
Deutsche Oper 56, 84
Deutsche Staatsoper 113
Deutscher Bundestag 10, 38, 43
Deutscher Dom 114
Deutsches Historisches Museum (DHM) 12, 14–5, 39, 46
Deutsches Technikmuseum 47, 103
Deutsches Theater 57
Diekmann im Chalet Suisse 93

die mitte 135
Dietrich, Marlene 12, 18, 50
Diplomatenviertel 97
Disabled Visitors 164
Discotheques
  Central Berlin: Scheunenviertel 128
  Gay & Lesbian 59
  Prenzlauer Berg 143
Döblin, Alfred 131
Doedens, Bruno 19, 35
Dorotheenstädtischer Friedhof 124
Dressler Kurfürstendamm 81, 87
Dressler Unter den Linden 121
Düppel 91
Dutschke, Rudi 43
DZ Bank 8, 41

E
East Germany
  Capital 131
  Design 142
  Fall 141
  Government 13, 115, 116–7, 141
  750-Jahr-Feier Berlin 140
  State Security Service 141, 145, 147
East Side Gallery 146
Economic Miracle 108
Edict of Potsdam 42, 114
Ehrenhalle 82
Eichmann, Adolf 89
Eiermann, Egon 26–7
Eierschale Haus Zenner 149
Eiffel 87
Einstein, Albert 50
Einstein Coffeeshop 86
Eisenman, Peter 115
Embassies 160
  Austria 97, 160
  Estonia 100
  France 9
  Great Britain 116
  India 97
  Italy 97
  Japan 97
  Mexico 97
  Nordic 41, 97
  Russia 13, 118
  Switzerland 160
  USA 9
Emergencies 166
Ende, Hermann 99
Endell, August 39, 123
Engelhart, Ludwig 132
Englischer Garten 100
Entrecôte 109
Ephraim-Palais 133

Equestrian Statue of Frederick the Great 13, 113
Ermisch, Richard 82
Erotik-Museum 84
Erzgebirgischer Weihnachtsmarkt 135
Estonian Embassy 100
Ethnologisches Museum 89
Eugen-Guttmann-Haus 9
Europa-Center 24
Excursions & Days Out 167

F

Facil 75
Fairs 62–3
Famous Berliners **50–51**
Fasanenplatz 81
Fasanenstraße 25, 80–81
Fashion Week 63
Fassbender & Rausch 119
Federal District 96–7
Federal Ministry of Defence 98
Federal Ministry of Finance 116
Federal President 38, 43
Felix 54
Festivals & Fairs **62–3**
Fichte, Johann Gottlieb 124
Filmmuseum Berlin 16, 18
Filmmuseum Potsdam 155
Filmpark Babelsberg 64–5, 155
First Floor 87
Fischers Fritz 75
Fitness Centres 69
Flavin, Dan 113
Florian 87
Flussbad Köpenick 145
Fontane, Theodor 51
Forsthaus Paulsborn 93
40 Seconds 54
Forum Fridericianum 12–13, 42, 113
Foster, Norman Sir 10, 92
Franco-Prussian War 14, 79, 97
Frankfurt/Oder 167
Frankfurter Allee 42–3, 133
Francucci's 87
Franziskanerkirche 134
Französische Kirche 156
Französischer Dom 45, 114
Frederick II (the Great) 12–13, 15, 29, 30, 31, 42, 47, 113, 152–3
Freie Universität (FU) 92
freiheit fünfzehn 149
Freilichtmuseum (Düppel) 91
French Community 45, 114
Friedrich I 30, 31, 145
Friedrich von Hohenzollern 31
Friedrich Wilhelm I 29, 31, 42
    see also Great Elector

Friedrich Wilhelm II 29, 30, 70
Friedrich Wilhelm III 29, 31
Friedrich Wilhelm IV 31, 154
Friedrichsfelde 147
Friedrichshagen 146, 147
Friedrichshain 146
Friedrichstadtkirche 114
Friedrichstadtpalast 57, 115
Friedrichstadtpassagen 115
Friedrichstraße 57, 118, 170
Friedrichswerdersche Kirche 45
Friedrich-Wilhem (restaurant) 157
Funkturm 82
Furtwänglerstraße 90

G

Galeria Kaufhof 131, 135
Galerie Brusberg 25
Galeries Lafayette 60, 119
Galopprennbahn Hoppegarten 68
Gandino, Francesco Chiaramelle de 79
Gardens
    see Parks & Gardens
Gasometer Schöneberg 106
Gay & Lesbian Attractions **58–9**
    Christopher Street Day 62
    Information 163
    Nazi Persecution 104
Gedenkstätte Normannenstraße 145
Gehry, Frank O. 8, 41
Gemäldegalerie 32, 34, 48
Gendarmenmarkt 73, 114, 120
Georg-Kolbe-Museum 84
German Empire 15, 116
Gethsemanekirche 141
Getting Around Berlin 162
Gipssammlung Staatliche Museen 61
Goldener Greif in Schloss Klein-Glienicke 91, 93
Golgatha 108
Gontard, Carl von 153, 156
Good Old Germany 135
Gorgonzola Club 109
Grand Hyatt 19, 72
Graves
    Brecht, Bertolt 124
    Fichte, Johann Gottlieb 124
    Hegel, Georg W.F. 124
    Kleist, Heinrich von 92
    Liebermann, Max 140
    Mann, Heinrich 124
    Mendelssohn, Moses 125
    Meyerbeer, Giacomo 140
    Schadow, Johann G. 124
    Schinkel, Karl F. 124
    Stüler, Friedrich A. 124
    Vogel, Henriette 92

Great Elector 15, 31, 42, 114
Great Wheel Berlin 79
Green's 136
Green Door 52
Grill Royal 121
Grimm, Wilhelm 51
Grimm, Jacob 51
Grips-Theater 64
Grober Unfug Comics 107
Gropius, Walter 99
Große Hamburger Straße 125, 140
Großer Bunkerberg 146
Großer Müggelsee 146
Großer Tiergarten 69, 70, 97
Großer Wannsee 88–9, 93, 146
Grüne Woche 63
Grunewald 70, 88, 91, 92
Grunewald & Dahlem **88–93**
Grunewaldturm 92
Grunewaldturm-Restaurant 93
Gugelhof 143
"Guest Workers" 104
Guided Tours **168**
Guy 121

H

Hackesche Höfe 38–9, 123, 129
Hackescher Hof 129
Hackescher Markt 73
Hallhuber 85
Hamburger Bahnhof 48, 98
Hansa-Viertel 99
Hartmanns Restaurant 109
Hasir 109
Hauptbahnhof 41, 161
Haus am Checkpoint Charlie 47, 103
Haus der Wannsee-Konferenz 89
Haus Liebermann 9
Haus Sanssouci 93
Havel 156
Health 166
Heat (restaurant) 137
Hebbel am Ufer 57
Heckmann-Höfe 127, 129
Hegel, Georg W.F. 51, 124
Heiliger See 154, 157
Heiliggeistkapelle 134
Hellmann Menswear 85
Helmholtzplatz 142
Henry-Ford-Bau 92
Hertha BSC 68
High-Lite 107
Historic Buildings **38–9**
Historic Events **42–3**
Historic Port 134
Historische Weinstuben 136
Hitler, Adolf 11, 98, 116
Hochbunker 126

Hof Joachimstraße 127
Hohenschönhausen 147
Hohenzollern 26, 31
Holländisches Viertel 154–5
Holocaust 89, 115
Holocaust-Denkmal 115
Hotel Adlon Berlin 8, 72
Hotel Savoy 73
Hotels 72–3, **172–9**
  & Guesthouses with Charm 178
  Budget Hotels and hostels 177
  Designer Hotels 174
  Famous Hotels 72–3
  for Business Travellers 175
  in Green Surroundings 176
  Luxury Hotels 179
  Medium-Priced Hotels 173
  Modest Hotels & Hostels 171, 172
House Boats 100
Hugenotten 42, 45, 114, 156
Hugo's 74
Humann, Carl 23
Humboldt, Wilhelm von 13
Humboldt-Forum 117
Humboldt-Universität 13, 113
Husemannstraße 140

I

Iduna-Haus 25
Information & Advice 163
Inline Skating 69
Insel 148
Internationale Funkausstellung 62
Internationale Tourismusbörse 63
Internationales Congress Centrum (ICC) 62–3, 82
Isherwood, Christopher 104
Ishtar Gate 20

J

Jack Wolfskin 119
Jagdschloss Grunewald 91
Jahn, Helmut 16, 19, 25
Jil Sander 85
Jews
  Cemeteries 125, 140
  Große Hamburger Straße 125
  Holocaust Memorial 115
  Neue Synagoge 123
  Old People's Home 125
  Oranienburger Straße 123
  Scheunenviertel 122–129
  Synagoge Rykestraße 141
Jüdischer Friedhof Schönhauser Allee 140
Jüdisches Gemeindehaus 80–81, 84
Jüdisches Museum 46, 103
Juliusturm 79

K

KaDeWe (Kaufhaus des Westens) 60, 170
Käfer im Reichstag 101
Kaffee Burger 128
Kaiser-Wilhelm-Gedächtnis-Kirche 7, 24, **26–7**, 45
Kamala 129
Kammergericht 106
Kammermusiksaal 33, 41
Kant-Dreieck 41, 81
Kantstraße 80–81
Karajan, Herbert von 50
Karl-Marx-Allee 133
Karneval der Kulturen 63
Kartoffelhaus No. 1 137
Käthe-Kollwitz-Museum 81, 83
Kempinski Hotel Bristol Berlin 72, 81, 179
Kennedy, John F. 43, 106
Kennedys (museum) 8, 118
Keyzer Soze 125, 129
Kleihues, Josef Paul 41
Klein-Glienicke 89
Kleist, Heinrich von 92
Klipper Schiffsrestaurant 149
Knaack-Club 143
Knobelsdorff, Georg Wenzeslaus von 12–13, 29, 113, 153
Knoblauchhaus 132
Knut (polar bear) 36
Koch, Robert 51, 126
Kollhoff, Hans 19
Kollhoff-Tower 19
Kollwitz, Käthe 13, 51, 83, 139
Kollwitz Monument 139
Kollwitzplatz 139
Komische Oper 118
Königs-Wusterhausen 167
Konnopke 142
Konzerthaus see Schauspielhaus
Koons, Jeff 17, 98
Köpenick 144–5
Koppenplatz 126
Kottbusser Tor 106
KPM (Königliche Porzellan-Manufaktur) 61
Kreuzberg & Schöneberg **102–9**
Krokodil 149
Kronprinzenpalais 13
Krumme Lanke 67
Kuchi 87
Ku'damm 7, **24–5**, 78–9
Ku'damm-Eck 25
Kulturbrauerei 139
Kulturforum 7, **32–5**, 40–41, 97
Kulturkaufhaus Dussmann 115, 119
Kumpelnest 3000 53

Kunst- und Antikmarkt Straße des 17. Juni 60, 85
Kunstbibliothek 33
Kunstgewerbemuseum 33, 47
Kunsthof 127
Künstlerhaus Bethanien 106
Kunstwerke (Galerie) 127
Kupferstichkabinett 33, 49
Kurfürsten 25, 31, 70, 91
Kurfürstendamm (Ku'damm) 7, **24–5**, 78–9

L

Label 205 im Q 205 (bar) 120
Labyrinth Kindermuseum 64
Lakes, Rivers & Canals **66–7**
  Großer Müggelsee 66, 146
  Großer Wannsee 66, 88–9, 93, 146
  Landwehrkanal 67
  Lietzensee 67
  Neuer See 67
  Schlachtensee 66
  Spree 66
  Tegeler See 67
  Teufelssee 66
Landwehrkanal 67, 100
Lange Nacht der Museen 62–3
Langhans Carl Gotthard 8, 29, 118, 132, 154
La Siesta 136
Le-Corbusier-Haus 84
Le Provencal 137
Leander 149
LebensArt 120
Legoland 65
Lehmofen 149
Lehniner Platz 25
Lenné Peter Joseph 29, 70, 89, 90, 97, **98**, 146
Leydicke, E. & M. 52
Liebermann, Max 9, 140
Lietzensee 67
Lindenthaler Allee 90
Linie 1 (Musical) 64
Literaturhaus 81
Lochner 101
Lorenz Adlon 121
Lortzing Monument 100
Lost Property 166
Löwenbrücke 100
Lubitsch 87
Ludwig-Erhard-Haus 40, 81
Luise 93
Lustgarten 39
Lutter & Wegner Gendarmenmarkt 75
Lutter & Wegner Potsdamer Platz 101

M

MaaßenZehn 107
Mach, Werner 68
Mächtig, Hermann 105
Madeleine 157
Maison Charlotte 157
Mann-o-Meter 58
Malatesta 121
Mao Thai 143
Marcellino 137
Märchenbrunnen 147
Margaux 121
Marheineke-Markthalle 107
Mariannenplatz 106
Marienkirche 44, 132
Markets **60–61**
    Marheineke-Markthalle 107
    Türkenmarkt Maybachufer 107
    Winterfeldtplatz 107
Märkisches Museum 132
Märkisches Ufer 134
Markttor von Milet 20
Marlene-Dietrich-Platz 17, 72
Marstall 155
Massimo 18 155, 157
Martin-Gropius-Bau 105
Marx-Engels-Forum 132
Matrix 148
Mauerpark 142
Max & Moritz 108
Max-Schmeling-Halle 142
Maxim-Gorki-Theater 118
Maxwell 129
Mehringplatz 106
Memorials
    Brecht-Weigel-Gedenkstätte 124
    Deutscher Widerstand 98
    Große Hamburger Straße 125
    Haus der Wannsee-Konferenz 89
    Hohenschönhausen 147
    Memorial for Members of the
      Reichstag 11
    Memorial for Victims of
      the Wall 11
    Neue Wache 13
    Normannenstraße 145
    Sowjetisches Ehrenmal 98
Memorial for Victims of the Wall 11
Mendelssohn, Moses 51, 125
Mendelssohn-Bartholdy, Felix
    51, 106
Merhaba 109
Messegelände 82
Metropoltheater 104, 118
Mexikoplatz 90
Meyerbeer, Giacomo 140
Mister Hu 108
Modern buildings **40–41**

Molotow 107
Monbijoupark 126
Money 160, 165
Monsieur Vuong 129
Monster Ronson's Ichiban Karaoke
    Bar 148
Monuments
    Alois Senefelder 142
    Benno Ohnesorg 84
    Equestrian Statue of Frederick
      the Great 13, 113
    Great Elector 29
    Holocaust 115
    Käthe Kollwitz 139
    Marx-Engels-Forum 132
    Sowjetisches Ehrenmal
      (Tiergarten) 98
    Sowjetisches Ehrenmal
      (Treptow) 71, 146
Mosse-Palais 106
Motorways 161
Müggelsee
    see Großer Müggelsee
Müggelturm 146
Münze 134
Münzstrasse 135
Museums **46–7**
    Alliiertenmuseum 90
    (Alte) Nationalgalerie 48, 114
    Altes Museum 39, 114
    Bauhaus-Archiv 49
    Berlinische Galerie 49
    Brecht-Weigel-Gedenkstätte
      50, 124
    Bröhan-Museum 49
    Dahlem Museums 46, 89
    Dalí Museum 118
    DDR Museum 118
    Deutsch-Russisches Museum 145
    Deutsche Guggenheim 49, 113
    Deutscher Dom 114
    Deutsches Historisches
      Museum 12, 14–15, 39, 46
    Deutsches Technikmuseum
      47, 64, 103
    Domäne Dahlem 65
    Ephraim-Palais 133
    Erotik-Museum 84
    Ethnologisches Museum 89
    Filmmuseum Berlin 16, 18
    Filmpark Babelsberg 64–5, 155
    Gemäldegalerie 23, 34, 48
    Georg-Kolbe-Museum 84
    Gestaltung 142
    Hamburger Bahnhof 48
    Haus am Checkpoint Charlie
      47, 103
    Historic Port 134

Museums (cont.)
    Jagdschloss Grunewald 91
    Jüdisches Museum 46, 103
    Käthe-Kollwitz-Museum 81, 83
    Knoblauchhaus 132
    Kulturforum 7, **32–5**
    Kunstgewerbemuseum 33, 47, 145
    Kupferstichkabinett 33, 49
    Labyrinth Kindermuseum 64
    Märkisches Museum 132
    Martin-Gropius-Bau 105
    Museum Berggruen 28, 29, 49
    Museum der Gegenwart
      (Hamburger Bahnhof) 48, 98
    Museum für Islamische Kunst
      23
    Museum für Kommunikation 117
    Museum für Naturkunde 64, 124
    Museum für Ostasiatische
      Kunst 89
    Museum für Pathologie 126
    Museumsinsel 7, 23, 114
    Musikinstrumentenmuseum
      33, 47
    Neue Nationalgalerie 32, 40, 48
    Neues Museum 114
    Newton-Sammlung 82–3
    Nikolaikirche (Mitte) 132
    Open Air Museum Domäne
      Dahlem 92
    Pergamonmuseum 7, **20–23**,
      46, 114
    Potsdam-Museum 156
    Prenzlauer Berg Museum 142
    Puppentheatermuseum 65
    Sammlung Industrielle
    Schwules Museum 59
    The Story of Berlin 25
    Topographie des Terrors 103
    Vitra Design Museum 139
Mutter Hoppe 137

N

National Museums 163
Nationalgalerie siehe Museen
Nazism
    Architecture 116
    Concentration Camps 14, 125, 140
    Enabling Act 11
    Film 18
    Gestapo 103
    Olympic Games 68, 23
    Resistance 98, 141
    SA 15, 141
    Seizing Power 11, 15
    SS 15, 125
    War Criminals 154
Nefertiti 46

Neptunbrunnen 133
Nering, Johann Arnold 15, 28, 134, 145
Neue Nationalgalerie 32, 40, 48
Neue Reichskanzlei 116
Neue Schönhauser Str. 126
Neue Synagoge 45, 123, 132
Neue Wache 13, 51
Neuer Flügel, Schloss Charlottenburg 28–30
Neuer Pavillon, Schloss Charlottenburg 29
Neuer See 53, 67, 100, 101
Neues Kranzler-Eck 25
Neues Palais 153
Newton-Bar 52, 120
Newton-Sammlung 82–3
Nicholas I, Tsar 92
Nightlife 122–3
Nikolaikirche (Mitte) 45, 132
Nikolaikirche (Potsdam) 155
Nikolaikirche (Spandau) 79
Nikolaiviertel 44, 132
No. 52 109
Nola's am Weinberg 129
Nollendorfplatz 104
Nordic Embassies 41, 97
Normannenstraße 145
Nouvel, Jean 115
November (Café) 143

O
O2 World 145
O & G (bar) 128
Oberbaumbrücke 10
Oderberger Straße 142
Oderquelle 143
Ohnesorg, Benno 84
Old Town (Köpenick) 145
Olympiastadion 68, 84
Olympic Games 1936 23, 68
Olympic Games 2000 142
Onkel-Tom-Siedlung 92
Open Air Museum Domäne Dahlem 92
Opening Hours 170
Opera
 see Deutsche Oper and Staatsoper Unter den Linden
Opera Court 120
Opernpalais 120
Operntreff 120
Orangerie (Sanssouci) 154
Oranienburger Straße 123
Oranienplatz 107
Oranienstraße 104, 107
Osteria No. 1 109
Oxymoron 128

P
Palace of Mshatta 21
Palaces
 Friedrichsfelde 147
 Jagdschloss Grunewald 91
 Köpenicker Schloss 145
 Marmorpalais 154
 Neues Palais 153
 Schloss Babelsberg 156
 Schloss Bellevue 38
 Schloss Britz 71
 Schloss Cecilienhof 154, 158
 Schloss Charlottenburg 7, **28–31**, 38, 70
 Schloss Charlottenhof 154
 Schloss Friedrichsfelde 71, 146
 Schloss Klein-Glienicke 89, 93
 Schloss Rheinsberg 167
 Schloss Sanssouci 152–3, 163
 Schlossruine Pfaueninsel 70, 89
 Stadtschloss 116
Palais am Festungsgraben 118
Palais am Pariser Platz 9
Palais Podewil 134
Pan Asia 129
Paris-Moskau 101
Pariser Platz 6, 8–9, 41
Parks & Gardens **70–71**, 169
 Babelsberg 156
 Botanischer Garten 70–71
 Großer Tiergarten 70, 97
 Grunewald 70–71, 88–9
 Monbijoupark 126
 Pfaueninsel 70, 89
 Schloss Britz und Park 71
 Schlosspark Charlottenburg 29, 70
 Schlosspark Sanssouci 153–4
 Thälmannpark 142
 Treptower Park 71, 146
 Viktoriapark 71, 105
 Volkspark Friedrichshain 71, 146–7
Parochialkirche 134
Pasternak 143
Peek & Cloppenburg 85
Pei, Ieoh Ming 15, 39
Performing Arts Venues **56–7**
Pergamon Altar 20, 22–3
Pergamonmuseum 7, **20–23**, 46, 114
Persephone, Goddess 21
Pesne, Antoine 153
Pfaueninsel 70, 89
Pfefferberg 142
Philharmonie 32, 35, 41, 56
Piano, Renzo 19
Piscator, Erwin 104
Planning your Trip 160

Podewil 134
Popkomm 62
Portzamparc, Christian de 9
Porzellankabinett 28
Post Offices 165
Postfuhramt 123, 125
Potsdam & Sanssouci **152–8**, 163
Potsdam Conference 154
Potsdam-Museum 156
Potsdamer Platz 6, **16–19**
Prater 139, 143
Prenzlauer Berg **138–43**
Prenzlauer Berg Museum 142
Prinz-Eisenherz-Buchhandlung 59
Prussia
 Architecture 31, 90, 152–3
 Hohenzollern 31
 Kulturbesitz (Stiftung) 99
 Sanssouci 152–5
 Wars 71, 97
Public conveniences 164
Pubs **52–3**
 Central Berlin: Around Alexanderplatz 136
 Central Berlin: Scheunenviertel 128
 Central Berlin: Unter den Linden 120
 Prenzlauer Berg 143
Puppenstube 135
Puppentheatermuseum 65

Q
Quadriga 8, 132
Quadriga (Restaurant) 73
Quartier 205 115, 119
Quartier 206 115, 119
Quartier 207 115

R
Radio Stations 163
Railway Stations
 Anhalter 104
 Ostbahnhof 161
 Zoo 161
Railways 161
Rathaus Schöneberg 43, 106
Ratskeller Köpenick 149
Rattle, Simon Sir 32
Rauch, Daniel Christian 13, 113
Rauschgold 108
Red Rooster Bar 148
Refugium 121
Regent Berlin 72
Regierender Bürgermeister 131
Reich Ministry of Aviation 116
Reichskanzlei 98, 116
Reichskristallnacht 123, 141

General Index

Reichstag 6, **10–11**, 38, 43
Reingold 128
Reinhard's 137
Reinhardt, Max 57, 126
Reservations 169
Restaurant Juliette 157
Restaurant Käfer 11
Restaurants **74–5**
  Berlin's Southeast 149
  Central Berlin: Around
    Alexanderplatz 135
  Central Berlin: Scheunenviertel 129
  Central Berlin: Unter den Linden 120
  Charlottenburg & Spandau 87
  Grunewald & Dahlem 93
  Kreuzberg & Schöneberg 109
  Potsdam & Sanssouci 157
  Prenzlauer Berg 143
Restaurants & Beer Gardens 93
Restauration 1900 143
Ribbeckhaus 134
Riehmers Hofgarten 105
Ritter Sport 119
Ritz-Carlton Berlin 73
Riva (Bar) 128
Riva, La (Restaurant) 137
Rogers, Richard Sir 19
Rohe, Mies van der 35, 40, 49
Römische Bäder (Sanssouci) 154
Rosenthaler Str. No. 37 127
Rosenthaler Straße 123
Russian Embassy 13, 118
Rykestraße 45, 141

S
S-Bahn Stations
  Alexanderplatz 131
  Friedrichstraße 115, 118
  Mexikoplatz 90
  Nollendorfplatz 104
  Savignyplatz 80
SA 15, 141
Sachsenhausen (concentration
  camp) 167
Sacrow 167
Safety 166
Sage Club 54
Sagebiel, Ernst 106, 116
Sale e Tabacchi 109
San Nicci 121
Sander, Jil 108
St-Annen-Kirche 92
St-Hedwigskathedrale 12, 44, 113
St-Matthäuskirche 33
St-Peter-und-Paul-Kirche 92, 156
Sanssouci 31, 152–55
Savignypassage 80
Savignyplatz 80

Schadow, Johann Gottfried 8, 124
Scharoun, Hans 33, 35, 41
Schauspielhaus 38, 114
Scheibe, Richard 98
Scheunenviertel 73, **122–9**
Schinkel, Karl Friedrich 13, 29, 38,
  39, 45, 90, 105, 124, 154, 155, 156
Schleusenbrücken 100
Schleusenkrug 101
Schliemann, Heinrich 29
Schloss Cecilienhof 157
Schlosshotel im Grunewald 72
Schlossinsel (Köpenick) 145
Schlossplatz 116–17
Schlüter, Andreas 14, 15, 29
Schönefeld, Airport 161
Schönhauser Allee 139
Schrörs Biergarten 149
Schüler, Ralf 82
Schüler-Witte, Ursulina 82
Schultes, Axel 40
Schultheiss-Brauerei 139
Schüßlerplatz 145
Schwarzes Café 86
Schwechten, Franz 104, 139
Schwules Museum 59
SchwuZ 58
Security 166
SED 133
Seeling, Heinrich 126
Seerestaurant Hotel
  Müggelsee/Rübezahl 148
Senefelder, Alois 142
Senefelderplatz 139, 142
Sergijewski, Nikolai 98
750-Year Anniversary 140
17 June 1953 42–3, 84
Shopping **60–61**, 170
  Alexanderplatz 131, 135
  Central Berlin:
    Around Alexanderplatz 135
  Central Berlin:
    Unter den Linden 119
  Charlottenburg & Spandau 85
  Fasanenstraße 81
  Friedrichstraße 115, 119, 170
  Galeries Lafayette 115, 119
  Kreuzberg & Schöneberg 107
  Kurfürstendamm 24–5, 170
  Potsdamer Platz Arkaden
    17, 170
  Quartier 206 115, 119
Shops & Markets **60–61**
  see also Shopping
Siegessäule 39, 97
Siegessäule (Magazine) 58
SO 36 (Disco) 59, 108
Sofitel Berlin Gendarmenmarkt 73

Sony Center 6, 16, 19, 40
Sophie-Charlotte 28
Sophie-Gips-Höfe 127
Sophie-Luise (Queen) 123
Sophienclub 55
Sophienhöfe 127
Sophienkirche 123, 126
Sophienstraße 22a 127
Sophienstraße 123, 127
Soultrane 81
Souvenir Shops 132, 170
Sowjetisches Ehrenmal
  (Tiergarten) 98
Sowjetisches Ehrenmal
  (Treptow) 71, 146
Spandau 78–9
Spandauer Vorstadt (Mitte)
  122, 124
Speckers Landhaus 157
Speer, Albert 116
Spielbank Berlin 17
Spindel (Restaurant) 149
Spindler & Klatt 54
Sport & Fitness Venues **68–9**
Sport Oase 69
Sports Highlights 63
Spree 66
Spreewald 167
SS 15, 125
Staatsbibliothek 33
Staatsoper Unter den Linden
  12, 42, 56
Staatsratsgebäude 116–17
Stadtbad Neukölln 69
Stadtbad Prenzlauer Berg 142
Stadtgericht 134
Stadtmauer 134
Stadtschloss 116
Stalin, Joseph 154
Ständige Vertretung 120
Stasi-Gefängnis 147
State Security Service (Stasi)
  141, 145, 147
Stauffenberg, Claus Schenk Graf
  von 98
Stiftung Preußischer Kulturbesitz
  99
Stilwerk 60–61, 85
Strandbad Rahnsdorf 146
Strandbad Wannsee 66, 90
Students (Reductions) 160
Stüler, Friedrich A. 33, 35, 92, 124,
  154, 156
Synagogues **44–5**
  Jüdisches Gemeindehaus
    80–81, 84
  Neue Synagoge 45, 123, 132
  Rykestraße 45, 141

T

Tacheles 124
Tadschikische Teestube 121
Taxis 162
Technische Universität 84
Teddy's 135
Tee Gschwendner 85
Teeladen 135
Tegel, Airport 161
Tegeler See 67
Telecafé 131, 136
Telegrafenberg 156
Telephones 165
Teltower Damm 92
Tempodrom 104
Tenement blocks 92, 138–9
Teufelsberg 70, 92
Teufelssee 66, 70, 92
Thälmannpark 142
The Story of Berlin 25
Theater am Potsdamer Platz 17
Theater des Westens 57
Theft 166
Theodor Tucher 8, 120
Tiergarten 96–7, 99
Tiergarten & Federal District
  96–101
Tierpark Friedrichsfelde 71, 147
Tom's Bar 58–9
Toni-Lessler-Straße 90
Totentanz, Der 132
Tourist Information 163
Trabrennbahn Mariendorf 68
Treptow 144–5
Treptower Park 71, 146
Tresor Club 54
Treuhandanstalt 116
Tucholskystraße 126
Türkenmarkt am Maybachufer 107
Turks 104
20 July 1944 98
The Twenties 16, 18, 19, 24, 42,
  51, 118

U

U- and S-Bahnhof Alexanderplatz
  135
U-Bahn 162
UFA-Studios 64, 155
Ungers, O.M. 23
Universität der Künste 84
Unter den Linden 6, 12–13

V

Van Loon 108
Vau 74
Velodrom 68
Velotaxis 162, 168
Victoria, Goddess of Victory 97
Victoria Bar 52
Vienna Bar 53
Viktoriapark 71, 105, 108
Villa Grisebach 81
Villa Maren 90
Villa von der Heydt 99
Villas, Dahlem 90
Voigt, Wilhelm 145, 149
Volksbühne 57
Volkspark Friedrichshain 71, 146–7
Voßstraße 116
Vox 74
Vox Bar at Hyatt 108
V2 Rocket 14

W

Waage 157
Waesemann, Hermann F. 38, 131
Walks
  Berlin's Southeast 147
  Central Berlin: Around
    Alexanderplatz 133
  Central Berlin: Scheunenviertel
    125
  Central Berlin: Unter den
    Linden 115, 117
  Charlottenburg & Spandau 81, 83
  Grunewald & Dahlem 91
  Köpenick 147
  Kreuzberg & Schöneberg 105
  Potsdam & Sanssouci 155
  Prenzlauer Berg 141
Wannsee 88–9, 93
Wannsee Conference 89
Warhol, Andy 98
Wars of Liberation 105
Wasserturm 140–41
Wasserwerk Sanssouci 156
Watergate (club) 55
Watteau, Antoine 30, 34, 153
Weekend 54
Weigel, Helene 50, 124
Weinbar Rutz 74
Weinhaus Huth 16, 19
Weinstein 143
WelcomeCard 163, 171

Weltkugelbrunnen 24
Werder 167
When to go 160
Wilford, Michael 116
Wilhelm I, Kaiser 26–7, 92
Wilhelm II, Kaiser 31
Wilhelmstraße 116
Windhorst 120
Winterfeldtplatz 61, 104, 107
Wirtshaus Schildhorn 93
Wirtshaus zur Pfaueninsel 93
Wisniewski, Edgar 33, 35, 41
WMF-Haus 118
Workers' Uprising in East Germany
  (17 June 1953) 42–3, 84
World War II
  Destruction 23, 24, 26–7,
    28, 42, 131, 132, 146
  Planning 116
  Post-War Years 18, 42
  Potsdam Conference 154
  Surrender 42, 145
Würgeengel 108

Y

Yan Yan (Panda) 36
Yorckschlösschen 108
Yosoy 128

Z

Zander 143
Zar Nikolaus I. 92
Zehlendorf 88, 90, 92
ZEISS-Großplanetarium 65, 142
Zeughaus 12, 15, 39
Zille-Hof 85
Zillestube 137
Zionskirche 140
Zionskirchplatz 140
Zitadelle Spandau 79
ZOB (Zentraler Omnibusbahnhof)
  161
Zoos
  Tierpark Friedrichsfelde 71, 147
  Zoologischer Garten 7, 36–7,
    65, 79
Zum Fischerkietz 136
Zum Nußbaum 52
Zum Paddenwirt 137
Zur Gerichtslaube 137
Zur letzten Instanz 136
Zwiebelfisch 53

Acknowledgements

The Author
Historian Jürgen Scheunemann has published several documentary and photographic books on Berlin and other destinations. His award-winning articles are published in travel magazines and daily newspapers in Germany and the US, and have appeared in the Berlin daily *Tagesspiegel*, among others.

For Dorling Kindersley Verlag, Munich:
Publishing Director
Dr. Jörg Theilacker
Editors Brigitte Maier, Gerhard Bruschke
Design & Layout Ulrike Meyer
Proofreader Linde Wiesner
Editorial Assistants Jasmin Jouhar, Robert Kocon
Photography Jürgen Scheunemann
Additional Photography Dorota and Mariusz Jarymowicz, Britta Jaschinski, Günter Schneider
Artwork www.chrisorr.com
Cartography Dominic Beddow, Simonetta Siori (Draughtsman Ltd)

For Dorling Kindersley, London:
Translation & Editing Sylvia Goulding/Silva Editions
Senior Publishing Manager
Louise Lang
Publishing Manager Kate Poole
Senior Art Editor Marisa Renzullo
Director of Publishing Gillian Allan
Publisher Douglas Amrine
Cartography Co-ordinator
Casper Morris
DTP Jason Little, Conrad van Dyk
Production Sarah Dodd
Revisions Claudia Himmelreich, Claire Jones, Petra Krischok, Maite Lantaron, Carly Madden, Nicola Malone, Marianne Petrou, Sands Publishing Solutions, Conrad van Dyk

Picture Credits
t-top; tc-top centre; tr-top right; cla-centre left above; ca-centre above; cra-centre right above; cl-centre left; c-centre; cr-centre right; clb-centre right below; cb-centre below; crb-centre right below; bl-below left; bc-below centre; br below right.

The publishers would like to thank the following individuals, companies and picture libraries for permission to reproduce their photographs: Alexander Plaza: 178tc; Ars vitalis: 69br; Art'otel Berlin: 174tl; Backpacker Hostel/Axbax: 177tl, 177tr; Bar jeder Vernunft: 57cla; Berliner Bäder-Betriebe: 69tl; Berliner Filmfestspiele: 62cl; Bleibtreu-Hotel: 173tl; Deutsche Guggenheim: 113clb; Dorint am Gendarmenmarkt: 179tl; Estrel Residence Congress Hotel: 175tr; Funpool: 68tr; Galeries Lafayette: 119tc; Heckers Hotel: 174tc; Hertha BSC: 68bl; Hotel Adlon: 8crb, 116cb; Hotel Hackescher Markt: 173tr; Hotel Künstlerheim Luise: 172tr; Hotel zur Bleiche: 176tc; Jüdisches Museum: 102tr; Margaux: 74b; Kempinski Hotel Bristol Berlin: 86c; Museum für Kommunikation: Herbert Schlemmer: 117b; Propeller City Island: 178tr; Quartier 206 Department Store: 60tl, 115tl; Relexa Hotel Cecilienhof: 176tr; Rocco Forte Hotel de Rome: 120tc; Schlossparkhotel: 176tl; Sorat Hotel Spreebogen: 174tl; Siegessäule: 58b; Tourismusverband Spreewald e.V.: Rainer Weisflog 167tr; Trabrennbahn Mariendorf: 68tc; Trenta sei: Benjamin Hüter 120tc; Jens Gläser 121tr; Zoologischer Garten: 36-7c.

40 SECONDS: Nela König 54clb; ALAMY IMAGES: Absorbme 148tc; David Crossland 36bc; Iain Masterton 20tl; ALPENSTÜCK: 129tr; ANKERKLAUSE: 108tr; ARENA CLUB: 148tl; ASPRIA: 69tr; BERLIN STORY: 119tc; BERLIN TOURISMUS MARKETING GMBH: 161tl; Wolfgang Scholvien 20cb, 21tl; BERLINER KAFFEERÖSTEREI: 86tc; BILDARCHIV PREUSSISCHER KULTURBESITZ, Berlin: 20tl, 31tr, 35c; Ägyptisches Museum/Margarete Büsing 4c; Antikensammlung 7tl, 22c, 22t, 46tl, 114c; Antikensammlung/Ingrid Geske-Heiden 114b; Ethnologisches Museum 30br; Gemäldegalerie, *Madonna in Church* by Jan van Eyck (c1425) 32t, *Portrait of the Merchant Georg Gisze* by Hans Holbein (1532) 34tr, *Venus and the Organ Player* by Titian (1550–2) 34tc, *Portrait of Hieronymus Holz-schuher* by Albrecht Dürer (1529) 34tr,

Madonna with the Child and Singing Angels by Botticelli (c1477) 34c, *Victorious Eros* by Caravaggio (1602) 34bl, 48tc, *Adoration of the Shepherds* by Hugo van der Goes (1470) 48tl, *The Glass of Wine* by Jan Vermeer (c1658–61) 48bu; Kunstgewerbemuseum 7cb, 33t, 46tr, 47c; Kupferstichkabinett, *Portrait of Dürer's Mother* by Albrecht Dürer 114c; Nationalgalerie, *Farm in Daugart* by Karl Schmidt-Rottluff (1910) © DACS, London 2006 32b, *Mao* by Andy Warhol (1973) © Licensed by The Andy Warhol Foundation for the Visual Arts Inc. / ARS, NY & DACS, London 2006 48cra; Nationalgalerie, Berggruen Collection, *Head of a Faun* by Pablo Picasso (1937) © Succession Picasso / DACS, London 2006 49tl; Vorderasiatisches Museum 20cbr, 22bl, 23c, 23b, 23t; BOCCA DI BACCO: 74tl; BRECHT-WEIGEL-GEDENKSTÄTTE Berlin: 50cr; BRIDGEMAN ART LIBRARY: National-galerie, Berlin, *Portrait of Georg Wilhelm Friedrich Hegel* (1770–1831) by Jacob Schlesinger (1792–1855) 50tl; BROEHAN MUSEUM: 49c; BYTEPARK GMBH – INTERMEDIALE KOMMUNIKATION: 172tc; CAFÉ EINSTEIN STAMMHAUS: 101tr; CASSIOPEIA. Berlin: 148tr; CLARCHEN'S BALLHAUS: Bernd Schoenberger 54tl; CLUB WATERGATE: Mike Breeuwer 55c; CORBIS: dpa/A3464 Rainer Jensen 20br; Terra/Stefano Amantini 20-21c; DDR MUSEUM: Bastian Werner 118tl; DEDERICHS REINECKE & PARTNER: Eventpress Herrmann/Henry H. Herrmann 65cr; DEUTSCHE PRESSEAGENTUR: 9b, 42tr, 50tc, 50tr, 50bl, 51tl, 51b, 62tc, 62tr, 62c, 63tl, 63tr, 63cr; DEUTSCHES HISTORISCHES MUSEUM: 15t, 18cl, 42cr; *Gloria Victis* by Antonin Mercie 14c; *Pieta Sculpture at the Neue Wache*, Kathe Kollwitz © DACS, London 2006 51c; *Martin Luther* by Lucas Cranach the Elder (1529) 14b; *Opening of the German Reichstag* (1871) 15b; DEUTSCHES TECHNIK-MUSEUM: 103bl; FELIX CLUB-RESTAURANT: 54tr; FIT OT PRINT, Berlin: 166tc; GALERIA KAUFHOF GMBH: 135tl; GETTY IMAGES: Andreas Rentz 21cr; GORGONZOLA CLUB: 109;

GRAND HYATT BERLIN: 75crb, 108tc; GREEN DOOR: diephotodesigner.de 52c, 53tl; GUGELHOF: 143tl; HENRY MOORE FOUNDATION: *Three Way Piece Nr. 2. (The) Archer* (1964–5) 35t; HOTEL PENSION FUNK: 172tl; HOTEL VILLA KASTANIA: 178tl.; INTERCONTINENTAL, BERLIN: 74bc; KÄTHE-KOLLWITZ-MUSEUM: *Mother and Child* by Käthe Kollwitz © DACS, London 2006 83bl; KOMISCHE OPER BERLIN: Hanns Joosten 118tc, Arwid Lagenpusch 112tr; KU'DAMM 101 HOTEL: 174tr; MUSEUM BERGGRUEN: Jens Ziehe 29br; MUSEUM FÜR NATURKUNDE: 47tr; PAN ASIA: Christopher Michaelis 129tl; PRESSE- UND INFORMATIONSAMT DES LANDES Berlin: BTM/Drewes 17bl; BTM/Koch 17cra LOLA LOUNGE: Nela Koenig 54tl; POPKOMM: 62tl; ROCCO FORTE HOTEL DE ROME: 120tc; SAN NICCI: Florian Bolk 121tr; KARSTEN SCHIRMER: 56cl; GÜNTER SCHNEIDER: 42tl, 95–6; JÜRGEN SCHEUNEMANN: 121tc, 128tl; SPINDLER & KLATT: 54tc; STAATLICH MUSEEN ZU BERLIN, PREUSSISCHER KULTUR-BESITZ KUNSTGEWERBE-MUSEUM: Hans Joachim Bartsch 47c; STIFTUNG STADTMUSEUM BERLIN: 14t; Peter Straube 130tr; STIFTUNG PREUS-SISCHE SCHLÖSSER UND GÄRTEN BERLIN-BRANDENBURG: 30c, 152tl, 153br, *Frederick's Watteau Paintings* by Antoine Watteau (1720) 30tc; *Frederick the Great* by Antoine Pesne 31cl, *Frederick Playing the Flute* by Adolf von Menzel 42b, 152cl; STRANDBAR MITTE: 52tc; ANDREAS TAUBER: 101tc; TEEGSCH WENDNER: 85tr; TV TURM ALEXAN-DERPLATZ GASTRONOMIEG-ESELLSCHAFT MBH: 136tr; VICTORIA BAR: Christian Gahl 53crb; HAUS DER WANNSEE-KONFERENZ: 89cb; WERNER OTTO BILDARCHIV, OBERHAUSEN: 76–7; www.csd-berlin.de: 160tr.

All other images © Dorling Kindersley London. For further information see: www.dkimages.com

Phrase Book

In an Emergency

Where is the telephone?	Wo ist das Telefon?	voh ist duss tel-e-fone?
Help!	Hilfe!	hilf-uh
Please call a doctor	Bitte rufen Sie einen Arzt	bitt-uh roof'n zee ine-en artst
Please call the police	Bitte rufen Sie die Polizei	bitt-uh roof'n zee dee poli-tsy
Please call the fire brigade	Bitte rufen Sie die Feuerwehr	bitt-uh roof'n zee dee foyer-vayr
Stop!	Halt!	hult

Communication Essentials

Yes	Ja	yah
No	Nein	nine
Please	Bitte	bitt-uh
Thank you	Danke	dunk-uh
Excuse me	Verzeihung	fair-tsy-hoong
Hello (good day)	Guten Tag	goot'n tahk
Goodbye	Auf Wiedersehen	owf-veed-er-zay-ern
Good evening	Guten Abend	goot'n ahb'nt
Good night	Gute Nacht	goot-uh nukht
Until tomorrow	Bis morgen	biss morg'n
See you	Tschüss	chooss
What is that?	Was ist das?	voss ist duss
Why?	Warum?	var-room
Where?	Wo?	voh
When?	Wann?	vunn
today	heute	hoyt-uh
tomorrow	morgen	morg'n
month	Monat	mohn-aht
night	Nacht	nukht
afternoon	Nachmittag	nahkh-mit-tahk
morning	Morgen	morg'n
year	Jahr	yar
there	dort	dort
here	hier	hear
week	Woche	vokh-uh
yesterday	gestern	gest'n
evening	Abend	ahb'nt

Useful Phrases

How are you? (informal)	Wie geht's?	vee gayts
Fine, thanks	Danke, es geht mir gut	dunk-uh, es gayt meer goot
Where is/are?	Wo ist/sind...?	voh ist/sind
How far is it to...?	Wie weit ist es...?	vee vite ist ess
Do you speak English?	Sprechen Sie Englisch?	shpresh'n zee eng-glish
I don't understand	Ich verstehe nicht	ish fair-shtay-uh nisht
Could you speak more slowly?	Könnten Sie langsamer sprechen?	kurnt-en zee lung-zam-er shpresh'n

Useful Words

large	gross	grohss
small	klein	kline
hot	heiss	hyce
cold	kalt	kult
good	gut	goot
bad	böse/schlecht	burss-uh/shlesht
open	geöffnet	g'urff-nett
closed	geschlossen	g'shloss'n
left	links	links
right	rechts	reshts
straight ahead	geradeaus	g'rah-der-owss

Making a Telephone Call

I would like to make a phone call	Ich möchte telefonieren	ish mer-shtuh tel-e-fon-eer'n
I'll try again later	Ich versuche noch ein mal später	ish fair-zookh-uh nokh ine-mull shpay-ter
Can I leave a message?	Kann ich eine Nachricht hinterlassen?	kan ish ine-uh nakh-risht hint-er-lahss-en
answer phone	Anrufbeantworter	an-roof-be-ahnt-vort-er
telephone card	Telefonkarte	tel-e-fohn-kart-uh
receiver	Hörer	hur-er
mobile	Handi	han-dee
engaged (busy)	besetzt	b'zetst
wrong number	Falsche Verbindung	falsh-uh fair-bin-doong

Sight-Seeing

library	Bibliothek	bib-leo-tek
entrance ticket	Eintrittskarte	ine-tritz-kart-uh
cemetery	Friedhof	freed-hofe
train station	Bahnhof	barn-hofe
gallery	Galerie	gall-er-ree
information	Auskunft	owss-koonft
church	Kirche	keersh-uh
garden	Garten	gart'n
palace/castle	Palast/Schloss	pallast/shloss
place (square)	Platz	plats
bus stop	Haltestelle	hal-te-shtel-uh
national holiday	Nationalfeiertag	nats-yon-ahl-fire-tahk
theatre	Theater	tay-aht-er
free admission	Eintritt frei	ine-tritt fry

Shopping

Do you have/ Is there...?	Gibt es...?	geept ess
How much does it cost?	Was kostet das?	voss kost't duss?
When do you open/ close?	Wann öffnen Sie? schliessen Sie?	vunn off'n zee shlees'n zee
this	das	duss
expensive	teuer	toy-er
cheap	preiswert	price-vurt
size	Grösse	gruhs-uh
number	Nummer	noom-er
colour	Farbe	farb-uh
brown	braun	brown
black	schwarz	shvarts
red	rot	roht
blue	blau	blau
green	grün	groon
yellow	gelb	gelp

Types of Shop

antique shop	Antiquariat	antik-var-yat
chemist (pharmacy)	Apotheke	appo-tay-kuh
bank	Bank	bunk
market	Markt	markt
travel agency	Reisebüro	rye-zer-boo-roe
department store	Warenhaus	vahr'n-hows
chemist's, drugstore	Drogerie	droog-er-ree
hairdresser	Friseur	freezz-er
newspaper kiosk	Zeitungskiosk	tsytoongs-kee-osk

bookshop	Buchhandlung	**bookh**-hant-loong
bakery	Bäckerei	beck-er-**eye**
post office	Post	posst
shop/store	Geschäft/Laden	gush-**eft/lard**'n
film processing shop	Photogeschäft	**fo**-to-gush-**eft**
self-service shop	Selbstbedienungs-laden	selpst-bed-**ee**-nungs-lard'n
shoe shop	Schuhladen	shoo-lard'n
clothes shop	Kleiderladen, Boutique	klyder-lard'n boo-**teek**-uh
food shop	Lebensmittel-geschäft	**lay**-bens-mittel-gush-eft
glass, porcelain	Glas, Porzellan	**glars, Port**-sellahn

Staying in a Hotel

Do you have any vacancies?	Haben Sie noch Zimmer frei?	harb'n zee nokh **tsimm**-er-fry
with twin beds?	mit zwei Betten?	mitt tsvy bett'n
with a double bed?	mit einem Doppelbett?	mitt ine'm **dopp**'lbet
with a bath?	mit Bad?	mitt **bart**
with a shower?	mit Dusche?	mitt **doosh**-uh
I have a reservation	Ich habe eine Reservierung	ish **harb**'n ine-uh rez-er-**veer**-oong
key	Schlüssel	shlooss'l
porter	Pförtner	**pfert**-ner

Eating Out

Do you have a table for...?	Haben Sie einen Tisch für...?	harb'n zee **ine**-uhn tish foor
I would like to reserve a table	Ich möchte eine Reservierung machen	ish **mer**-shtuh ine-uh rezer-**veer**-oong makh'n
I'm a vegetarian	Ich bin Vegetarier	ish bin vegg-er-**tah**-ree-er
Waiter!	Herr Ober!	hair **oh**-bare!
The bill (check), please	Die Rechnung, bitte	dee **resh**-noong bitt-uh
breakfast	Frühstück	**froo**-shtock
lunch	Mittagessen	**mit**-targ-ess'n
dinner	Abendessen	**arb**'nt-ess'n
bottle	Flasche	**flush**-uh
dish of the day	Tagesgericht	**tahg**-es-gur-isht
main dish	Hauptgericht	**howpt**-gur-isht
dessert	Nachtisch	**nahkh**-tish
cup	Tasse	**tass**-uh
wine list	Weinkarte	vine-kart-uh
tankard	Krug	khroog
glass	Glas	**glars**
spoon	Löffel	**lerff**'l
teaspoon	Teelöffel	tay-lerff'l
tip	Trinkgeld	**trink**-gelt
knife	Messer	**mess**-er
starter (appetizer)	Vorspeise	**for**-shpize-uh
the bill	Rechnung	**resh**-noong
plate	Teller	**tell**-er
fork	Gabel	**gahb**'l

Menu Decoder

Aa	**arl**	eel
Apfel	**upf**'l	apple
Apfelschorle	**upf**'l-shoorl-uh	apple juice with sparkling mineral water
Apfelsine	**upf**'l-seen-uh	orange
Aprikose	upri-**kawz**-uh	apricot

Artischocke	arti-**shokh**-uh	artichoke
Aubergine	or-ber-jeen-uh (eggplant)	aubergine
Banane	bar-**narn**-uh	banana
Beefsteack	**beef**-stayk	steak
Bier	beer	beer
Bockwurst	**bokh**-voorst	a type of sausage
Bohnensuppe	burn-en-zoop-uh	bean soup
Branntwein	brant-vine	spirits
Bratkartoffeln	brat-kar-toff'ln	fried potatoes
Bratwurst	brat-voorst	fried sausage
Brötchen	bret-tchen	bread roll
Brot	brot	bread
Brühe	bruh-uh	broth
Butter	**boot**-ter	butter
Champignon	**shum**-pin-yong	mushroom
Currywurst	**kha**-ree-voorst	sausage with curry sauce
Dill	**dill**	dill
Ei	**eye**	egg
Eis	**ice**	ice/ ice cream
Ente	**ent**-uh	duck
Erdbeeren	ayrt-**beer**'n	strawberries
Fisch	**fish**	fish
Forelle	for-**ell**-uh	trout
Frikadelle	Frika-dayl-uh	rissole/ hamburger
Gans	ganns	goose
Garnele	**gar**-nayl-uh	prawn/shrimp
gebraten	g'**braat**'n	fried
gegrillt	g'**grilt**	grilled
gekocht	g'**kokht**	boiled
geräuchert	g'**rowk**-ert	smoked
Geflügel	g'**floog**'l	poultry
Gemüse	g'**mooz**-uh	vegetables
Grütze	**grurt**-ser	groats, gruel
Gulasch	**goo**-lush	goulash
Gurke	**goork**-uh	gherkin
Hammelbraten	hamm'l-**braat**'n	roast mutton
Hähnchen	haynsh'n	chicken
Hering	**hair**-ing	herring
Himbeeren	him-beer'n	raspberries
Honig	**hoe**-nikh	honey
Kaffee	kaf-**fay**	coffee
Kalbfleisch	kalp-flysh	veal
Kaninchen	ka-**neensh**'n	rabbit
Karpfen	**karpf**'n	carp
Kartoffelpüree	kar-toff'l-poor-ay	mashed potatoes
Käse	**kayz**-uh	cheese
Kaviar	**kar**-vee-ar	caviar
Knoblauch	k'**nob**-lowkh	garlic
Knödel	**k'nerd**'l	noodle
Kohl	**koal**	cabbage
Kopfsalat	**kopf**-zal-aat	lettuce
Krebs	**krayps**	crab
Kuchen	**kookh**'n	cake
Lachs	**lahkhs**	salmon
Leber	**lay**-ber	liver
mariniert	mari-neert	marinated
Marmelade	marmer-**lard**-uh	marmalade, jam
Meerrettich	may-re-tish	horseradish
Milch	**milsh**	milk
Mineralwasser	minn-er-**arl**-vuss-er	mineral water
Möhre	**mer**-uh	carrot
Nuss	**nooss**	nut
Öl	**erl**	oil
Olive	o-**leev**-uh	olive

Petersilie	payt-er-**zee**-li-uh	parsley
Pfeffer	**pfeff**-er	pepper
Pfirsich	**pfir**-zish	peach
Pflaumen	**pflow**-men	plum
Pommes frites	pomm-**fritt**	chips/ French fries
Quark	kvark	soft cheese
Radieschen	ra-**deesh**'n	radish
Rinderbraten	**rind**-er-brat'n	joint of beef
Rinderroulade	**rind**-er-roo-lard-uh	beef olive
Rindfleisch	**rint**-flysh	beef
Rippchen	**rip**-sh'n	cured pork rib
Rotkohl	roht-koal	red cabbage
Rüben	rhoob'n	turnip
Rührei	**rhoo**-er-eye	scrambled eggs
Saft	**zuft**	juice
Salat	zal-aat	salad
Salz	**zults**	salt
Salzkartoffeln	zults-kar-toff'l	boiled potatoes
Sauerkirschen	zow-er-**keersh**'n	cherries
Sauerkraut	zow-er-krowt	sauerkraut
Sekt	**zekt**	sparkling wine
Senf	**zenf**	mustard
scharf	sharf	spicy
Schaschlik	shash-lik	kebab
Schlagsahne	shlahgg-zarn-uh	whipped cream
Schnittlauch	shnit-lowkh	chives
Schnitzel	**shnitz**'l	veal or pork cutlet
Schweinefleisch	**shvine**-flysh	pork
Spargel	**shparg**'l	asparagus
Spiegelei	shpeeg'l-eye	fried egg
Spinat	shpin-art	spinach
Tee	**tay**	tea
Tomate	tom-art-uh	tomato
Wassermelone	vuss-er-me-lohn-uh	watermelon
Wein	**vine**	wine
Weintrauben	**vine**-trowb'n	grapes
Wiener Würstchen	**veen**-er voorst-sh'n	frankfurter
Zander	**tsan**-der	pike-perch
Zitrone	tsi-trohn-uh	lemon
Zucker	**tsook**-er	sugar
Zwieback	tsvee-bak	rusk
Zwiebel	**tsvee**b'l	onion

Numbers

0	null	**nool**
1	eins	**eye'ns**
2	zwei	**tsvy**
3	drei	**dry**
4	vier	**feer**
5	fünf	**foonf**
6	sechs	**zex**
7	sieben	**zeeb**'n
8	acht	**uhkht**
9	neun	**noyn**
10	zehn	**tsayn**
11	elf	**elf**
12	zwölf	**tserlf**
13	dreizehn	**dry**-tsayn
14	vierzehn	**feer**-tsayn
15	fünfzehn	**foonf**-tsayn
16	sechzehn	**zex**-tsayn
17	siebzehn	**zeep**-tsayn
18	achtzehn	**uhkht**-tsayn
19	neunzehn	**noyn**-tsayn
20	zwanzig	**tsvunn**-tsig
21	einundzwanzig	**ine**-oont-tsvunn-tsig
30	dreissig	**dry**-sig
40	vierzig	**feer**-sig
50	fünfzig	**foonf**-tsig
60	sechzig	**zex**-tsig
70	siebzig	**zeep**-tsig
80	achtzig	**uhkht**-tsig
90	neunzig	**noyn**-tsig
100	hundert	**hoond**'t
1000	tausend	**towz**'nt
1,000,000	eine Million	**ine**-uh **mill**-yon

Time

one minute	eine Minute	**ine**-uh min-**oot**-uh
one hour	eine Stunde	**ine**-uh **shtoond**-uh
half an hour	eine halbe Stunde	**ine**-uh hullb-uh **shtoond**-uh
Monday	Montag	**mohn**-targ
Tuesday	Dienstag	**deens**-targ
Wednesday	Mittwoch	**mitt**-vokh
Thursday	Donnerstag	**donn**-ers-targ
Friday	Freitag	**fry**-targ
Saturday	Samstag/ Sonnabend	**zums**-targ zonn-ah-bent
Sunday	Sonntag	**zon**-targ
January	Januar	**yan**-ooar
February	Februar	**fay**-brooar
March	März	**mairts**
April	April	april
May	Mai	my
June	Juni	**yoo**-ni
July	Juli	**yoo**-lee
August	August	ow-**goost**
September	September	zep-**tem**-ber
October	Oktober	ok-toh-ber
November	November	no-**vem**-ber
December	Dezember	day-**tsem**-ber
spring	Frühling	**froo**-ling
summer	Sommer	**zomm**-er
autumn (fall)	Herbst	**hairpst**
winter	Winter	**vint**-er